# Contents

BERLITZ®

# ITALIAN
## for travellers

By the staff of Editions Berlitz

# How best to use this phrase book

● We suggest that you start with the **Guide to pronunciation** (pp. 6–8), then go on to **Some basic expressions** (pp. 9–15). This gives you not only a minimum vocabulary, but also helps you get used to pronouncing the language. The phonetic transcription throughout the book enables you to pronounce every word correctly.

● Consult the **Contents** pages (3–5) for the section you need. In each chapter you'll find travel facts, hints and useful information. Simple phrases are followed by a list of words applicable to the situation.

● Separate, detailed contents lists are included at the beginning of the extensive **Eating out** and **Shopping guide** sections (Menus, p. 39, Shops and services, p. 97).

● If you want to find out how to say something in Italian, your fastest look-up is via the **Dictionary** section (pp. 164–189). This not only gives you the word, but is also cross-referenced to its use in a phrase on a specific page.

● If you wish to learn more about constructing sentences, check the **Basic grammar** (pp. 159–163).

● Note the **colour margins** are indexed in Italian and English to help both listener and speaker. And, in addition, there is also an **index in Italian** for the use of your listener.

● Throughout the book, this symbol ☛ suggests phrases your listener can use to answer you. If you still can't understand, hand this phrase book to the Italian-speaker to encourage pointing to an appropriate answer. The English translation for you is just alongside the Italian.

---


Library of Congress Catalog Card No. 85-81373

Second revised edition - 1st printing
Printed in Switzerland

Acknowledgments

We are particularly grateful to Francesca Grazzi Rahimi for her help in the preparation of this book, and to Dr. T. J. A. Bennett who devised the phonetic transcription.

# Guide to pronunciation

This and the following chapter are intended to make you familiar with the phonetic transcription we devised and to help you get used to the sounds of Italian. As a minimum vocabulary for your trip, we've selected a number of basic words and phrases under the title "Some Basic Expressions" (pages 9–15).

### An outline of the spelling and sounds of Italian

You'll find the pronunciation of the Italian letters and sounds explained below, as well as the symbols we're using for them in the transcriptions. Note that Italian has some diacritical letters—letters with accent marks—which we don't use in English.

The imitated pronunciation should be read as if it were English except for any special rules set out below. It is based on Standard British pronunciation, though we have tried to take account of General American pronunciation also. Of course, the sounds of any two languages are never exactly the same; but if you follow carefully the indications supplied here, you'll have no difficulty in reading our transcriptions in such a way as to make yourself understood.

Letters written in **bold** should be stressed (pronounced louder).

### Consonants

| Letter | Approximate pronunciation | Symbol | Example | |
|---|---|---|---|---|
| **b, d, f, k, l, m, n, p, q t, v** | are pronounced as in English | | | |
| **c** | 1) before **e** and **i**, like **ch** in **chip** | ch | **cerco** | **chayr**koa |
| | 2) elsewhere, like **c** in **cat** | k | **conto** | **koan**toa |

| | | | | |
|---|---|---|---|---|
| **ch** | like **c** in **cat** | k | **che** | kay |
| **g** | 1) before **e** and **i**, like **j** in **jet** | j | **valigia** | vah**lee**jah |
| | 2) elsewhere, like **g** in **go** | g | **grande** | **grahn**day |
| **gh** | like **g** in **go** | g | **ghiaccio** | gee**aht**choa |
| **gl** | like **lli** in **million** | ly | **gli** | lyee |
| **gn** | like **ni** in **onion** | ñ | **bagno** | **bah**ñoa |
| **h** | always silent | | **ha** | ah |
| **r** | trilled like a Scottish **r** | r | **deriva** | deh**ree**vah |
| **s** | 1) generally like **s** in **sit** | s | **questo** | koo**ay**stoa |
| | 2) sometimes like **z** in **zoo** | z | **viso** | **vee**zoa |
| **sc** | 1) before **e** and **i**, like **sh** in **shut** | sh | **uscita** | oo**shee**tah |
| | 2) elsewhere, like **sk** in **skin** | sk | **scarpa** | **skahr**pah |
| **z/zz** | 1) generally like **ts** in hits | ts | **grazie** | **graa**tseeay |
| | 2) sometimes like **ds** in roads | dz | **romanzo** | roa**mahn**dzoa |

## Vowels

| | | | | |
|---|---|---|---|---|
| **a** | 1) short, like **a** in **father**, but shorter | ah | **gatto** | **gaht**toa |
| | 2) long, like **a** in **father** | aa | **casa** | **kaa**sah |
| **e** | 1) can always be pronounced like **ay** in **way** | ay | **sera** | **say**rah |
| | 2) in correct speech, it is sometimes pronounced like **e** in **get** or, when long, more like **ai** in **said** | eh | **bello** | **behl**loa |
| | | ai | **bene** | **bai**nay |
| **i** | like **ee** in **meet** | ee | **vini** | **vee**nee |
| **o** | 1) can always be pronounced like **oa** in **goat** | oa | **sole** | **soa**lay |
| | 2) in correct speech, it is sometimes pronounced like **o** in **got**, or when long, more like **aw** in **law** | o | **notte** | **not**tay |
| | | aw | **rosa** | **raw**zah |
| **u** | like **oo** in **foot** | oo | **fumo** | **foo**moa |

### Two or more vowels

In groups of vowels **a, e,** and **o** are strong vowels, and **i** and **u** are weak vowels. When two strong vowels are next to each other, they are pronounced as two separate syllables, e.g., *beato* = bay**ah**toa. When a strong and weak vowel are next to each other, the weak one is pronounced more quickly and with less stress (less loudly) than the strong one, e.g., *piede* = pee**ay**day; such sounds are diphthongs and constitute only one syllable. If the weak vowel is stressed, then it is pronounced as a separate syllable, e.g., *due* = **doo**ay. Two weak vowels together are pronounced as a diphthong, and it is generally the second one that is more strongly stressed, e.g., *guida* = goo**ee**dah.

### Stressing of words

Generally, the vowel of the next to last syllable is stressed. When a final vowel is stressed, it has an accent written over it *(più)*. Normally an accent is used only when the stress falls on a final vowel, and not when it falls on syllables before the next to last one.

### Pronunciation of the Italian alphabet

| | | | | | | | |
|---|---|---|---|---|---|---|---|
| **A** | ah | **H** | ah**k**kah | **O** | o | **V** | vee |
| **B** | bee | **I** | ee | **P** | pee | **W** | vee **doap**peeah |
| **C** | chee | **J** | ee **loong**gah | **Q** | koo | **X** | eeks |
| **D** | dee | **K** | **kah**ppah | **R** | **eh**rray | **Y** | ee **gray**kah |
| **E** | ay | **L** | **eh**llay | **S** | **eh**ssay | **Z** | **dzay**tah |
| **F** | **eh**ffay | **M** | **eh**mmay | **T** | tee | | |
| **G** | jee | **N** | **eh**nnay | **U** | oo | | |

# Some basic expressions

| | | |
|---|---|---|
| Yes. | **Sì.** | see |
| No. | **No.** | no |
| Please. | **Per favore/ Per piacere.** | pair fah**voa**ray/ pair peeah**chay**ray |
| Thank you. | **Grazie.** | **graa**tseeay |
| Thank you very much. | **Molte grazie/ Tante grazie.** | **moal**tay **graa**tseeay/ **tahn**tay **graa**tseeay |
| You're welcome. | **Prego.** | **pray**goa |
| That's all right/ Don't mention it. | **Non c'è di che.** | noan chai dee kay |

**Greetings** *Saluti*

| | | |
|---|---|---|
| Good morning. | **Buon giorno.** | bwon **joar**noa |
| Good afternoon. | **Buon giorno.** | bwon **joar**noa |
| Good evening. | **Buona sera.** | **bwo**nah **say**rah |
| Good night. | **Buona notte.** | **bwo**nah **not**tay |
| Good-bye. | **Arrivederci.** | ahrreevay**dair**chee |
| So long! | **Ciao!** | **chaa**oa |
| See you later. | **A più tardi.** | ah pee**oo tahr**dee |
| This is Mr./Mrs./ Miss ... | **Le presento il Signor/la Signora/la Signorina ...** | lay pray**zayn**toa eel see**ñoar**/lah see**ñoa**rah/ lah seeñoa**ree**nah |
| How do you do? (Pleased to meet you.) | **Molto lieto(a).*** | **moal**toa lee**ay**toa(ah) |
| How are you? | **Come sta?** | **koa**may stah |
| Very well, thanks. And you? | **Molto bene, grazie. E lei?** | **moal**toa **bai**nay **graa**tseeay. ay **lai**ee |

* In the case where there are masculine and feminine forms of a word, we give the masculine first, with the feminine in brackets afterwards; in this example, a woman would say **Molto lieta.**

| | | |
|---|---|---|
| | **Come va?** | koamay vah |
| | **Bene.** | bainay |
| pardon? | **Prego?** | praygoa |
| e. | **Mi scusi.** | mee skoozee |
| Ex me. (May get past?) | **Permesso?** | pairmaissoa |
| Sorry! | **Mi dispiace.** | mee deespeeahchay |

## Questions *Domande*

| | | |
|---|---|---|
| Where? | **Dove?** | doavay |
| How? | **Come?** | koamay |
| When? | **Quando?** | kwahndoa |
| What? | **Che cosa/Che?** | kay kawsah/kay |
| Why? | **Perchè?** | pehrkay |
| Who? | **Chi?** | kee |
| Which? | **Quale?** | kwaalay |
| Where is ...? | **Dov'è/Dove si trova ...?** | doavai/doavay see trawvah |
| Where are ...? | **Dove sono/ Dove si trovano ...?** | doavay soanoa/doavay see trawvahnoa |
| Where can I find/ get ...? | **Dove posso trovare ...?** | doavay possoa trovaaray |
| How far? | **Quanto dista?** | kwahntoa deestah |
| How long? | **Quanto tempo?** | kwahntoa tehmpoa |
| How much/How many? | **Quanto/Quanti?** | kwahntoa/kwahntee |
| How much does this cost? | **Quanto costa questo?** | kwahntoa kostah kooaystoa |
| When does ... open/ close? | **A che ora apre/ chiude ...?** | ah kay oarah aapray/ keeooday |
| What do you call this/that in Italian? | **Come si chiama questo/quello in italiano?** | koamay see keeaamah kooaystoa/kooaylloa een eetahleeaanoa |
| What does this/that mean? | **Che cosa significa questo/quello?** | kay kawsah seeñeefeekah kooaystoa/kooaylloa |

## Do you speak ...? *Parla ...?*

| | | |
|---|---|---|
| Do you speak English? | **Parla inglese?** | **pah**rlah eeng**glay**say |
| Is there anyone here who speaks ...? | **C'è qualcuno qui che parla ...?** | chai kwahl**koo**noa kooee kay **pahr**lah |
| I don't speak (much) Italian. | **Non parlo (bene) l'italiano.** | noan **pahr**loa (**bai**nay) leetahlee**aa**noa |
| Could you speak more slowly? | **Può parlare più lentamente, per favore?** | pwo pahr**laa**ray pee**oo** layntah**mayn**tay pair fah**voa**ray |
| Could you repeat that? | **Vuol ripetere, per favore?** | vwol ree**pai**tayray pair fah**voa**ray |
| Could you spell it? | **Può sillabarlo?** | pwo seellah**baar**loa |
| Please write it down. | **Per favore, me lo scriva.** | pair fah**voa**ray may loa **skree**vah |
| Can you translate this for me? | **Può tradurmi questo?** | pwo trah**door**mee koo**ay**stoa |
| Please point to the word/phrase/ sentence in the book. | **Per favore, mi indichi la parola/ l'espressione/ la frase nel libro.** | pair fah**voa**ray mee **een**deekee lah pah**ro**lah/ laysprehssee**oa**nay/ lah **fraa**zay nehl **lee**broa |
| Just a minute. I'll see if I can find it in this book. | **Un attimo. Guardo se posso trovarla in questo libro.** | oon **aht**teemoa. **gwahr**doa say **pos**soa troa**vaar**lah een koo**ay**stoa **lee**broa |
| It's on page ... | **È a pagina ...** | ai ah **paa**jeenah |
| I understand. | **Capisco.** | kah**pee**skoa |
| I don't understand. | **Non capisco.** | noan kah**pee**skoa |
| Do you understand? | **Capisce?** | kah**pee**shay |

## Can/May ...? *Posso ...?*

| | | |
|---|---|---|
| Can I have ...? | **Posso avere ...?** | **pos**soa ah**vay**ray |
| Can we have ...? | **Possiamo avere ...?** | possee**aa**moa ah**vay**ray |
| Can you show me ...? | **Può mostrarmi ...?** | pwo moa**straar**mee |
| I can't. | **Non posso.** | noan **pos**soa |
| Can you tell me ...? | **Può dirmi ...?** | pwo **deer**mee |

| | | |
|---|---|---|
| Can you help me? | **Può aiutarmi?** | pwo aheeoo**taar**mee |
| Can I help you? | **Posso aiutarla?** | **pos**soa aheeoo**taar**lah |
| Can you direct me to ...? | **Può indicarmi la direzione per ...?** | pwo eendee**kahr**mee lah deeraytsee**oa**nay pair |

## Wanting ... *Vorrei ...*

| | | |
|---|---|---|
| I'd like ... | **Vorrei ...** | vor**rai**ee |
| We'd like ... | **Vorremmo ...** | vor**rehm**moa |
| What do you want? | **Che cosa desidera?** | kay **kaw**sah day**zee**dayrah |
| Give me ... | **Mi dia ...** | mee **dee**ah |
| Give it to me. | **Me lo dia.** | may loa **dee**ah |
| Bring me ... | **Mi porti ...** | mee **por**tee |
| Bring it to me. | **Me lo porti.** | may loa **por**tee |
| Show me ... | **Mi mostri ...** | mee **moa**stree |
| Show it to me. | **Me lo mostri.** | may loa **moa**stree |
| I'm looking for ... | **Cerco ...** | **chayr**koa |
| I'm hungry. | **Ho fame.** | oa **faa**may |
| I'm thirsty. | **Ho sete.** | oa **say**tay |
| I'm tired. | **Sono stanco(a).** | **soa**noa **stahng**koa(ah) |
| I'm lost. | **Mi sono perduto(a).** | mee **soa**noa pehr**doo**toa(ah) |
| It's important. | **È importante.** | ai eempor**tahn**tay |
| It's urgent. | **È urgente.** | ai oor**jehn**tay |
| Hurry up! | **Presto!** | **preh**stoa |

## It is/There is ... *È/C'è ...*

| | | |
|---|---|---|
| It is/It's ... | **È ...** | ai |
| Is it ...? | **È ...?** | ai |
| It isn't ... | **Non è ...** | noan ai |
| Here it is. (masc./fem.) | **Eccolo/Eccola.** | **ehk**koaloa/**ehk**koalah |
| Here they are. (masc./fem.) | **Eccoli/Eccole.** | **ehk**koalee/**ehk**koalay |

| | | |
|---|---|---|
| There it is. | **Eccolo/Eccola.** | **ehk**koaloa/**ehk**koalah |
| There they are. | **Eccoli/Eccole.** | **ehk**koalee/**ehk**koalay |
| There is/There are ... | **C'è/Ci sono ...** | chai/chee **soa**noa |
| Is there/Are there ...? | **C'è/Ci sono ...?** | chai/chee **soa**noa |
| There isn't/aren't ... | **Non c'è/Non ci sono ...** | noan chai/noan chee **soa**noa |
| There isn't/aren't any. | **Non ce n'è/Non ce ne sono.** | noan chay nai/noan chay nay **soa**noa |

## It's ... *È ...*

| | | |
|---|---|---|
| big/small | **grande/piccolo*** | **grahn**day/**peek**koaloa |
| quick/slow | **rapido/lento** | **raa**peedoa/**lehn**toa |
| hot/cold | **caldo/freddo** | **kahl**doa/**frayd**doa |
| full/empty | **pieno/vuoto** | pee**ay**noa/**vwaw**toa |
| easy/difficult | **facile/difficile** | **faa**cheelay/deef**fee**cheelay |
| heavy/light | **pesante/leggero** | pay**sahn**tay/lay**djai**roa |
| open/shut | **aperto/chiuso** | ah**pehr**toa/kee**oo**soa |
| right/wrong | **giusto/sbagliato** | **joo**stoa/zbah**lyaa**toa |
| old/new | **vecchio/nuovo** | **vehk**keeoa/**nwaw**voa |
| old/young | **anziano/giovane** | ahntsee**aa**noa/**joa**vahnay |
| beautiful/ugly | **bello/brutto** | **bail**loa/**broot**toa |
| free (vacant)/ occupied | **libero/occupato** | **lee**bayroa/okkoo**paa**toa |
| good/bad | **buono/cattivo** | **bwaw**noa/kaht**tee**voa |
| better/worse | **migliore/peggiore** | mee**lyoa**ray/pay**djoa**ray |
| here/there | **qui/là** | koo**ee**/lah |
| early/late | **presto/tardi** | **preh**stoa/**tahr**dee |
| cheap/expensive | **buon mercato/caro** | bwawn mayr**kah**toa/**kaa**roa |
| near/far | **vicino/lontano** | vee**chee**noa/lon**taa**noa |
| first/last | **primo/ultimo** | **pree**moa/**ool**teemoa |

* For feminine and plural forms, see grammar section page 160 (adjectives).

## Quantities *Quantità*

| | | |
|---|---|---|
| a little/a lot | **un po'/molto** | oon po/**moal**toa |
| few/a few | **pochi/alcuni** | **po**kee/ahl**koo**nee |
| much | **molto** | **moal**toa |
| many | **molti** | **moal**tee |
| more/less | **più/meno** | pee**oo**/**mai**noa |
| more than/less than | **più di/meno di** | pee**oo** dee/**mai**noa dee |
| enough/too | **abbastanza/troppo** | ahbbah**stahn**tsah/**trop**poa |
| some/any | **del, della, dei, degli, delle** | dayl **dayl**lah **dai**ee **day**lyee **dayl**lay |

## Some prepositions ... *Alcune preposizioni ...*

| | | |
|---|---|---|
| at | **a*** | ah |
| on | **su** | soo |
| in | **in** | een |
| to | **a** | ah |
| after | **dopo** | **daw**poa |
| before (time) | **prima di** | **pree**mah dee |
| before (place) | **davanti a** | dah**vahn**tee ah |
| for | **per** | pair |
| from | **da** | dah |
| with | **con** | kon |
| without | **senza** | **sayn**tsah |
| through | **per, attraverso** | pair ahttrah**vehr**soa |
| towards | **verso** | **vehr**soa |
| until | **fino a** | **fee**noa ah |
| during | **durante** | doo**rahn**tay |
| next to | **accanto a** | ahk**kahn**toa ah |
| near | **vicino a** | vee**chee**noa ah |
| behind | **dietro** | dee**ay**troa |

* See also grammar section page 163 (prepositions).

| | | |
|---|---|---|
| between | **tra, fra** | trah frah |
| since | **da** | dah |
| above | **sopra** | **soa**prah |
| below | **al di sotto** | ahl dee **sott**oa |
| under | **sotto** | **sott**oa |
| inside | **dentro** | **dayn**troa |
| outside | **fuori** | **fwaw**ree |
| up | **su, in alto** | soo een ahltoa |
| upstairs | **di sopra** | dee **soa**prah |
| down | **giù** | joo |
| downstairs | **di sotto** | dee **sott**oa |

## ... and a few more useful words ... *e qualche altra parola utile*

| | | |
|---|---|---|
| and | **e** | ay |
| or | **o** | oa |
| not | **non** | noan |
| never | **mai** | **mah**ee |
| nothing | **nulla/niente** | **nool**lah/nee**ayn**tay |
| something | **qualcosa** | kwahl**kaw**sah |
| none | **nessuno** | nays**soo**noa |
| very | **molto** | **moal**toa |
| too, also | **anche** | **ahng**kay |
| yet | **ancora** | ahng**koa**rah |
| but | **ma, però** | mah pay**ro** |
| at once | **subito** | **soo**beetoa |
| soon | **presto** | **preh**stoa |
| now | **adesso** | ah**dehs**soa |
| then | **poi, in seguito** | **poa**ee een **say**gooeetoa |
| again | **ancora** | ahng**koa**rah |
| perhaps | **forse** | **for**say |
| only | **soltanto** | sol**tahn**toa |

# Arrival

**CONTROLLO DEI PASSAPORTI**
PASSPORT CONTROL

| | | |
|---|---|---|
| Here's my passport. | **Ecco il passaporto.** | **ehk**koa eel pahssah**port**oa |
| I'll be staying ... | **Resterò ...** | raystay**roa** |
| a few days<br>a week<br>a month | **qualche giorno<br>una settimana<br>un mese** | **kwahl**kay **joar**noa<br>**oo**nah saytee**maa**nah<br>oon **mai**zay |
| I don't know yet. | **Non so ancora.** | noan soa ahng**koa**rah |
| I'm here on holiday. | **Sono qui in vacanza.** | **soa**noa koo**ee** een vah**kahn**tsah |
| I'm here on business. | **Sono qui per affari.** | **soa**noa koo**ee** pair ahf**faa**ree |
| I'm just passing through. | **Sono di passaggio.** | **soa**noa dee pahs**sad**joa |

## If things become difficult:

| | | |
|---|---|---|
| I'm sorry, I don't understand. | **Mi dispiace, non capisco.** | mee deespee**ah**chay noan kah**pee**skoa |
| Is there anyone here who speaks English? | **C'è qualcuno qui che parla inglese?** | chai kwahl**koo**noa koo**ee** kay **pahr**lah eeng**glay**say |

**DOGANA**
CUSTOMS

After collecting your baggage at the airport *(l'aeroporto)* you have a choice: follow the green arrow if you have nothing to declare. Or leave via a doorway marked with a red arrow if you have items to declare (in excess of those allowed).

**MERCI DA DICHIARARE**
GOODS TO DECLARE

**NULLA DA DICHIARARE**
NOTHING TO DECLARE

The chart below shows what you can bring in duty-free.*

| | Cigarettes | | Cigars | | Tobacco | Spirits | | Wine |
|---|---|---|---|---|---|---|---|---|
| Italy 1) | 400 | or | 100 | or | 500 g. | ¾ l. | or | 2 l. |
| 2) | 300 | or | 75 | or | 400 g. | 1½ l. | or | 5 l. |
| 3) | 200 | or | 50 | or | 250 g. | ¾ l. | or | 2 l. |
| Switzerland | 200 | or | 50 | or | 250 g. | 1 l. | and | 2 l. |

1) residents of countries outside Europe
2) residents of countries within Europe and entering from an EEC country
3) residents of countries within Europe and entering from another country

| | | |
|---|---|---|
| I've nothing to declare. | **Non ho nulla da dichiarare.** | noan oa **nool**lah dah deekeeah**raa**ray |
| I've a carton of cigarettes/bottle of whisky. | **Ho una stecca di sigarette/bottiglia di whisky.** | oa **oo**nah **stayk**kah dee seegah**rayt**tay/ bot**tee**lyah dee "whisky" |
| Must I pay on this? | **Devo pagare per questo?** | **day**voa pah**gaa**ray pair koo**ay**stoa |
| It's for my personal use. | **È per mio uso personale.** | ai pair **mee**oa **oo**zoa pairsoa**naa**lay |

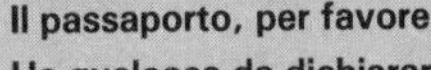

| | |
|---|---|
| **Il passaporto, per favore.** | Your passport, please. |
| **Ha qualcosa da dichiarare?** | Do you have anything to declare? |
| **Per favore, apra questa borsa.** | Please open this bag. |
| **Deve pagare il dazio per questo.** | You'll have to pay duty on this. |
| **Ha altri bagagli?** | Do you have any more luggage? |

* All allowances subject to change without notice.

## Baggage—Porter *Bagagli—Facchino*

These days porters are only available at airports or the railway stations of large cities. Where no porters are available you'll find luggage trolleys for the use of the passengers.

| | | |
|---|---|---|
| Porter! | **Facchino!** | fahk**kee**noa |
| Please take my ... | **Per favore, prenda ...** | pair fah**voa**ray **prehn**dah |
| bag<br>luggage<br>suitcase | **la mia borsa**<br>**i miei bagagli**<br>**la mia valigia** | lah **mee**ah **bor**sah<br>ee mee**ai**ee bah**gaa**lyee<br>lah **mee**ah vah**lee**jah |
| That's mine. | **Quella è mia.** | koo**ayl**lah ai **mee**ah |
| Take this luggage ... | **Porti questi bagagli ...** | **por**tee koo**ay**stee bah**gaa**lyee |
| to the bus<br>to the luggage lockers | **all'autobus**<br>**alla custodia automatica dei bagagli** | ahl**low**toabooss<br>**ahl**lah koo**staw**deeah owtoa**maa**teekah **dai**ee bah**gaa**lyee |
| How much is that? | **Quant'è?** | kwahn**tai** |
| There's one piece missing. | **Manca un collo.** | **mahng**kah oon **kol**loa |
| Where are the luggage trolleys (carts)? | **Dove sono i carrelli portabagagli?** | **doa**vay **soa**noa ee kahr**rehl**lee portahbah**gaa**lyee |

## Changing money *Cambio*

| | | |
|---|---|---|
| Where's the currency exchange? | **Dove si trova l'ufficio cambio?** | **doa**vay see **traw**vah loof**fee**choa **kahm**beeoa |
| Can you change these traveller's cheques (checks)? | **Può cambiare questi traveller's cheques?** | pwo kahmbee**aa**ray koo**ay**stee "traveller's cheques" |
| I want to change some dollars/pounds. | **Vorrei cambiare dei dollari/delle sterline.** | vor**rai**ee kahmbee**aa**ray **dai**ee **dol**lahree/**dayl**lay stayr**lee**nay |
| Can you change this into lire/Swiss francs? | **Può cambiare questo in lire/franchi svizzeri?** | pwo kahmbee**aa**ray koo**ay**stoa een **lee**ray/**frahng**kee **sveet**tsayree |
| What's the exchange rate? | **Qual è il corso del cambio?** | kwahl ai eel **kor**soa dayl **kahm**beeoa |

BANK—CURRENCY, see page 129

## Where is ...? *Dov'è ...?*

| | | |
|---|---|---|
| Where is the ...? | **Dov'è ...?** | doa**vai** |
| booking office | **l'ufficio prenotazioni** | loo**ffee**choa praynoatahtseeo**a**nee |
| car hire | **l'autonoleggio** | lowtoanoa**layd**joa |
| duty-free shop | **il negozio duty-free** | eel nay**go**tseeoa "duty-free" |
| newsstand | **l'edicola** | lay**dee**kolah |
| restaurant | **il ristorante** | eel reestoa**rahn**tay |
| shopping area | **la zona dei negozi** | lah **dzo**anah **dai**ee nay**go**tsee |
| How do I get to ...? | **Come posso andare a ...?** | **koa**may **pos**soa ahn**daa**ray ah |
| Is there a bus into town? | **C'è un autobus per la città?** | chai oon **ow**toabooss pair lah cheet**tah** |
| Where can I get a taxi? | **Dove posso prendere un taxi?** | **doa**vay **pos**soa **prehn**dayray oon "taxi" |
| Where can I hire a car? | **Dove posso noleggiare una macchina?** | **doa**vay **pos**soa noalayd**jaa**ray **oo**nah **mahk**keenah |

## Hotel reservation *Prenotazione d'albergo*

| | | |
|---|---|---|
| Do you have a hotel guide? | **Ha una guida degli alberghi?** | ah **oo**nah **gwee**dah **dai**lyee ahl**bayr**gee |
| Could you reserve a room for me at a hotel/boarding-house? | **Potrebbe prenotarmi una camera in un albergo/una pensione?** | poa**trehb**bay praynoa**taar**mee **oo**nah **kaa**mayrah een oon ahl**bayr**goa/**oo**nah paynsee**oa**nay |
| in the centre | **in centro** | een **chayn**troa |
| near the railway station | **vicino alla stazione** | vee**chee**noa **ahl**lah stahtsee**oa**nay |
| a single room | **una camera singola** | **oo**nah **kaa**mayrah **seeng**goalah |
| a double room | **una camera doppia** | **oo**nah **kaa**mayrah **doap**peeah |
| not too expensive | **non troppo cara** | noan **troap**poa **kaa**rah |
| Where is the hotel/boarding house? | **Dov'è l'albergo/la pensione?** | doa**vai** lahl**bayr**goa/lah paynsee**oa**nay |
| Do you have a street map? | **Ha una pianta della città?** | ah **oo**nah pee**ahn**tah **dayl**lah cheet**tah** |

HOTEL/ACCOMMODATION, see page 22

## Car hire (rental) *Autonoleggio*

To hire a car you must produce a valid driving licence (held for at least one year) and your passport. Some firms set a minimum age at 21, other 25. Holders of major credit cards are normally exempt from deposit payments, otherwise you must pay a substantial (refundable) deposit for a car. Third-party insurance is usually automatically included.

| | | |
|---|---|---|
| I'd like to hire (rent) a car. | **Vorrei noleggiare una macchina.** | vor**rai**ee noalayd**jaa**ray **oo**nah **mahk**keenah |
| small | **piccola** | **peek**koalah |
| medium-sized | **di media grandezza** | dee **may**deeah grahn**dayt**tsah |
| large | **grande** | **grahn**day |
| automatic | **automatica** | owtoa**mah**teekah |
| I'd like it for a day/a week. | **La vorrei per un giorno/una settimana.** | lah vor**rai**ee pair oon **joar**noa/**oo**nah saytteem**maa**nah |
| Are there any week-end arrangements? | **Vi sono condizioni speciali per il week-end?** | vee **soa**noa koandeetsee**oa**nee spay**chaa**lee pair eel "week-end" |
| Do you have any special rates? | **Avete tariffe particolari?** | ah**vay**tay tah**reef**fay pahrteekoa**laa**ree |
| What's the charge per day/week? | **Qual è la tariffa giornaliera/settimanale?** | kwahl ai lah tah**reef**fah joarnahlee**ay**rah/saytteemahn**aa**lay |
| Is mileage included? | **È compreso il chilometraggio?** | ai koam**pray**soa eel keelomay**trahd**joa |
| What's the charge per kilometre? | **Qual è la tariffa al chilometro?** | kwahl ai lah tah**reef**fah ahl kee**law**maytroa |
| I want to hire the car here and leave it in ... | **Vorrei noleggiare la macchina qui e renderla a ...** | vor**rai**ee noalayd**jaa**ray lah **mahk**keenah koo**ee** ay **rayn**dayrlah ah |
| I want full insurance. | **Voglio l'assicurazione completa.** | **vol**yoa lahsseekooraht-see**oa**nay koam**play**tah |
| What's the deposit? | **Quanto è la cauzione?** | **kwahn**toa ai lah kowtsee**oa**nay |
| I've a credit card. | **Ho una carta di credito.** | oa **oo**nah **kahr**tah dee **kray**deetoa |
| Here's my driving licence. | **Ecco la mia patente.** | **ehk**koa lah **mee**ah pah**tehn**tay |

CAR, see page 75

## **Taxi** *Taxi*

Taxis are clearly marked and available in all the larger towns. If the cab is unmetered, or you have a fair distance to go, ask the fare beforehand. Special rates for night journeys, baggage, etc. should be posted on an official fare chart.

| | | |
|---|---|---|
| Where can I get a taxi? | **Dove posso trovare un taxi?** | doavay possoa trawvaaray oon "taxi" |
| Please get me a taxi. | **Per favore, mi trovi un taxi.** | pair fahvoaray mee trawvee oon "taxi" |
| What's the fare to ...? | **Qual è il prezzo della corsa fino a ...?** | kwahl ai eel prehttsoa dayllah korsah feenoa ah |
| How far is it to ...? | **Quanto dista ...?** | kwahntoa deestah |
| Take me to ... | **Mi conduca ...** | mee koandookah |
| this address | **a questo indirizzo** | ah kooaystoa eendeereettsoa |
| the airport | **all'aeroporto** | ahllahayroportoa |
| the town centre | **in centro città** | een chayntroa cheettah |
| the ... Hotel | **all'albergo ...** | ahllahlbayrgoa |
| the railway station | **alla stazione** | ahllah stahtseeoanay |
| Turn ... at the next corner. | **Al prossimo angolo giri ...** | ahl prosseemoa ahnggoloa jeeree |
| left/right | **a sinistra/a destra** | ah seeneestrah/ah dehstrah |
| Go straight ahead. | **Vada sempre diritto.** | vahdah sehmpray deereettoa |
| Please stop here. | **Per favore, si fermi qui.** | pair fahvoaray see fayrmee kooee |
| I'm in a hurry. | **Ho fretta.** | oa frayttah |
| Could you drive more slowly? | **Può andare più lentamente?** | pwo ahndaaray peeoo layntahmayntay |
| Could you help me carry my luggage? | **Può aiutarmi a portare i miei bagagli?** | pwo aheeootaarmee ah portaaray ee meeaiee bahgaalyee |
| Could you wait for me? | **Può aspettarmi?** | pwo ahspehttaarmee |
| I'll be back in 10 minutes. | **Tornerò fra 10 minuti.** | tornayro frah 10 meenootee |

TIPPING, see inside back-cover

# Hotel—Other accommodation

Early reservation (and confirmation) is essential in most major tourist centres during the high season. Most towns and arrival points have a tourist information office (*azienda di soggiorno e turismo*—ahdzee**ehn**dah dee sod**joar**noa ay too**ree**smoa), or *ufficio turistico* (oof**fee**choa too**ree**steekoa), and that's the place to go if you're stuck without a room.

The Italian tourist organization, E.N.I.T., publishes an annual directory of all hotels in Italy with details of minimum and maximum prices and facilities.

**albergo/hotel** (ahl**bayr**goa/oa**tehl**)

Hotels in Italy are classified as *di lusso* (international luxury class), or *prima, seconda, terza, quarta categoria* (first, second, third, fourth class).

*Note:* Especially near railway stations, one often finds *alberghi diurni* (ahl**bayr**gee dee**oor**nee—"daytime hotels"). These have no sleeping accommodation, but provide bathrooms, rest rooms, hairdressers, and other similar services. Most close at midnight.

**motel** (mo**tehl**)

Increasing in number, improving in service, the Automobile Association of Italy has a list of recommended motels.

**locanda** (lo**kahn**dah)

A country inn.

**pensione** (paynsee**oa**nay)

Corresponds to a boarding house; it usually offers *pensione completa* (full board) or *mezza pensione* (half board). Meals are likely to be from a set menu. *Pensioni* are classified first, second or third class.

**ostello della gioventù** (oa**stehl**loa **dayl**lah joavayn**too**)

Youth hostel. They are open to holders of membership cards issued by the International Youth Hostel Association.

**appartamento ammobiliato** (ahppahrtah**mayn**toa ahmmoabeelee**ah**toa)

Furnished flat (apartment). Contact a specialized travel agent if this is the type of arrangement you're looking for.

CAMPING, see page 32

## Checking in—Reception *Ufficio ricevimento*

| | | |
|---|---|---|
| My name is ... | **Mi chiamo ...** | mee kee**aa**moa |
| I've a reservation. | **Ho fatto una prenotazione.** | oa **faht**toa **oo**nah praynoatahtsee**oa**nay |
| We've reserved two rooms. | **Abbiamo prenotato due camere.** | ahbbee**aa**moa praynoa**tah**toa **doo**ay **kaa**mayray |
| Here's the confirmation. | **Ecco la conferma.** | **ehk**koa lah kon**fehr**mah |
| Do you have any vacancies? | **Avete camere libere?** | ah**vay**tay **kaa**mayray **lee**bayray |
| I'd like a ... room ... | **Vorrei una camera ...** | vor**rai**ee **oo**nah **kaa**mayrah |
| single | **singola** | **seeng**goalah |
| double | **doppia** | **doap**peeah |
| with twin beds | **con due letti** | kon **doo**ay **leht**tee |
| with a double bed | **con un letto matrimoniale** | kon oon **leht**toa mahtreemoanee**aa**lay |
| with a bath | **con bagno** | kon **baa**ñoa |
| with a shower | **con doccia** | kon **dot**chah |
| with a balcony | **con balcone** | kon bahl**koa**nay |
| with a view | **con vista** | kon **vee**stah |
| We'd like a room ... | **Vorremmo una camera ...** | vor**rehm**moa **oo**nah **kaa**mayrah |
| in the front | **sul davanti** | sool dah**vahn**tee |
| at the back | **sul retro** | sool **rai**troa |
| facing the sea | **sul mare** | sool **maa**ray |
| It must be quiet. | **Deve essere tranquilla.** | **day**vay **ehs**sayray trahngkoo**eel**lah |
| Is there ...? | **C'è ...?** | chai |
| air conditioning | **l'aria condizionata** | **laa**reeah kondeetseeo**naa**tah |
| heating | **il riscaldamento** | eel reeskahldah**mayn**toa |
| a radio/television in the room | **la radio/il televisore nella stanza** | lah **raa**deeoa/eel taylayvee**zoa**ray **nayl**lah **stahn**tsah |
| laundry service | **il servizio di lavanderia** | eel sayr**vee**tseeoa dee lahvahnday**ree**ah |
| room service | **il servizio nella stanza** | eel sayr**vee**tseeoa **nayl**lah **stahn**tsah |
| hot water | **l'acqua calda** | **lahk**kwah **kahl**dah |
| running water | **l'acqua corrente** | **lahk**kwah kor**rain**tay |
| a private toilet | **il gabinetto privato** | eel gahbee**nayt**toa pree**vaa**toa |

CHECKING OUT, see page 31

| | | |
|---|---|---|
| Could you put an extra bed in the room? | **Può mettere un altro letto nella camera?** | pwo **may**ttehray oon **ahl**troa **leh**ttoa **nayl**lah **kaa**mayrah |

## How much? *Quanto?*

| | | |
|---|---|---|
| What's the price ...? | **Qual è il prezzo ...?** | kwahl ai eel **preh**ttsoa |
| per night | **per una notte** | pair **oo**nah **no**ttay |
| per week | **per una settimana** | pair **oo**nah saytteemaanah |
| for bed and breakfast | **per la camera e la colazione** | pair lah **kaa**mayrah ay lah koalahtseeoanay |
| excluding meals | **pasti esclusi** | **paa**stee ay**skloo**zee |
| for full board (A.P.) | **per la pensione completa** | pair lah paynseeoanay koam**play**tah |
| for half board (M.A.P.) | **per mezza pensione** | pair **meh**dzah paynseeoanay |
| Does that include ...? | **Il prezzo comprende ...?** | eel **preh**ttsoa koam**prayn**day |
| breakfast | **la colazione** | lah koalahtsee**oa**nay |
| service | **il servizio** | eel sayr**vee**tseeoa |
| value-added tax (VAT)* | **l'I.V.A.** | **lee**vah |
| Is there any reduction for children? | **C'è una riduzione per i bambini?** | chai **oo**nah reedootsee-**oa**nay pair ee bahm**bee**nee |
| Do you charge for the baby? | **Fate pagare per il bambino?** | **faa**tay pah**gaa**ray pair eel bahm**bee**noa |
| That's too expensive. | **È troppo caro.** | ai **tro**ppoa **kaa**roa |
| Haven't you anything cheaper? | **Non ha nulla di meno caro?** | noan ah **nool**lah dee **mai**noa **kaa**roa |

## How long *Quanto tempo?*

| | | |
|---|---|---|
| We'll be staying ... | **Resteremo ...** | raystay**ray**moa |
| overnight only | **una notte** | **oo**nah **no**ttay |
| a few days | **qualche giorno** | **kwahl**kay **joar**noa |
| a week (at least) | **una settimana (come minimo)** | **oo**nah saytte**e**maanah (**koa**may **mee**neemoa) |
| I don't know yet. | **Non ho ancora deciso.** | noan oa ahng**koa**rah day**chee**soa |

* Americans note: a type of sales tax in Italy.

NUMBERS, see page 147

## Decision *Decisione*

| | | |
|---|---|---|
| May I see the room? | **Posso vedere la camera?** | possoa vay**day**ray lah **kaa**mayrah |
| That's fine. I'll take it. | **Va bene, la prendo.** | vah **bai**nay lah **prehn**doa |
| No, I don't like it. | **No, non mi piace.** | noa noan mee pee**ah**chay |
| It's too ... | **È troppo ...** | ai **trop**poa |
| cold/hot<br>dark/small<br>noisy | **fredda/calda**<br>**buia/piccola**<br>**rumorosa** | **frayd**dah/**kahl**dah<br>**boo**eeah/**peek**koalah<br>roomoa**roa**zah |
| I asked for a room with a bath. | **Ho chiesto una camera con bagno.** | oa kee**eh**stoa **oo**nah **kaa**mayrah kon **baa**ñoa |
| Do you have anything ...? | **Ha qualcosa ...?** | ah kwahl**kaw**sah |
| better<br>bigger<br>cheaper<br>quieter | **migliore**<br>**più grande**<br>**meno caro**<br>**più tranquillo** | mee**lyoa**ray<br>pee**oo grahn**day<br>**mai**noa **kaa**roa<br>pee**oo** trahngkoo**eel**loa |
| Do you have a room with a better view? | **Ha una camera con una vista più bella?** | ah **oo**nah **kaa**mayrah kon **oo**nah **vee**stah pee**oo bail**lah |

## Registration *Registrazione*

Upon arrival at a hotel or boarding house you'll be asked to fill in a registration form (*una scheda*—**oo**nah **skay**dah).

| | |
|---|---|
| **Cognome/Nome** | Name/First name |
| **Domicilio/Strada/N°** | Home address/Street/Number |
| **Cittadinanza/Professione** | Nationality/Profession |
| **Data/Luogo di nascita** | Date/Place of birth |
| **Proveniente da .../Diretto a ...** | From .../To ... |
| **Numero di passaporto** | Passport number |
| **Luogo/Data** | Place/Date |
| **Firma** | Signature |

| | | |
|---|---|---|
| What does this mean? | **Cosa significa questo?** | **kaw**sah see**ñee**feekah koo**ay**stoa |

| | |
|---|---|
| **Mi può mostrare il passaporto?** | May I see your passport? |
| **Vuol compilare la scheda, per cortesia?** | Would you mind filling in this registration form? |
| **Firmi qui, per favore.** | Sign here, please. |
| **Quanto tempo si trattiene?** | How long will you be staying? |

| | | |
|---|---|---|
| What's my room number? | **Qual è il numero della mia stanza?** | kwahl ai eel **noo**mayroa **dayl**lah **mee**ah **stahn**tsah |
| Will you have our luggage sent up? | **Può far portare su i nostri bagagli?** | pwo faar por**taa**ray soo ee **no**stree bah**gaa**lyee |
| Where can I park my car? | **Dove posso parcheggiare la macchina?** | **doa**vay **pos**soa pahrkayd**jaa**ray lah **mahk**keenah |
| Does the hotel have a garage? | **L'albergo ha il garage?** | lahl**bayr**goa ah eel gah**raazh** |
| I'd like to leave this in your safe. | **Vorrei depositare questo nella vostra cassaforte.** | vor**rai**ee daypozee**taa**ray koo**ay**stoa **nayl**lah **vo**strah kahssah**for**tay |

## Hotel staff *Personale d'albergo*

| | | |
|---|---|---|
| hall porter | **il portiere** | eel pawrtee**ay**ray |
| maid | **la cameriera (nelle camere)** | lah kahmayree**ay**rah (**nayl**lay **kaa**mayray) |
| manager | **il direttore** | eel deereht**toa**ray |
| page (bellboy) | **il fattorino** | eel fahtto**ree**noa |
| porter | **il facchino** | eel fahk**kee**noa |
| receptionist | **il capo ricevimento** | eel **kah**poa reechayvee**mayn**toa |
| switchboard operator | **il (la) centralinista** | eel (lah) chayntrahlee**nee**stah |
| waiter | **il cameriere** | eel kahmayree**ay**ray |
| waitress | **la cameriera** | lah kahmayree**ay**rah |

## General requirements *Richieste generali*

| | | |
|---|---|---|
| The key, please. | **La chiave, per favore.** | lah kee**aa**vay pair fah**voa**ray |
| Will you please wake me at ...? | **Potrebbe svegliarmi alle ...?** | poa**trehb**bay zvay**lyaar**mee **ahl**lay |

TELLING THE TIME, see page 153

| | | |
|---|---|---|
| Is there a bath on this floor? | **C'è un bagno a questo piano?** | chai oon **baa**ñoa ah koo**ay**stoa pee**aa**noa |
| What's the voltage here? | **Qual è il voltaggio?** | kwahl ai eel voal**tahd**joa |
| Where's the outlet for the shaver? | **Dov'è la presa per il rasoio?** | doa**vai** lah **pray**zah pair eel rah**zoa**eeoa |
| Can we have breakfast in our room? | **Possiamo avere la colazione in camera?** | possee**aa**moa ah**vay**ray lah koalahtsee**oa**nay een **kaa**mayrah |
| Can you find me a ...? | **Può trovarmi ...?** | pwo traw**vahr**mee |
| babysitter | **una babysitter** | **oo**nah "babysitter" |
| secretary | **una segretaria** | **oo**nah saygray**taa**reeah |
| typewriter | **una macchina per scrivere** | **oo**nah **mahk**keenah pair **skree**vayray |
| May I have a/an/some ...? | **Posso avere ...?** | **pos**soa ah**vay**ray |
| ashtray | **un portacenere** | oon portah**chay**nayray |
| bath towel | **un asciugamano** | oon ahshoogah**maa**noa |
| (extra) blanket | **una coperta (in più)** | **oo**nah ko**pehr**tah (een pee**oo**) |
| envelopes | **delle buste** | **dayl**lay **boo**stay |
| (more) hangers | **degli attaccapanni (in più)** | **day**lyee ahttahkkah**pahn**nee (een pee**oo**) |
| hot-water bottle | **una borsa dell'acqua calda** | **oo**nah **boar**sah dehl**lahk**-kwah **kahl**dah |
| ice cubes | **dei cubetti di ghiaccio** | **dai**ee koo**beht**tee dee gee**aht**choa |
| needle and thread | **un ago e del filo** | oon **aa**goa ay dayl **fee**loa |
| (extra) pillow | **un guanciale (in più)** | oon gwahn**chaa**lay (een pee**oo**) |
| reading-lamp | **una lampada** | **oo**nah **lahm**pahdah |
| soap | **una saponetta** | **oo**nah sahpoa**neht**tah |
| writing-paper | **della carta da lettere** | **dayl**lah **kahr**tah dah **leht**tayray |
| Where's the ...? | **Dov'è ...?** | doa**vai** |
| bathroom | **il bagno** | eel **baa**ñoa |
| dining-room | **la sala da pranzo** | lah **saa**lah dah **prahn**dzoa |
| emergency exit | **l'uscita di sicurezza** | loo**shee**tah dee seekoo**reht**sah |
| hairdresser's | **il parrucchiere** | eel pahrrookkee**ay**ray |
| lift (elevator) | **l'ascensore** | lahshayn**soa**ray |
| Where are the toilets? | **Dove sono i gabinetti?** | **doa**vay **soa**noa ee gahbee**neht**tee |

BREAKFAST, see page 38

## Telephone—Mail—Messages *Telefono—Posta—Messaggi*

| | | |
|---|---|---|
| Can you get me Rome 123-45-67? | **Può passarmi Roma 123-45-67?** | pwo pahs**sahr**mee **roa**mah 123-45-67 |
| How much are my telephone charges? | **Quanto devo pagare per la telefonata?** | **kwahn**toa **day**voa pah**gaa**ray pair lah taylayfoa**naa**tah |
| Do you have stamps? | **Ha dei francobolli?** | ah **dai**ee frahngkoa**boal**lee |
| Would you please mail this for me? | **Può spedirmi questo, per favore?** | pwo spay**deer**mee koo**ay**stoa pair fah**voa**ray |
| Are there any messages for me? | **Vi sono messaggi per me?** | vee **soa**noa mays**sah**djee pair mai |
| Is there any mail for me? | **C'è posta per me?** | chai **pos**tah pair mai |

## Difficulties *Difficoltà*

| | | |
|---|---|---|
| The... doesn't work. | **... non funziona.** | ... noan foontsee**oa**nah |
| air conditioner | **il condizionatore d'aria** | eel koandeetseeoanah**toa**ray **daa**reeah |
| fan | **il ventilatore** | eel vaynteelah**toa**ray |
| heating | **il riscaldamento** | eel reeskahldah**mayn**toa |
| light | **la luce** | lah **loo**chay |
| radio | **la radio** | lah **raa**deeoa |
| television | **il televisore** | eel taylayvee**zoa**ray |
| The water tap is dripping. | **Il rubinetto sgocciola.** | eel roobee**neht**toa **zgot**choalah |
| There's no hot water. | **Non c'è acqua calda.** | noan chai **ahk**kwah **kahl**dah |
| The wash-basin is clogged. | **Il lavabo è otturato.** | eel lah**vaa**boa ai ottoo**raa**toa |
| The window is jammed. | **La finestra è incastrata.** | lah fee**neh**strah ai eengkah**straa**tah |
| The curtains are stuck. | **Le tende sono bloccate.** | lay **tayn**day **soa**noa blok**kaa**tay |
| The bulb is burned out. | **La lampadina è bruciata.** | lah lahmpah**dee**nah ai broo**chaa**tah |
| My room has not been made up. | **La mia camera non è stata rifatta.** | lah **mee**ah **kaa**mayrah noan ai **staa**tah ree**faht**tah |

POST OFFICE AND TELEPHONE, see page 132

| | | |
|---|---|---|
| The ... is broken. | **... è rotto(a).** | ... ai **rot**toa(ah) |
| blind | **la persiana** | lah pairsee**aa**nah |
| lamp | **la lampada** | lah **lahm**pahdah |
| plug | **la spina** | lah **spee**nah |
| shutter | **l'imposta** | leem**poa**stah |
| switch | **l'interruttore** | leentayrroot**toa**ray |
| Can you get it repaired? | **Può ripararlo(la)?** | pwo reepah**rahr**loa(lah) |

## Laundry—Dry cleaner's *Lavanderia—Lavanderia a secco*

| | | |
|---|---|---|
| I want these clothes ... | **Voglio far ... questi abiti.** | **vo**lyoa faar ... koo**ay**stee **aa**beetee |
| cleaned | **pulire** | poo**lee**ray |
| ironed | **stirare** | stee**raa**ray |
| pressed | **stirare a vapore** | stee**raa**ray ah vah**poa**ray |
| washed | **lavare** | lah**vaa**ray |
| When will they be ready? | **Quando saranno pronti?** | **kwahn**doa sah**rahn**noa **proan**tee |
| I need them ... | **Ne ho bisogno ...** | nay oa bee**zoa**ñoa |
| tonight | **stasera** | stah**say**rah |
| tomorrow | **domani** | doa**maa**nee |
| before Friday | **prima di venerdì** | **pree**mah dee vaynayr**dee** |
| Can you ... this? | **Mi può ... questo?** | mee pwo ... koo**ay**stoa |
| mend | **rammendare** | rahmmayn**daa**ray |
| patch | **rappezzare** | rappeht**tsaa**ray |
| stitch | **cucire** | koo**chee**ray |
| Can you sew on this button? | **Può attaccare questo bottone?** | pwo ahttahk**kaa**ray koo**ay**stoa boat**toa**nay |
| Can you get this stain out? | **Mi può togliere questa macchia?** | mee pwo **to**lyayray koo**ay**stah **mahk**keeah |
| Can this be invisibly mended? | **Mi può fare un rammendo invisibile?** | mee pwo **faa**ray oon rahm**mayn**doa eenvee**zee**beelay |
| Is my laundry ready? | **È pronta la mia biancheria?** | ai **pron**tah lah **mee**ah beeahngkay**ree**ah |
| This isn't mine. | **Questo non è mio.** | koo**ay**stoa noan ai **mee**oa |
| There's something missing. | **Manca un capo.** | **mahng**kah oon **kaa**poa |
| There's a hole in this. | **C'è un buco in questo.** | chai oon **boo**koa een koo**ay**stoa |

## Hairdresser—Barber *Parrucchiere—Barbiere*

| | | |
|---|---|---|
| Is there a hairdresser/ beauty salon in the hotel? | **C'è il parrucchiere/ l'istituto di bellezza nell'albergo?** | chai eel pahrrookkee**ay**ray/ leestee**too**toa dee behl**leht**tsah nayllahl**bayr**goa |
| Can I make an appointment for Thursday? | **Posso avere un appuntamento per giovedì?** | **pos**soa ahv**ay**ray oon ahppoontah**mayn**toa pair joavay**dee** |
| I'd like it cut and shaped. | **Vorrei il taglio e la messa in piega.** | vor**rai**ee eel **taal**yoa ay lah **mays**sah een pee**ay**gah |
| I want a haircut, please. | **Voglio il taglio dei capelli, per favore.** | **vol**yoa eel **taal**yoa **dai**ee kah**pehl**lee pair fah**voa**ray |
| bleach | **una decolorazione** | **oo**nah daykoaloaraht**see**oanay |
| blow-dry | **l'asciugatura col fono** | lashoogah**too**rah kol **faw**no |
| colour rinse | **un cachet** | oon kah**shay** |
| dye | **una tintura** | **oo**nah teen**too**rah |
| face-pack | **la maschera di bellezza** | lah **mah**skayrah dee behl**leht**tsah |
| manicure | **la manicure** | lah mahnee**koor** |
| permanent wave | **la permanente** | lah pairmah**nayn**tay |
| setting lotion | **un fissatore** | oon feessah**toa**ray |
| shampoo and set | **shampoo e messa in piega** | "shampoo" ay **mays**sah een pee**ay**gah |
| with a fringe (bangs) | **con la frangia** | kon lah **frahn**jah |
| I'd like a shampoo for ... hair. | **Vorrei uno shampoo per capelli ...** | vor**rai**ee **oo**noa "shampoo" pair kah**pehl**lee |
| normal/dry/ greasy (oily) | **normali/secchi/ grassi** | noar**maa**lee/**sayk**kee/ **grahs**see |
| Do you have a colour chart? | **Avete una tabella dei colori?** | ah**vay**tay **oo**nah tah**bayl**lah **dai**ee koa**loa**ree |
| Don't cut it too short. | **Non li tagli troppo corti.** | noan lee **taal**yee **trop**poa **koar**tee |
| A little more off the ... | **Ancora un po'...** | ahng**koa**rah oon po |
| back | **dietro** | dee**ay**troa |
| neck | **sul collo** | sool **kol**loa |
| sides | **ai lati** | **ahee laa**tee |
| top | **in cima** | een **chee**mah |
| I don't want any hairspray. | **Non voglio lacca.** | noan **vol**yoa **lahk**kah |

DAYS OF THE WEEK, see page 151

| | | |
|---|---|---|
| I'd like a shave. | **Vorrei che mi radesse.** | vor**rai**ee kay mee rah**days**say |
| Would you please trim my ...? | **Per favore, vuole spuntarmi ...?** | pair fah**voa**ray **vwaw**lay spoon**tahr**mee |
| beard | **la barba** | lah **bahr**bah |
| moustache | **i baffi** | ee **bahf**fee |
| sideboards (sideburns) | **le basette** | lay bah**zayt**tay |

## **Checking out** *Partenza*

| | | |
|---|---|---|
| May I please have my bill? | **Posso avere il conto, per favore?** | **pos**soa ah**vay**ray eel **koan**toa pair fah**voa**ray |
| I'm leaving early in the morning. Please have my bill ready. | **Partirò domani mattina presto. Mi prepari il conto, per favore.** | pahrtee**roa** doa**maa**nee maht**tee**nah **preh**stoa. mee pray**paa**ree eel **koan**toa pair fah**voa**ray |
| We'll be checking out around noon. | **Partiremo verso mezzogiorno.** | pahrtee**ray**moa **vehr**soa mehdzoa**joar**noa |
| I must leave at once. | **Devo partire immediatamente.** | **day**voa pahr**tee**ray eemmaydeeahtah**mayn**tay |
| Is everything included? | **È tutto incluso?** | ai **toot**toa eeng**kloo**zoa |
| Can I pay by credit card? | **Posso pagare con la carta di credito?** | **pos**soa pah**gaa**ray kon lah **kahr**tah dee **kray**deetoa |
| You've made a mistake in this bill, I think. | **Ha fatto un errore nel conto, credo.** | ah **faht**toa oon ehr**roa**ray nayl **koan**toa **kray**doa |
| Can you get us a taxi? | **Può chiamarci un taxi?** | pwo keeah**mahr**chee oon "taxi" |
| Would you send someone to bring down our luggage? | **Può mandare qualcuno a portare giù i nostri bagagli?** | pwo mahn**daa**ray kwahl**koo**noa ah por**taa**ray joo ee **no**stree bah**gaa**lyee |
| Here's the forwarding address. | **Ecco il mio prossimo indirizzo.** | **ehk**koa eel **mee**oa **pros**seemoa eendee**reet**tsoa |
| You have my home address. | **Avete il mio indirizzo abituale.** | ah**vay**tay eel **mee**oa eendee**reet**tsoa ahbeetoo**aa**lay |
| It's been a very enjoyable stay. | **È stato un soggiorno molto piacevole.** | ai **staa**toa oon soad**joar**noa **moal**toa peeah**chay**voalay |

TIPPING, see inside back-cover

## Camping *Campeggio*

In Italy there are many authorized camping sites with excellent facilities. Most camp sites are equipped with water, electricity and toilets. You will find them listed in the telephone directory, under *Campeggio*. The local tourist office has a list of sites, tariffs and facilities available. The Touring Club Italiano also publish a list of campsites and touristic villages. It is on sale in bookshops.

| | | |
|---|---|---|
| Is there a camp site near here? | **C'è un campeggio qui vicino?** | chai oon kahm**payd**joa kooee vee**chee**noa |
| Can we camp here? | **Possiamo campeggiare qui?** | possee**aa**moa kahmpay**djaa**ray koo**ee** |
| Have you room for a tent/caravan (trailer)? | **C'è posto per una tenda/una roulotte?** | chai **poa**stoa pair **oo**nah **tain**dah/**oo**nah roo**lot** |
| What's the charge...? | **Quanto si paga ...?** | **kwahn**toa see **paa**gah |
| per day | **al giorno** | ahl **joar**noa |
| per person | **per persona** | pair payr**soa**nah |
| for a car | **per una macchina** | pair **oo**nah **mahk**keenah |
| for a tent | **per una tenda** | pair **oo**nah **tain**dah |
| for a caravan (trailer) | **per una roulotte** | pair **oo**nah roo**lot** |
| Is the tourist tax included? | **È compresa la tassa di soggiorno?** | ai koam**pray**sah lah **tahs**sah dee soa**djoar**noa |
| Is there/Are there (a) ...? | **C'è/Ci sono ...?** | chai/chee **soa**noa |
| drinking water | **l'acqua potabile** | **lahk**kwah poa**taa**beelay |
| electricity | **l'elettricità** | laylehttreechee**tah** |
| playground | **il parco giochi** | eel **pahr**koa **joa**kee |
| restaurant | **il ristorante** | eel reestoa**rahn**tay |
| shopping facilities | **dei negozi** | **dai**ee nay**go**tsee |
| swimming pool | **la piscina** | lah pee**shee**nah |
| Where are the showers/toilets? | **Dove sono le docce/i gabinetti?** | **doa**vay **soa**noa lay **dot**chay/ee gahbee**nayt**tee |
| Where can I get butane gas? | **Dove posso trovare del gas butano?** | **doa**vay **pos**soa tro**vaa**ray dayl gahz boo**taa**noa |
| Is there a youth hostel near here? | **C'è un ostello della gioventù qui vicino?** | chai oon oa**stehl**loa **dayl**lah joavayn**too** koo**ee** vee**chee**noa |

CAMPING EQUIPMENT, see page 106

# Eating out

There are various types of places to eat and drink in Italy. Here are some of them:

**Autogrill** (**ow**toagreel) — large restaurant on a motorway (expressway); usually table and cafeteria service available.

**Bar** (bahr) — bar; can be found on virtually every street corner; coffee and drinks served. In most of them you first have to get a ticket from the cashier. Then you go to the counter and order what you want. Only a few bars have tables and chairs. If you want to be served at a table, the charge for your drinks and food will be somewhat higher.

**Caffè** (kahf**fai**) — coffee shop; generally food isn't served there except for breakfast. If it offers *panini o toasts* you'll be able to get a snack. Coffee shops always serve alcoholic beverages.

**Gelateria** (jaylahtay**ree**ah) — ice-cream parlour; Italian ice-cream is very tasty, rich and creamy, often reminiscent of old-fashioned, homemade ice-cream.

**Locanda** (lo**kahn**dah) — simple restaurants serving local dishes.

**Osteria** (oastay**ree**ah) — inn; wine and simple food are served.

**Paninoteca** (pahneenoa**tay**kah) — a sort of coffee shop where you can find a great variety of sandwiches *(panini)* served hot or cold.

**Pizzeria** (peettsay**ree**ah) — pizza parlour; often other dishes are served, too.

**Ristorante** (reestoa**rahn**tay) — You'll encounter restaurants classified by stars, forks and knives and endorsed by everyone including travel agencies, automobile associations and gastronomic guilds. Bear in mind that any form of classification is relative. Some restaurants are judged according to their fancy décor while others—linen and chandeliers aside—are rated merely by the quality of their cooking.

**Rosticceria** (roasteetchay**ree**ah) — originally, it was a shop specializing in grilled meats, chicken and fish. But today *rosticcerie* often have tables where you eat grilled food on the premises.

**Sala da tè** (**saa**lah dah tai) — serves ice-cream and pastries.

**Taverna** (tah**vehr**nah) — a more modest type of *trattoria.*

**Tavola calda** (**taa**voalah **kahl**dah) — "hot table"; a cafeteria-style restaurant serving hot dishes at fairly low prices. They're usually crowded but quick; you may have to eat standing up.

**Trattoria** (trahttoa**ree**ah) — a medium-priced restaurant serving meals and drink. The food is simple but can be surprisingly good if you happen to hit upon the right place.

Most restaurants display a menu in the window. Many offer a tourist menu *(menù turistico),* a fixed-price three- or four-course meal with limited choice, or the speciality of the day *(piatto del giorno).*

All restaurants, no matter how modest, must now issue a formal bill *(la ricevuta fiscale)* with VAT, or sales tax *(I.V.A.).* A customer may actually be stopped outside the premises and fined if he cannot produce this receipt. The bill usually includes cover *(il coperto)* and service *(il servizio)* charges as well.

### Meal times *Orari dei pasti*

Breakfast (*la colazione*—lah kolahtsee**oa**nay) at the hotel is normally served from 7 to 10 a.m. (See page 38 for a breakfast menu.)

Lunch (*il pranzo*—eel **prahn**dzoa) is served from 12.30 to 2 p.m.

Dinner (*la cena*—lah **chay**nah) begins at 7 or 8 p.m., but hotels tend to open their dining rooms earlier for the foreign tourists.

TIPPING, see inside back-cover

*Note:* The names of meals can be confusing. Lunch is sometimes called *colazione* and dinner *pranzo,* especially in towns. If you are invited out, make sure of the time, so you don't turn up at the wrong meal.

### **Italian cuisine** *Cucina italiana*

To many foreigners, Italian cooking means *spaghetti, macaroni, tagliatelle*... in other words, pasta. In fact, you will be amazed at the rich variety available: tasty hors d'œuvres, long-simmered soups, traditional meat dishes, fresh fish and shellfish, high-quality poultry, an incredible number of cheeses, not to mention the magnificent cakes and ice-cream.

Each region has its own speciality, never lacking in flavour or originality, inspired by sun-drenched fruit and vegetables. Italian cooking is like the country itself: colourful, happy, generous, exuberant.

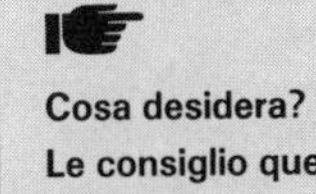

| | |
|---|---|
| **Cosa desidera?** | What would you like? |
| **Le consiglio questo.** | I recommend this. |
| **Cosa desidera da bere?** | What would you like to drink? |
| **Non abbiamo ...** | We haven't got ... |
| **Vuole ...?** | Do you want ...? |

### **Hungry?** *Ha fame?*

| | | |
|---|---|---|
| I'm hungry/I'm thirsty. | **Ho fame/Ho sete.** | oa **faa**may/oa **say**tay |
| Can you recommend a good restaurant? | **Può consigliarmi un buon ristorante?** | pwo koanseel**yaar**mee oon bwon reestoa**rahn**tay |
| Are there any inexpensive restaurants around here? | **Vi sono dei ristoranti economici qui vicino?** | vee **soa**noa **dai**ee reestoa**rahn**tee aykoa**naw**meechee koo**ee** vee**chee**noa |

If you want to be sure of getting a table in a well-known restaurant, it may be better to telephone in advance.

| | | |
|---|---|---|
| I'd like to reserve a table for 4. | **Vorrei riservare un tavolo per 4.** | vorr**aiee** reesehr**vaa**ray oon **taa**voala pair 4 |
| We'll come at 8. | **Verremo alle 8.** | vayr**ray**moa **ahl**lay 8 |
| Could we have a table ...? | **Potremmo avere un tavolo ...?** | poa**traym**moa ah**vay**ray oon **taa**voaloa |
| in the corner | **d'angolo** | **dahng**goaloa |
| by the window | **vicino alla finestra** | vee**chee**noa **ahl**lah fee**nay**strah |
| outside | **all'aperto** | ahllah**pehr**toa |
| on the terrace | **sulla terrazza** | **sool**lah tayr**raht**tsah |
| in a non-smoking area | **nel settore per non fumatori** | nayl seht**toa**ray pair noan foomah**toa**ree |

## Asking and ordering *Chiedere e ordinare*

| | | |
|---|---|---|
| Waiter/Waitress! | **Cameriere/ Cameriera!** | kahmayree**ai**ray/kahmayree**ai**rah |
| I'd like something to eat/drink. | **Vorrei mangiare/bere qualcosa.** | vorr**aiee** mahn**jaa**ray/ **bay**ray kwahl**kaw**sah |
| May I have the menu, please? | **Posso avere il menù?** | **pos**soa ah**vay**ray eel may**noo** |
| Do you have a set menu/local dishes? | **Avete un menù a prezzo fisso/dei piatti locali?** | ah**vay**tay oon may**noo** ah **preht**tsoa **fees**soa/**dai**ee pee**aht**tee loa**kaa**lee |
| What do you recommend? | **Cosa consiglia?** | **kaw**sah kon**see**lyah |
| I'd like ... | **Vorrei ...** | vorr**aiee** |
| Could we have a/ an ..., please? | **Potremmo avere ..., per favore?** | poa**traym**moa ah**vay**ray ... pair fah**voa**ray |
| ashtray | **un portacenere** | oon portah**chay**nayray |
| cup | **una tazza** | **oo**nah **taht**tsah |
| extra chair | **una sedia in più** | **oo**nah **sai**deeah een pee**oo** |
| fork | **una forchetta** | **oo**nah for**keht**tah |
| glass | **un bicchiere** | oon beekkee**ai**ray |
| knife | **un coltello** | oon koal**tehl**loa |
| napkin (serviette) | **un tovagliolo** | oon toavah**lyaw**loa |
| plate | **un piatto** | oon pee**aht**toa |
| spoon | **un cucchiaio** | oon kookkee**aa**eeoa |
| May I have some ...? | **Potrei avere ...?** | poa**trai**ee ah**vay**ray |
| bread | **del pane** | dayl **paa**nay |
| butter | **del burro** | dayl **boor**roa |

NUMBERS, see page 147

| | | |
|---|---|---|
| lemon | **del limone** | dayl lee**moa**nay |
| mustard | **della senape** | **dayl**lah **say**nahpay |
| oil | **dell'olio** | **dayl**lolyoa |
| pepper | **del pepe** | dayl **pay**pay |
| salt | **del sale** | dayl **saa**lay |
| seasoning | **del condimento** | dayl koandee**mayn**toa |
| sugar | **dello zucchero** | **dayl**loa **tsook**kayroa |
| vinegar | **dell'aceto** | dayllah**chay**toa |

Some useful expressions for dieters or those with special requirements:

| | | |
|---|---|---|
| I'm on a diet. | **Sono a dieta.** | **soa**noa ah dee**ay**tah |
| I mustn't eat food containing ... | **Non devo mangiare cibi che contengono ...** | noan **day**voa mahn**jaa**ray **chee**bee kay koan**tayng**goanoa |
| flour/fat | **farina/grasso** | fah**ree**nah/**grahs**soa |
| salt/sugar | **sale/zucchero** | **saa**lay/**tsook**kayroa |
| Do you have ... for diabetics? | **Avete ... per diabetici?** | ah**vay**tay ... pair deeah**bai**teechee |
| cakes | **dei dolci** | **daiee doal**chee |
| fruit juice | **del succo di frutta** | dayl **sook**koa dee **froot**tah |
| special menu | **un menù speciale** | oon may**noo** spay**chaa**lay |
| Do you have vegetarian dishes? | **Avete dei piatti vegetariani?** | ah**vay**tay **daiee** pee**aht**tee vayjaytahree**aa**nee |
| Could I have ... instead of the dessert? | **Potrei avere ... invece del dessert?** | po**trai**ee ah**vay**ray ... een**vay**chay dayl day**ssehr** |
| Can I have an artificial sweetener? | **Posso avere del dolcificante?** | **pos**soa ah**vay**ray dayl doalcheefee**kahn**tay |

## And ...

| | | |
|---|---|---|
| I'd like some more. | **Ne vorrei ancora.** | nai vor**rai**ee ahng**koa**rah |
| Can I have more ..., please. | **Posso avere ancora un po' di ...?** | **pos**soa ah**vay**ray ahng**koa**rah oon po dee |
| Just a small portion. | **Una piccola porzione.** | **oo**nah **peek**koalah poart**see**oanay |
| Nothing more, thanks. | **Nient'altro, grazie.** | neeayn**tahl**troa **graat**seeay |
| Where are the toilets? | **Dove sono i gabinetti?** | **doa**vay **soa**noa ee gahbee**nayt**tee |

## Breakfast *Colazione*

Italians just have a *cappuccino* and a brioche for breakfast. Hotels usually propose coffee or tea, bread, butter and jam. You can ask for fruit juice, an egg and toast, if you like a more copious breakfast.

| | | |
|---|---|---|
| I'd like breakfast, please. | **Vorrei fare colazione.** | vor**rai**ee **faa**ray kolah-tsee**oa**nay |
| I'll have a/an/ some ... | **Desidero ...** | day**zee**dayroa |
| bacon and eggs | **uova e pancetta** | **waw**vah ay pahn**cheht**tah |
| boiled egg | **un uovo alla coque** | oon **waw**voa **ahl**lah kok |
| soft/hard | **molle/sodo** | **mol**lay/**so**doa |
| cereal | **dei cereali** | **dai**ee chehreh**aa**lee |
| eggs | **delle uova** | **day**llay **waw**vah |
| fried eggs | **delle uova fritte** | **day**llay **waw**vah **freet**tay |
| scrambled eggs | **delle uova strapazzate** | **day**llay **waw**vah strahpahtt**saa**tay |
| fruit juice | **un succo di frutta** | oon **sook**koa dee **froot**tah |
| grapefruit | **pompelmo** | pom**payl**moa |
| orange | **arancia** | ah**rahn**chah |
| ham and eggs | **uova e prosciutto** | **waw**vah ay proa**shoot**toa |
| jam | **della marmellata** | **dayl**lah mahrmayl**laa**tah |
| marmalade | **della marmellata d'arance** | **dayl**lah mahrmayl**laa**tah dah**rahn**chay |
| toast | **del pane tostato** | dayl **paa**nay tos**taa**toa |
| May I have some ...? | **Posso avere ...?** | **pos**soa ah**vay**ray |
| bread | **del pane** | dayl **paa**nay |
| butter | **del burro** | dayl **boor**roa |
| (hot) chocolate | **una cioccolata (calda)** | **oo**nah choakkoa**laa**tah (**kahl**dah) |
| coffee | **un caffè** | oon kahf**fai** |
| caffein-free | **decaffeinato** | daykahffehee**naa**toa |
| black | **nero** | **nay**roa |
| with milk | **macchiato** | mahkkee**aa**toa |
| honey | **del miele** | dayl mee**ay**lay |
| milk | **del latte** | dayl **laht**tay |
| cold/hot | **freddo/caldo** | **frayd**doa/**kahl**doa |
| rolls | **dei panini** | **dai**ee pah**nee**nee |
| tea | **del tè** | dayl tai |
| with milk | **con latte** | kon **laht**tay |
| with lemon | **con limone** | kon lee**moa**nay |
| (hot) water | **dell'acqua (calda)** | dayl**lahk**kwah (**kahl**dah) |

**What's on the menu?** *Che c'è sul menù?*

Under the headings below you'll find alphabetical lists of dishes that might be offered on an Italian menu with their English equivalent. You can simply show the book to the waiter. If you want some cheese, for instance, let *him* point to what's available on the appropriate list. Use pages 36 and 37 for ordering in general.



*Note:* Italian cooking remains essentially regional. Each of the nation's 18 regions has its own specialities. There are, of course, many well-known dishes that are common to all Italy. But here again the terminology may vary from place to place. (There are at least half a dozen names for octopus or squid!) So in the lists that follow, be prepared for regional variations.

## Reading the menu *Per leggere il menù*

| | |
|---|---|
| **Menù a prezzo fisso** | Set menu |
| **Piatto del giorno** | Dish of the day |
| **Lo chef consiglia ...** | The chef recommends ... |
| **Specialità della casa** | Specialities of the house |
| **Specialità locali** | Local specialities |
| **Contorno a scelta** | Choice of vegetables |
| **I nostri piatti di carne sono serviti con contorno** | Our meat dishes are accompanied by vegetables |
| **Su ordinazione** | Made to order |
| **Supplemento** | Extra charge |
| **Verdure di stagione** | Vegetables in season |
| **Attesa: 15 minuti** | Waiting time: 15 minutes |
| **Pane, grissini e coperto L. ...** | Bread, *grissini* and cover L. ... |
| **A scelta** | Choice |
| **Piatti freddi** | Cold dishes |

| | | |
|---|---|---|
| **antipasti** | ahnteepahstee | hors d'œuvres |
| **bevande** | bayvahnday | drinks |
| **cacciagione** | kahtchahjoanay | game |
| **carne** | kahrnay | meat |
| **carne ai ferri** | kahrnay ahee fehrree | grilled meat |
| **crostacei** | kroastahchayee | shellfish |
| **dessert** | dayssehr | dessert |
| **formaggi** | foarmahdjee | cheese |
| **frutta** | froottah | fruit |
| **frutti di mare** | froottee dee maaray | seafood |
| **gelati** | jaylaatee | ice-cream |
| **insalate** | eensahlaatay | salads |
| **minestre** | meenehstray | soups |
| **pastasciutta** | pahstahshoottah | pasta |
| **pesci** | payshee | fish |
| **pollame** | poallaamay | poultry |
| **primi piatti** | preemee peeahttee | first course |
| **riso** | reezoa | rice |
| **secondi piatti** | saykoandee peeahttee | second (main) course |
| **verdure** | vehrdooray | vegetables |
| **vini** | veenee | wines |

## Appetizers *Antipasti*

| | | |
|---|---|---|
| I'd like an appetizer. | **Vorrei un antipasto.** | vorr**aiee** oon ahntee**pah**stoa |
| **acciughe** | aht**choo**gay | anchovies |
| **affettati misti** | ahffayt**taa**tee **mee**stee | cold cuts of pork |
| **antipasto assortito** | ahntee**pah**toa ahssoar**tee**toa | assorted appetizer |
| **carciofi** | kahr**cho**fee | artichokes |
| **caviale** | kahvee**aa**lay | caviar |
| **coppa** | **koa**ppah | cured pork shoulder |
| **frutti di mare** | **froo**ttee dee **maa**ray | mixed seafood |
| **gamberetti** | gahmbay**ray**ttee | shrimps |
| **mortadella** | moartah**deh**llah | Bologna sausage |
| **olive** | o**lee**vay | olives |
| **ostriche** | **os**treekay | oysters |
| **prosciutto** | proa**shoo**ttoa | ham |
| **cotto** | **ko**ttoa | cooked ham |
| **crudo di Parma** | **kroo**doa dee **pahr**mah | cured ham from Parma |
| **salame** | sah**laa**may | salami |
| **salmone affumicato** | sahl**moa**nay affoomee**kaa**toa | smoked salmon |
| **sardine all'olio** | sahr**dee**nay ahl**lo**lyoa | sardines in oil |
| **sottaceti** | soattah**chay**tee | pickled vegetables |
| **tonno** | **to**nnoa | tunny in oil |

**bagna cauda** (baa**ñ**ah ka**hoo**dah) raw vegetables accompagnied by a hot sauce made from anchovies, garlic, oil, butter and sometimes truffles (Northern Italy)

**carciofini sottolio** (kahrcho**fee**nee soatt**o**lyoa) artichoke hearts in olive oil

**insalata di frutti di mare** (eensah**laa**tah dee **froot**tee dee **maa**ray) prawns and squid with lemon, pickles and olives

**insalata di pollo** (eensah**laa**tah dee **poa**lloa) chicken salad with green salad, lemon, cream

**insalata russa** (eensah**laa**tah **roo**ssah) diced boiled vegetables in mayonnaise

**mozzarella con pomodori** (motsah**ray**llah kon poamoa**daw**ree) mozzarella cheese with tomatoes, basilic, pepper and olive oil

| | |
|---|---|
| **prosciutto crudo con melone** (proa**shoot**toa **kroo**doa kon may**loa**nay) | sliced melon with cured ham from Parma |

## Pizza

*Pizza* (plural *pizze*) is surely one of Italy's best-known culinary exports. And the variety of toppings is endless, from simple cheese and tomato to assorted seafood. A *calzone* has basically the same ingredients, but the pastry forms a sort of sealed sandwich, with the filling inside.

Here are the best known variations on the theme:

| | |
|---|---|
| **capricciosa** (kahpreet**choa**sah) | the cook's speciality |
| **margherita** (mahrgay**ree**tah) | named after Italy's first queen, the *pizza* ingredients, tomato, cheese and basil, reflect the national colours |
| **napoletana** (nahpoalay**taa**nah) | the classic *pizza* with anchovies, ham, capers, tomatoes, cheese and oregano |
| **quattro stagioni** (**kwaht**troa stah**joa**nee) | "four seasons" – containing a variety of vegetables: tomatoes, artichoke, mushrooms, olives, plus cheese, ham and bacon |
| **siciliana** (seecheelee**aa**nah) | with black olives, capers and cheese |

## Omelets *Frittate*

| | | |
|---|---|---|
| I'd like an omelet. | **Vorrei una frittata.** | vor**rai**ee **oo**nah freet**taa**tah |
| **frittata** | freet**taa**tah | omelet |
| **di asparagi** | dee ah**spaa**rahjee | asparagus |
| **di carciofi** | dee kahr**cho**fee | artichokes |
| **di cipolle** | dee chee**poal**lay | onions |
| **di spinaci** | dee spee**naa**chee | spinach |
| **di zucchine** | dee tsook**kee**nay | dried baby marrow (zucchini) |
| **frittata campagnola** | freet**taa**tah kahmpah**ñoa**lah | an omelet with onion, grated cheese, milk and cream |
| **frittata primaverile** | freet**taa**tah preemahvay**ree**lay | omelet with vegetables |

**Soups** *Minestre, zuppe*

In Italy, soup goes by many names, as the following list shows. Some of them are sufficient for a main course. An Italian meal always includes a soup or a dish of *pastasciutta*.

| | | |
|---|---|---|
| **brodo** | **braw**doa | bouillon, broth, soup |
| **di manzo** | dee **mahn**dzoa | meat broth |
| **di pollo** | dee **poal**loa | chicken broth |
| **busecca** | boo**zayk**kah | thick tripe, vegetable and bean soup |
| **cacciucco** | kaht**chook**koa | spicy seafood stew (chowder) |
| **crema di legumi** | **kreh**mah dee lay**goo**mee | vegetable cream soup |
| **crema di pomodori** | **kreh**mah dee poamoa**daw**ree | tomato cream soup |
| **minestra** | mee**neh**strah | soup |
| **in brodo** | een **braw**doa | bouillon with noodles or rice |
| **di funghi** | dee **foong**gee | cream of mushroom |
| **minestrone** | meeneh**stroa**nay | a thick vegetable soup (sometimes with noodles) sprinkled with parmesan cheese |
| **passato di verdura** | pahs**saa**toa dee vehr**doo**rah | mashed vegetable soup, generally with croutons |
| **pasta e fagioli** | **pah**stah ay fah**joa**lee | noodles and beans |
| **pastina in brodo** | pah**stee**nah een **braw**doa | broth with little noodles |
| **zuppa** | **tsoop**pah | soup |
| **alla cacciatora** | **ahl**lah kahtchah**toa**rah | meat with mushrooms |
| **alla marinara** | **ahl**lah mahree**naa**rah | spicy fish stew (chowder) |
| **alla pavese** | **ahl**lah pah**vay**zay | consommé with poached egg, croutons and grated cheese |
| **alla veneta** | **ahl**lah **vay**naytah | vegetables with white wine and noodles |
| **di datteri di mare** | dee **daht**tayree dee **maa**ray | sea dates (kind of mussel) |
| **di frutti di mare** | dee **froot**tee dee **maa**ray | seafood |
| **di pesce** | dee **pay**shay | spicy fish stew (chowder) |
| **di vongole** | dee **vong**goalay | clams and white wine |

## Pasta

*Pasta* (or *pastasciutta*), the generic name for a wide range of noodles and noodle-related dishes, constitutes the traditional Italian first course. In addition to the well-known *spaghetti,* pasta comes in a bewildering variety of sizes and shapes—ribbons, strings, tubes, shells or stars—known under as many different appellations. It can be served on its own, in broth, with butter or tomato sauce, stuffed with meat, cheese or vegetables, and is often accompanied by a highly flavoured sauce such as those described below.

**agnolotti** (ahñoa**lot**tee) — a round pasta parcel with a filling of chopped meat, vegetables and cheese

**cannelloni** (kahnnay**llaw**nee) — tubular dough stuffed with meat, cheese or vegetables, covered with a white sauce and baked

**cappelletti** (kahppay**llayt**tee) — small ravioli filled with meat, herbs, ham, cheese and eggs

**fettuccine** (fayttoot**chee**nay) — narrow flat noodles

**lasagne** (lah**zaa**ñay) — thin layers of white or green *(lasagne verdi)* dough alternating with tomato sauce and sausage meat, white sauce and grated cheese; baked in the oven

**rigatoni** (reegah**taw**nee) — large macaroni, similar to *cannelloni* but smaller and ridged

**tagliatelle** (tahlyah**tehl**lay) — flat noodles

**tortellini** (toartehl**lee**nee) — rings of dough filled with seasoned minced meat and served in broth or with a sauce

## Sauces *Salse*

It's the sauce that makes spaghetti and macaroni so delicious—Italian cooks are masters of the art.

**aglio, olio, peperoncino** (**ah**lyoa **o**lyoa paypayroan**chee**noa) — garlic, olive oil, sweet peppers, anchovies and parmesan

| | |
|---|---|
| **al burro** (ahl **boor**roa) | with butter and grated parmesan |
| **al sugo** (ahl **soo**goa) | with tomato sauce and grated parmesan |
| **amatriciana** (ahmahtree**chaa**nah) | tomatoes, red peppers, bacon, onions, garlic and white wine |
| **bolognese** (boaloa**ñay**zay) | tomatoes, minced meat, onions and herbs |
| **carbonara** (kahrboa**naa**rah) | smoked ham, cheese, eggs and olive oil |
| **carrettiera** (kahrraytteea**ay**rah) | tuna, mushrooms, tomato purée, freshly ground pepper |
| **marinara** (mahree**naa**rah) | tomatoes, olives, garlic, clams and mussels |
| **pesto** (**pay**stoa) | basil leaves, garlic, cheese, and sometimes pine kernels and marjoram |
| **pommarola** (poammah**raw**lah) | tomatoes, garlic, basil |
| **puttanesca** (poottah**nay**skah) | capers, black olives, parsley, garlic, olive oil, black pepper |
| **ragù** (rah**goo**) | like *bolognese* |
| **con le vongole** (kon lay **voan**goalay) | clams, garlic, parsley, pepper, olive oil, sometimes tomatoes |

## Rice *Riso*

In Northern Italy, a rice dish is often offered as a first course to replace pasta. Cooked on its own or together with vegetables, meat, herbs, fish and/or seafood, rice may also be served with a sauce.

| | | |
|---|---|---|
| **risi e bisi** | **ree**see ay **bee**see | rice with peas and bacon |
| **riso in bianco** | **ree**soa een bee**ahng**koa | boiled rice with butter and grated parmesan |
| **risotto** | ree**sot**toa | rice casserole |
| **con fegatini** | kon faygah**tee**nee | with chicken livers |
| **con funghi** | kon **foong**gee | with mushrooms |
| **alla milanese** | **ahl**lah meelah**nai**say | marrow, white wine, saffron and parmesan |

### Fish and seafood *Pesci e frutti di mare*

Don't miss the opportunity to sample some of the wide variety of fresh fish and seafood in coastal areas. Some inland regions offer special preparations of fish from their rivers, lakes and streams. Fish is most commonly baked or poached until just done, then dressed with a delicate sauce.

| | | |
|---|---|---|
| I'd like some fish. | **Vorrei del pesce.** | vor**rai**ee dayl **pay**shay |
| What kind of seafood do you have? | **Che genere di frutti di mare avete?** | kay **jeh**nayray dee **froot**tee dee **maa**ray ah**vay**tay |
| **acciughe** | aht**choo**gay | anchovies |
| **aguglie** | ah**goo**lyay | garfish |
| **anguilla** | ahnggoo**eel**lah | eel |
| **aragosta** | ahrah**goa**stah | lobster |
| **aringa** | ah**reeng**gah | herring |
| **arselle** | ahr**sehl**lay | scallops |
| **baccalà** | bahkkah**lah** | dried salt cod |
| **bianchetti** | beeahng**kayt**tee | whitebait |
| **branzino** | brahn**dzee**noa | (sea) bass |
| **calamaretti** | kahlahmah**rayt**tee | baby squid |
| **calamari** | kahlah**maa**ree | squid |
| **carpa** | **kahr**pah | carp |
| **cozze** | **koat**say | mussels |
| **dentice** | **dehn**teechay | type of sea bream |
| **eperlano** | aypayr**laa**noa | smelt |
| **gamberetti** | gahmbay**rayt**tee | shrimps |
| **gamberi** | **gahm**bayree | crayfish |
| **granchi** | **grahng**kee | crabs |
| **gronghi** | **groang**gee | conger eel |
| **lamprede** | lahm**pray**day | lampreys |
| **luccio** | **loot**choa | pike |
| **lumache di mare** | loo**maa**kay dee **maa**ray | sea snails |
| **merlano** | mayr**laa**noa | whiting |
| **merluzzo** | mayr**loot**tsoa | cod |
| **nasello** | nah**sehl**loa | coal-fish |
| **orata** | oa**raa**tah | type of sea bream |
| **ostriche** | **o**streekay | oysters |
| **pesce persico** | **pay**shay **pehr**seekoa | perch |
| **pesce spada** | **pay**shay **spaa**dah | swordfish |
| **polpo** | **poal**poa | octopus |
| **razza** | **raht**tsah | ray |
| **ricci** | **reet**chee | sea urchins |
| **rombo** | **roam**boa | turbot |
| **salmone** | sahl**moa**nay | salmon |

| | | |
|---|---|---|
| **sardine** | sahr**dee**nay | sardines |
| **scampi** | **skahm**pee | prawns |
| **scorfano** | **skoar**fahnoa | sea-scorpion, sculpin |
| **sgombro** | **zgoam**broa | mackerel |
| **seppia** | **sayp**peeah | cuttlefish |
| **sogliola** | **saw**lyoalah | sole |
| **spigola** | **spee**goalah | sea bass |
| **storione** | stoaree**oa**nay | sturgeon |
| **tonno** | **toan**noa | tunny (tuna) |
| **triglie** | **tree**lyay | red mullet |
| **trota** | **traw**tah | trout |
| **vongole** | **vong**goalay | clams |

| | | |
|---|---|---|
| baked | **al forno** | ahl **for**noa |
| boiled | **lesso** | **lays**soa |
| (deep) fried | **(ben) fritto** | (bain) **freet**toa |
| grilled | **alla griglia** | **ahl**lah **gree**lyah |
| marinated | **marinato** | mahree**naa**toa |
| poached | **affogato** | ahffoa**gaa**toa |
| smoked | **affumicato** | ahffoomee**kaa**toa |
| steamed | **cotto a vapore** | **kot**toa ah vah**poa**ray |
| stewed | **in umido** | een **oo**meedoa |

## Fish specialities *Specialità di pesce*

**anguilla alla veneziana** (ahnggoo**eel**lah **ahl**lah vaynaytsee**aa**nah)
eel cooked in sauce made from tunny (tuna) and lemon

**baccalà alla vicentina** (bahkkah**lah ahl**lah veechayn**tee**nah)
cod cooked in milk with onion, garlic, parsley, anchovies and cinnamon

**fritto misto** (**freet**toa **mee**stoa)
a fry of various small fish and shellfish

**pesci in carpione** (**pay**shee een kahrpee**oa**nay)
boiled fish, cooked in vinegar, served cold with lemon

**pesci al cartoccio** (**pay**shee ahl kahr**tot**choa)
baked in a parchment envelope with onions, parsley and herbs

**sgombri in umido** (**zgoam**bree een **oo**meedoa)
stewed mackerel in white wine with green peas

**stoccafisso** (stoakkah**fees**soa)
dried cod cooked with tomatoes, olives and artichoke

| | |
|---|---|
| **sogliole alla mugnaia** (**saw**lyolay **ahl**lah moo**ñaa**eeah) | sole sautéed in butter, garnished with parsley and lemon |
| **triglie alla livornese** (**tree**lyay **ahl**lah leevoar**nay**say) | baked red mullet |

## Meat *Carne*

| | | |
|---|---|---|
| I'd like some ... | **Vorrei ...** | vor**rai**ee |
| beef | **del manzo** | dayl **mahn**dzoa |
| lamb | **dell'agnello** | dayllah**ñehl**loa |
| mutton | **del montone** | dayl moan**toa**nay |
| pork | **del maiale** | dayl maaee**aa**lay |
| veal | **del vitello** | dayl vee**tehl**loa |

| | | |
|---|---|---|
| **animelle di vitello** | ahnee**mehl**lay dee vee**tehl**loa | sweetbreads |
| **arrosto** | ahr**roa**stoa | roast |
| **bistecca** | bee**stayk**kah | steak |
| **di filetto** | dee fee**leht**toa | rib steak |
| **braciola** | brah**choa**lah | chop |
| **cosciotto** | koa**shawt**toa | leg |
| **costola** | **ko**stoalah | rib |
| **costoletta** | koastoa**layt**tah | cutlet |
| **cervello** | chayr**vehl**loa | brains |
| **fegato** | **fay**gahtoa | liver |
| **fesa** | **fay**sah | round cut from rump |
| **filetto** | fee**layt**toa | fillet |
| **lingua** | **leeng**gwah | tongue |
| **lombata/lombo** | loam**baa**tah/**loam**boa | loin |
| **medaglioni** | maydah**lyoa**nee | round fillet |
| **midollo** | mee**doal**loa | marrow |
| **nodini** | noa**dee**nee | veal chops |
| **pancetta affumicata** | pahn**cheht**tah ahffoo-mee**kaa**tah | bacon |
| **polpette** | poal**payt**tay | meatballs |
| **polpettone** | poalpayt**toa**nay | meat loaf of seasoned beef or veal |
| **porcellino da latte/ porchetta** | poarchayl**lee**noa dah **laht**tay/poar**kayt**tah | suck(l)ing pig |
| **prosciutto** | proa**shoot**toa | ham |
| **rognoni** | roa**ñoa**nee | kidneys |
| **rosbif** | **ros**beef | roast beef |
| **salumi** | sah**loo**mee | assorted pork products |
| **salsicce** | sahl**seet**chay | sausages |

| | | |
|---|---|---|
| **scaloppina** | skahloap**pee**nah | escalope |
| **spalla** | **spahl**lah | shoulder |
| **tripe** | **treep**pay | tripe |

## Meat dishes *Piatti di carne*

| | |
|---|---|
| **abbacchio** (ahb**bahk**keeoa) | roast lamb, often served in a casserole with anchovies |
| **bistecca alla fiorentina** (bee**stayk**kah **ahl**lah feeoarayn**tee**nah) | a grilled steak flavoured with pepper, lemon juice and parsley |
| **cima alla genovese** (**chee**mah **ahl**lah jaynoa**vay**say) | rolled veal stuffed with eggs, sausage and mushrooms |
| **costata al prosciutto** (koa**staa**tah ahl proa**shoot**toa) | a chop filled with ham, cheese and truffles; breaded and fried until golden brown |
| **costoletta alla milanese** (koastoa**layt**tah **ahl**lah meelah**nay**say) | breaded veal cutlet, flavoured with cheese |
| **fegato alla veneziana** (**fay**gahtoa **ahl**lah vaynaytsee**aa**nah) | thin slices of calf's liver fried with onions |
| **involtini** (eenvoal**tee**nee) | thin slices of meat (beef, veal or pork) rolled and stuffed |
| **ossi buchi** (ossee **boo**kee) | veal or beef knuckle braised and served in a highly flavoured sauce |
| **piccata al marsala** (peek**kaa**tah ahl mahr**saa**lah) | thin veal escalope braised in marsala sauce |
| **saltimbocca alla romana** (sahlteem**boak**kah **ahl**lah roa**maa**nah) | veal escalope braised in marsala wine with ham and sage |
| **scaloppina alla Valdostana** (skahloap**pee**nah **ahl**lah vahldoa**staa**nah) | veal escalope filled with cheese and ham |
| **spezzatino** (spaytsah**tee**noa) | meat or poultry stew |
| **spiedino** (speeay**dee**noa) | pieces of meat grilled or roasted on a skewer |

**stracotto** (strah**kot**toa) meat stew slowly cooked for several hours

**trippe alla fiorentina** (**treep**pay **ahl**lah feeorayn**tee**nah) tripe and beef braised in a tomato sauce, served with cheese

**vitello tonnato** (vee**tayl**loa toan**naa**toa) cold veal with tuna fish sauce

**zampone** (tsahm**poa**nay) pig's trotter filled with seasoned pork, boiled and served in slices

**How do you like your meat?** *Come vuole la carne?*

| | | |
|---|---|---|
| baked | **al forno** | ahl **for**noa |
| barbecued | **alla graticola/alla griglia** | **ahl**lah grah**tee**koalah/ **ahl**lah **gree**lyah |
| boiled | **lesso** | **lays**soa |
| braised | **brasato** | brah**saa**toa |
| broiled | **allo spiedo** | **ahl**loa spee**eh**doa |
| casseroled | **in casseruola** | een kassayr**wo**lah |
| fried | **fritto** | **freet**toa |
| grilled | **ai ferri** | **ahee fehr**ree |
| roast(ed) | **arrosto** | ahr**roa**stoa |
| spit-roasted | **allo spiedo** | **ahl**loa spee**eh**doa |
| stewed | **in umido** | een **oo**meedoa |
| stuffed | **farcito** | fahr**chee**toa |
| underdone (rare) | **al sangue** | ahl **sahng**gooay |
| medium | **a puntino** | ah poon**tee**noa |
| well-done | **ben cotto** | bain **kot**toa |

**Game and poultry** *Cacciagione e pollame*

Many small fowl not regarded as game birds in America or Britain are served as first or main courses in Italy. They're usually grilled or roasted. Among small fowl considered as gourmet dishes are lark, plover, thrush and ortolan.

| | | |
|---|---|---|
| I'd like some game. | **Vorrei della cacciagione.** | vor**raiee dayl**lah kahtchah**joa**nay |
| What poultry dishes do you serve? | **Che piatti di pollame servite?** | kay pee**aht**tee dee poal**laa**may sayr**vee**tay |

| | | |
|---|---|---|
| **allodola** | ahl**lo**doalah | lark |
| **anatra** | **aa**nahtrah | duck |
| **beccaccia** | bayk**kaht**chah | woodcock |
| **beccaccino** | baykkaht**chee**noa | snipe |
| **camoscio** | kah**mo**shoa | chamois |
| **cappone** | kahp**poa**nay | capon |
| **capretto** | kah**prayt**toa | kid goat |
| **capriolo** | kahpree**o**loa | roebuck |
| **cervo** | **chehr**voa | deer |
| **cinghiale** | cheenggee**aa**lay | wild boar |
| **coniglio** | koa**neel**yoa | rabbit |
| **fagiano** | fah**jaa**noa | pheasant |
| **faraona** | fahrah**oa**nah | guinea fowl |
| **gallina** | gahl**lee**nah | stewing fowl |
| **gallo cedrone** | **gahl**loa cheh**droa**nay | grouse |
| **lepre** | **lai**pray | hare |
| **oca** | **o**kah | goose |
| **ortolano** | oartoa**laa**noa | ortolan |
| **pernice** | payr**nee**chay | partridge |
| **piccione** | peet**choa**nay | pigeon |
| **piviere** | peevee**eh**ray | plover |
| **pollo** | **poal**loa | chicken |
| **pollo novello** | **poal**loa noa**vehl**loa | spring chicken |
| **quaglia** | **kwah**lyah | quail |
| **selvaggina** | saylvahd**jee**nah | venison |
| **tacchino** | tahk**kee**noa | turkey |
| **tordo** | **toar**doa | thrush |

**capretto ripieno al forno** (kah**prayt**toa reepee**ay**noa ahl **for**noa) — stuffed kid, oven-roasted

**galletto amburghese** (gahl**layt**toa ahmboor**gay**say) — young tender chicken, oven-roasted

**palombacce allo spiedo** (pahloam**baht**chay **ahl**loa spee**eh**doa) — wood pigeon, spit-roasted

**polenta e coniglio** (poa**lehn**tah ay koa**neel**yoa) — rabbit stew served with a mush made from maize flour (cornmeal mush)

**polenta e uccelli** (poa**lehn**tah ay oot**chehl**lee) — various small birds roasted on a spit and served with polenta (see immediately above)

**pollo alla diavola** (**poal**loa **ahl**lah dee**aa**voalah) — highly spiced and grilled chicken

## Vegetables—Salads *Verdure—Insalate*

| | | |
|---|---|---|
| What kind of vegetables have you got? | **Che genere di verdure avete?** | kay **jeh**nayray dee vehr**doo**ray ah**vay**tay |
| I'd like a (mixed) salad. | **Vorrei un'insalata (mista).** | vor**rai**ee ooneensah**laa**tah (**mee**stah) |

| | | |
|---|---|---|
| **asparagi** | ah**spaa**rahjee | asparagus |
| **barbabietola** | bahrbahbee**eh**toalah | beetroot |
| **broccoli** | **brok**kolee | broccoli |
| **carciofi** | kahr**cho**fee | artichokes |
| **carote** | kah**raw**tay | carrots |
| **cavolfiore** | kahvoalfee**oa**ray | cauliflower |
| **cavolo** | **kaa**voaloa | cabbage |
| **cavolini di Bruxelles** | kahvoa**lee**nee dee broos**sayl** | brussels sprouts |
| **ceci** | **chay**chee | chick-peas |
| **cetriolini** | chaytreeoa**lee**nee | gherkins |
| **cetriolo** | chaytree**o**loa | cucumber |
| **cicoria** | chee**ko**reeah | endive (Am. chicory) |
| **cipolle** | chee**pol**lay | onions |
| **fagioli** | fah**joa**lee | haricot beans |
| **fagiolini** | fahjoa**lee**nee | French (green) beans |
| **fave** | **faa**vay | broad beans |
| **finocchio** | fee**nok**keeoa | fennel |
| **funghi** | **foong**gee | mushrooms |
| **indivia** | een**dee**veeah | chicory (Am. endive) |
| **insalata (verde)** | eensah**laa**tah (**vayr**day) | (green) salad |
| **lattuga** | laht**too**gah | lettuce |
| **lenticchie** | layn**teek**keeay | lentils |
| **melanzane** | maylahnt**saa**nay | aubergine (eggplant) |
| **patate** | pah**taa**tay | potatoes |
| **peperoni** | paypay**roa**nee | sweet peppers |
| **piselli** | pee**sehl**lee | peas |
| **pomodoro** | poamoa**daw**roa | tomato |
| **porcini** | poar**chee**nee | boletus mushrooms |
| **porro** | **por**roa | leeks |
| **radicchio** | rah**deek**keeoa | a kind of bitter, red and white lettuce |
| **ravanelli** | rahvah**nehl**lee | radishes |
| **sedano** | **seh**dahnoa | celery |
| **spinaci** | spee**naa**chee | spinach |
| **tartufi** | tahr**too**fee | truffles |
| **verdura mista** | vehr**doo**rah **mee**stah | mixed vegetables |
| **verza** | **vehr**dzah | green cabbage |
| **zucca** | **tsook**kah | pumpkin, gourd |
| **zucchini** | tsook**kee**nee | zucchini |

## Spices and herbs *Spezie e odori*

| | | |
|---|---|---|
| **aglio** | ahlyoa | garlic |
| **basilico** | bahzeeleekoa | basil |
| **cannella** | kahnnehllah | cinnamon |
| **capperi** | kahppehree | capers |
| **chiodi di garofano** | keeodee dee gahrofahnoa | cloves |
| **cipollina** | cheepoalleenah | chive |
| **cumino** | koomeenoa | cumin |
| **lauro** | lahooroa | bay |
| **maggiorana** | madjoaraanah | marjoram |
| **menta** | mayntah | mint |
| **noce moscata** | noachay moaskaatah | nutmeg |
| **origano** | oareegahnoa | origan |
| **prezzemolo** | prehttsaymoaloa | parsley |
| **rosmarino** | roazmahreenoa | rosemary |
| **salvia** | sahlveeah | sage |
| **scalogno** | skahloañoa | shallot |
| **timo** | teemoa | thyme |
| **zafferano** | dzahffehraanoa | saffron |
| **zenzero** | dzehndzehroa | ginger |

## Cheese *Formaggio*

Italy produces a great variety of cheese, many of them little known outside the locality in which they're made.

**Bel Paese** (behl pahayzay) — smooth cheese with delicate taste

**caciocavallo** (kahchoakahvahlloa) — firm, slightly sweet cheese from cow's or sheep's milk

**gorgonzola** (goargoandzolah) — most famous of the Italian blue-veined cheese, rich with a tangy flavour

**mozzarella** (motsahrehllah) — soft, unripened cheese with a bland, slightly sweet flavour, made from buffalo's milk in southern Italy, elsewhere with cow's milk

**parmigiano (-reggiano)** (pahrmeejaanoa-raydjaanoa) — parmesan (also called *grana*), a hard cheese generally grated for use in hot dishes and pasta but also eaten alone

**pecorino** (paykoareenoa) — a hard cheese made from sheep's milk

**ricotta** (reekottah) — soft cow's or sheep's milk cheese

## Fruit *Frutta*

| | | |
|---|---|---|
| Do you have fresh fruit? | **Avete della frutta fresca?** | ah**vay**tay **day**llah **froo**ttah **fray**skah |
| I'd like a fresh fruit cocktail. | **Vorrei una macedonia di frutta.** | vor**rai**ee **oo**nah mahchay**do**neeah dee **froo**ttah |

| | | |
|---|---|---|
| **albicocca** | ahlbee**ko**kkah | apricot |
| **ananas** | **ah**nahnahss | pineapple |
| **anguria** | ahng**goo**reeah | watermelon |
| **arachide** | ah**rah**keeday | peanuts |
| **arancia** | ah**rahn**chah | orange |
| **banana** | bah**naa**nah | banana |
| **caco** | **kaa**koa | persimmon |
| **castagna** | kah**staa**ñah | chestnut |
| **cedro** | **chay**droa | lime |
| **ciliege** | cheelee**ay**jay | cherries |
| **cocomero** | koa**koa**mayroa | watermelon |
| **cotogna** | koa**toa**ñah | quince |
| **datteri** | **daht**tayree | dates |
| **fico** | **fee**koa | fig |
| **fragole** | **fraa**goalay | strawberries |
| **lamponi** | lahm**poa**nee | raspberries |
| **limone** | lee**moa**nay | lemon |
| **mandarino** | mahndah**ree**noa | tangerine |
| **mandorle** | **mahn**doarlay | almonds |
| **mela** | **may**lah | apple |
| **melone** | may**loa**nay | melon |
| **mirtilli** | meer**teel**lee | blueberries |
| **more** | **mo**ray | blackberries |
| **nocciole** | noat**cho**lay | hazelnuts |
| **noce di cocco** | **noa**chay dee **ko**kkoa | coconut |
| **noci** | **noa**chee | walnuts |
| **pera** | **pay**rah | pear |
| **pesca** | **peh**skah | peach |
| **pinoli** | pee**no**lee | pine kernels |
| **pompelmo** | poam**payl**moa | grapefruit |
| **prugna** | **proo**ñah | plum |
| **prugna secca** | **proo**ñah **sayk**kah | prune |
| **ribes** | **ree**bays | redcurrants |
| **ribes nero** | **ree**bays **nay**roa | blackcurrants |
| **susina** | soo**zee**nah | plum |
| **uva** | **oo**vah | grapes |
| **bianca/nera** | bee**ahng**kah/**nay**rah | white/black |
| **uva passa** | **oo**vah **pah**ssah | raisins |
| **uva spina** | **oo**vah **spee**nah | gooseberries |

## Dessert *Dolce*

You'll find a profusion of cakes and tarts to round off the meal. Among the more interesting is the *zuppa inglese*—not a soup at all but a kind of trifle (see below). *Granita* is a partially frozen dessert made with coffee or fruit juice. Or try some of the delicious ice-cream for which Italy is renown.

| | | |
|---|---|---|
| I'd like a dessert, please. | **Vorrei un dessert, per favore.** | vor**rai**ee oon days**sehr** pair fah**voa**ray |
| What do you recommend? | **Cosa consiglia?** | **kaw**sah koan**see**lyah |
| Something light, please. | **Qualcosa di leggero, per favore.** | kwahl**kaw**sah dee layd**jai**roa pair fah**voa**ray |
| I'd like a slice of cake. | **Vorrei una fetta di torta.** | vor**rai**ee **oo**nah **feht**tah dee **toar**tah |
| with/without (whipped) cream | **con/senza panna (montata)** | kon/**sayn**tsah **pahn**nah (moan**taa**tah) |

| | | |
|---|---|---|
| **budino** | boo**dee**noa | pudding |
| **crema** | **krai**mah | custard |
| **crostata di mele** | kroa**staa**tah dee **may**lay | apple pie |
| **dolce** | **doal**chay | cake |
| **gelato** | jay**laa**toa | ice-cream |
| **alla fragola** | **ahl**lah **fraa**goalah | strawberry |
| **al limone** | ahl lee**moa**nay | lemon |
| **alla vaniglia** | **ahl**lah vah**nee**lyah | vanilla |
| **misto** | **mee**stoa | mixed |
| **tartufi di cioccolata** | tahr**too**fee dee choakkoa**laa**tah | chocolate truffles |
| **torta** | **toar**tah | cake |
| **di cioccolata** | dee choakkoa**laa**tah | chocolate cake |
| **di frutta** | dee **froot**tah | fruit cake |

**cassata** (kas**saa**tah) — ice cream with candied fruit (Am. spumoni)

**cassata siciliana** (kas**saa**tah seecheelee**aa**nah) — sponge cake garnished with sweet cream cheese, chocolate and candied fruit

**zabaglione** (dzahbah**lyoa**nay) — a mixture of eggyolks, sugar and Marsala wine; served warm

**zuppa inglese** (**dzoop**pah eeng**glay**say) — sponge cake steeped in rum with candied fruit and custard or whipped cream

**Drinks** *Bevande*

**Aperitifs** *Aperitivi*

The average Italian is just as fond of his favourite *aperitivo* (ahpehreet**ee**voa) as we are of our cocktail or highball. Often bittersweet, some aperitifs have a wine and brandy base with herbs and bitters while others may have a vegetable base. Here are some aperitifs you may want to try:

| | |
|---|---|
| **Americano** (ahmayree**kaa**noa) | despite its name, one of the most popular Italian aperitifs; a vermouth to which bitters, brandy and lemon peel are added |
| **Aperol** (**ah**payroal) | a non-alcoholic bitters |
| **Campari** (kahm**paa**ree) | reddish-brown bitters, flavoured with orange peel and herbs, it has a quinine taste |
| **Cynar** (chee**naar**) | produced from artichoke |
| **Martini** (mahr**tee**nee) | a brand-name vermouth not to be confused with a martini cocktail |

| | | |
|---|---|---|
| neat (straight) | **liscio** | **lee**shoa |
| on the rocks | **con ghiaccio** | kon gee**ah**tchoa |
| with (seltzer) water | **con acqua (di seltz)** | kon **ah**kkwah (dee sehltz) |

**SALUTE!/CIN-CIN!**
(sah**loo**tay/cheen cheen)
YOUR HEALTH!/CHEERS!

**Wine** *Vino*

Italy is one of the most important wine producers in Europe. Vineyards are found all over the Italian peninsula and islands.

Some of the country's most reputed wines (like *Barbaresco, Barbera* and *Barolo*) come from the Piedmont in northwestern Italy. But most other regions have noted wine, too. This is your opportunity to sample local wine, some of which is of surprisingly good quality.

*Chianti* is doubtless Italy's best-known wine outside of its borders. The best of it is produced between Florence and Siena. The term *Chianti classico* on the label indicates that the production of this wine has been carefully supervised. A *Chianti* of superior quality carries the term *riserva* on the label.

Some restaurants list their wines in a corner of the menu while others have them marked up on the wall. As much of the nation's wine doesn't travel well, don't expect a *trattoria* to offer more than a few types of wine. Most of the wine must be drunk young so don't look too hard for vintage labels. In smaller places you might get *vino aperto* (open wine) or *vino della casa* (house wine) at a moderate price, served in one-quarter, one-half or one-litre carafes.

| | | |
|---|---|---|
| May I have the wine list, please. | **Per favore, mi porti la lista dei vini.** | pair fah**voa**ray mee **por**tee lah **lee**stah **dai**ee **vee**nee |
| I'd like a bottle of white/red wine. | **Vorrei una bottiglia di vino bianco/ rosso.** | vor**rai**ee **oo**nah bot**tee**lyah dee **vee**noa bee**ahng**koa/ **roas**soa |
| half a bottle | **mezza bottiglia** | **meh**dzah bot**tee**lyah |
| a carafe | **una caraffa** | **oo**nah kah**rahf**fah |
| half a litre | **mezzo litro** | **meh**dzoa **lee**troa |
| a glass | **un bicchiere** | oon beek**kee**ai**ray** |
| A bottle of champagne, please. | **Una bottiglia di champagne, per favore.** | **oo**nah bot**tee**lyah dee **sham**pahñ pair fah**voa**ray |
| Where does this wine come from? | **Da dove viene questo vino?** | dah **doa**vay vee**ay**nay koo**ay**stoa **vee**noa |

| | | |
|---|---|---|
| red | **rosso** | **roas**soa |
| white | **bianco** | bee**ahng**koa |
| rosé | **rosatello** | rawzah**tehl**loa |
| dry | **secco** | **sehk**koa |
| full-bodied | **pieno** | pee**ay**noa |
| light | **leggero** | layd**jai**roa |
| sparkling | **spumante** | spoo**mahn**tay |
| sweet | **dolce** | **doal**chay |

The following chart will help you to choose your wine if you want to do some serious wine-tasting.

| Type of wine | Examples | Accompanies |
|---|---|---|
| **sweet white wine** | *Orvieto* from Umbria (the export variety is usually dry), *Aleatico* and *Vino Santo* from Tuscany and the famed *Marsala* from Sicily. | desserts, especially custard, pudding, cake |
| **dry white wine** | *Frascati* from Latium or *Verdicchio dei Castelli di Jesi* from the Adriatic Marches; local white wine generally falls into this category | fish, seafood, cold or boiled meat, fowl (the unconventional Romans enjoy drinking *Frascati* with a heavy meal) |
| **rosé** | *Lagrein* from Trentino-Alto Adige | goes with almost anything but especially cold dishes, eggs, pork and lamb |
| **light-bodied red wine** | *Bardolino* and *Valpolicella* from the Lake of Garda; local red wine, including Italian- Swiss *Merlot,* usually fits this category | roast chicken, turkey, veal, lamb, steaks, ham, liver, quail, pheasant, soft-textured cheeses, stews and pasta |
| **full-bodied red wine** | *Barolo, Barbera* and *Barbaresco* from Piedmont | duck, goose, kidneys, most game, tangy cheese like *gorgonzola*—in short, any strong-flavoured dishes |
| **sparkling white wine** | *Asti spumante* (Italians like to refer to it as champagne but it's slightly sweet) | goes nicely with dessert and pastry; if it's dry, you might try *spumante* as an aperitif or with shellfish, nuts or dried fruit |

### Beer *Birra*

Beer is always available and growing in popularity. Italian brands are weaker than northern European beers.

| | | |
|---|---|---|
| I'd like a beer, please. | **Vorrei una birra, per favore.** | vorr**aiee** **oo**nah **beer**rah pair fah**voa**ray |
| Do you have ... beer? | **Avete della birra ...?** | ah**vay**tay **dayl**lah **beer**rah |
| bottled | **in bottiglia** | een bot**tee**lyah |
| draught | **alla spina** | **ahl**lah **spee**nah |
| foreign | **straniera** | strahnee**ay**rah |
| light/dark | **bionda/scura** | bee**oan**dah/**skoo**rah |

### Other alcoholic drinks *Altre bevande alcoliche*

Coffee shops and bars usually have a good stock of foreign and domestic liquor—even some of your favourite brands.

| | | |
|---|---|---|
| aperitif | **un aperitivo** | oon ahpayree**tee**voa |
| brandy | **un brandy** | oon "brandy" |
| cognac | **un cognac** | oon "cognac" |
| gin and tonic | **un gin e tonico** | oon "gin" ay **to**neekoa |
| liqueur | **un liquore** | oon loo**kwoa**ray |
| port | **un porto** | oon **por**toa |
| rum | **un rum** | oon room |
| vermouth | **un vermouth** | oon **vehr**moot |
| vodka | **una vodka** | **oo**nah **vod**kah |
| whisky (and soda) | **un whisky (e soda)** | oon "whisky" (ay **so**dah) |

| | | |
|---|---|---|
| glass | **un bicchiere** | oon beekkee**ai**ray |
| bottle | **una bottiglia** | **oo**nah bot**tee**lyah |
| double (a double shot) | **doppio** | **doap**peeoa |
| neat (straight) | **liscio** | **lee**shoa |
| on the rocks | **con ghiaccio** | kon gee**aht**choa |

You'll certainly want to take the occasion to sip an after-dinner drink. If you'd like something which approaches French cognac try *Vecchia Romagna*. If you feel a digestive is called for ask for an *amaro* (bitter), or a glass of *Fernet-Branca* should fit the bill.

| | | |
|---|---|---|
| I'd like to try a glass of ..., please. | **Vorrei assaggiare un bicchiere di ...** | vorr**aiee** ahssahdj**aa**ray oon beekke**ai**ray dee |
| Are there any local specialities? | **Avete specialità locali?** | ah**vay**tay spaychahlee**tah** loa**kaa**lee |

**Nonalcoholic drinks** *Bevande analcoliche*

The Italian *caffè espresso* has a rich aroma and is excellent everywhere. Served in demi-tasses, it's stronger than what we're used to at home. However, if you'd like to try a more concentrated cup of espresso coffee, ask for a *ristretto* (ree**strayt**toa). As against this, a *caffè lungo* (kahf**fay loong**goa) is a slightly weaker cup of espresso coffee.

For breakfast don't miss the opportunity to drink a *cappuccino* (kahppoot**chee**noa), a delicious mixture of coffee and hot milk, dusted with cocoa. In summer, iced tea and coffee are popular.

| | | |
|---|---|---|
| I'd like a/an ... | **Vorrei ...** | vorr**aiee** |
| chocolate | **un cioccolato** | oon choakkoa**laa**toa |
| coffee | **un caffè** | oon kahf**fai** |
| with cream | **con panna** | kon **pahn**nah |
| iced coffee | **un caffè freddo** | oon kahf**fay frayd**doa |
| fruit juice | **un succo di frutta** | oon **sook**koa dee **froot**tah |
| grapefruit | **di pompelmo** | dee poam**payl**moa |
| lemon | **di limone** | dee lee**moa**nay |
| orange | **d'arancia** | dah**rahn**chah |
| herb tea | **una tisana** | **oo**nah tee**zaa**nah |
| lemonade | **una limonata** | **oo**nah leemoa**naa**tah |
| milk | **del latte** | dayl **laht**tay |
| milkshake | **un frullato di latte** | oon frool**laa**toa dee **laht**tay |
| mineral water | **dell'acqua minerale** | dayl**lahk**kwah meenay**raa**lay |
| fizzy (carbonated) | **gasata** | gah**zaa**tah |
| still | **naturale** | nahtoo**raa**lay |
| orangeade | **un'aranciata** | oonahrahn**chaa**tah |
| tea | **un tè** | oon tai |
| with milk/lemon | **con latte/limone** | kon **laht**tay/leem**oa**nay |
| iced tea | **un tè freddo** | oon tai **frayd**doa |
| tomato juice | **un succo di pomodoro** | oon **sook**koa dee poamoa**daw**roa |
| tonic water | **dell'acqua tonica** | dayl**lahk**kwah **to**neekah |

## Complaints *Reclami*

| | | |
|---|---|---|
| There is a plate/glass missing. | **Manca un piatto/un bicchiere.** | **mahng**kah oon pee**aht**toa/oon beekkee**ai**ray |
| I have no knive/fork/ spoon. | **Non ho il coltello/ la forchetta/il cucchiaio.** | noan oa eel kol**tehl**loa/ lah for**keht**tah/eel kookkee**aa**eeoa |
| That's not what I ordered. | **Non è ciò che avevo ordinato.** | noan ai cho kay ah**vay**voa oardee**naa**toa |
| I asked for ... | **Avevo chiesto ...** | ah**vay**voa kee**eh**stoa |
| There must be some mistake. | **Ci deve essere un errore.** | chee **day**vay **ehs**sayray oon ehr**roa**ray |
| May I change this? | **Posso cambiare questo?** | **pos**soa kahmbee**aa**ray koo**ay**stoa |
| I asked for a small portion (for the child). | **Avevo chiesto una piccola porzione (per il bambino).** | ah**vay**voa kee**eh**stoa **oo**nah **peek**koalah poartsee**oa**nay (pair eel bahm**bee**noa) |
| The meat is ... | **La carne è ...** | lah **kahr**nay ai |
| overdone | **troppo cotta** | **trop**poa **kot**tah |
| underdone | **poco cotta** | **po**koa **kot**tah |
| too rare | **troppo al sangue** | **trop**poa ahl **sahng**gooay |
| too tough | **troppo dura** | **trop**poa **doo**rah |
| This is too ... | **Questo è troppo ...** | koo**ay**stoa ai **trop**poa |
| bitter/salty | **amaro/salato** | ah**maa**roa/sah**laa**toa |
| sweet | **dolce** | **doal**chay |
| I don't like it. | **Non mi piace.** | noan mee pee**ah**chay |
| The food is cold. | **Il cibo è freddo.** | eel **chee**boa ai **frayd**doa |
| This isn't fresh. | **Questo non è fresco.** | koo**ay**stoa noan ai **fray**skoa |
| What's taking you so long? | **Perchè impiegate tanto tempo?** | pehr**kai** eempeeay**gaa**tay **tahn**toa **tehm**poa |
| Have you forgotten our drinks? | **Ha dimenticato le nostre bevande?** | ah deemaynteek**kaa**toa lay **nos**tray bay**vahn**day |
| The wine tastes of cork. | **Il vino sa di tappo.** | eel **vee**noa sah dee **tahp**poa |
| This isn't clean. | **Questo non è pulito.** | koo**ay**stoa noan ai poo**lee**toa |
| Would you ask the head waiter to come over? | **Vuole chiedere al capo cameriere di venire qui?** | **vwo**lay kee**ay**dayray ahl **kaa**poa kahmayree**eh**ray dee vay**nee**ray koo**ee** |

### The bill (check) *Il conto*

Though the bill usually includes the service charge *(il servizio)*, it is customary to leave a tip *(la mancia)* for the waiter. Note that you will occasionally also find one or both of the following items added to your bill: *coperto* (cover charge), *supplemento* (surcharge).

| | | |
|---|---|---|
| I'd like to pay. | **Vorrei pagare.** | vorr**ai**ee pah**gaa**ray |
| We'd like to pay separately. | **Vorremmo pagare separatamente.** | vorr**ehm**moa pah**gaa**ray saypahrahtah**mayn**tay |
| I think you've made a mistake in this bill. | **Penso che abbiate fatto un errore nel conto.** | **pehn**soa kay ahbbee**aa**tay **faht**toa oon ayr**roa**ray nayl **koan**toa |
| What is this amount for? | **Per che cos'è questo importo?** | pair kay ko**zai** koo**ay**stoa eem**por**toa |
| Is service included? | **È compreso il servizio?** | ai koam**pray**soa eel sayr**vee**tseeoa |
| Is the cover charge included? | **È compreso il coperto?** | ai koam**pray**soa eel ko**pair**toa |
| Is everything included? | **È tutto compreso?** | ai **toot**toa koam**pray**soa |
| Do you accept traveller's cheques? | **Accettate i traveller's cheques?** | ahtchayt**taa**tay ee "traveller's cheques" |
| Can I pay with this credit card? | **Posso pagare con questa carta di credito?** | **pos**soa pah**gaa**ray kon koo**ay**stah **kahr**tah dee **kray**deetoa |
| Thank you, this is for you. | **Grazie, questo è per lei.** | **graa**tseeay koo**ay**stoa ai pair **leh**ee |
| Keep the change. | **Tenga il resto.** | **tayng**gah eel **reh**stoa |
| That was a delicious meal. | **È stato un pasto delizioso.** | ai **staa**toa oon **paa**stoa dayleetsee**oa**soa |
| We enjoyed it, thank you. | **Ci è piaciuto, grazie.** | chee ai peeah**choo**toa **graa**tseeay |

**SERVIZIO COMPRESO**
SERVICE INCLUDED

TIPPING, see inside back-cover

### Snacks—Picnic *Spuntini—Picnic*

Bars and snack bars stay open from early morning till late at night. Most have a selection of sandwiches *(panini imbottiti)* and pastries *(pasticcini),* inexpensive if you eat at the counter. There are, of course, *pizzerie* for a sit-down pizza or, if you're in a hurry, places selling pizza by the slice. In a *paninoteca,* you can find all sorts of *panini* to eat on the spot or to bring away. The same in a *rosticceria,* plus a great variety of food ready to eat at home or in a picnic.

| | | |
|---|---|---|
| I'll have one of those, please. | **Per favore, vorrei uno di quelli.** | pair fah**voa**ray vor**raiee** **oo**noa dee koo**ayl**lee |
| Give me two of these and one of those. | **Mi dia due di questi e uno di quelli.** | mee **dee**ah **doo**ay dee koo**ay**stee ay **oo**noa dee koo**ayl**lee |
| to the left/right | **a sinistra/a destra** | ah see**nee**strah/a **deh**strah |
| above/below | **sopra/sotto** | **soa**prah/**soat**toa |
| It's to take away. | **È da portare via.** | ai dah poar**taa**ray **vee**ah |
| How much is that? | **Quant'è?** | kwahn**tai** |
| I'd like a/some ... | **Vorrei ...** | vor**raiee** |
| chicken | **un pollo** | oon **poal**loa |
| half a roasted chicken | **metà pollo arrosto** | may**tah** **poal**loa ahr**roa**stoa |
| chips | **delle patatine fritte** | **dayl**lay pahtah**tee**nay **freet**tay |
| (slice of) pizza | **una (fetta di) pizza** | **oo**nah (**fayt**tah dee) **peet**tzah |
| sandwich | **un panino imbottito** | oon pah**nee**noa eembot**tee**toa |
| cheese | **al formaggio** | ahl foar**mad**joa |
| ham | **al prosciutto cotto** | ahl proa**shoot**toa **kot**toa |
| Parma ham | **al prosciutto crudo** | ahl proa**shoot**toa **kroo**doa |
| salami | **al salame** | ahl sah**laa**may |

Here's a basic list of food and drink that might come in useful when shopping for a picnic.

| | | |
|---|---|---|
| Please give me a/an/some ... | **Per favore, mi dia ...** | pair fah**voa**ray mee **dee**ah |
| apples | **delle mele** | **dayl**lay **may**lay |
| bananas | **delle banane** | **dayl**lay bah**naa**nay |

| | | |
|---|---|---|
| biscuits (Br.) | **dei biscotti** | **dai**ee bee**skoat**tee |
| beer | **della birra** | **dayl**lah **beer**rah |
| bread | **del pane** | dayl **paa**nay |
| butter | **del burro** | dayl **boor**roa |
| cake | **una torta** | **oo**nah **toar**tah |
| cheese | **del formaggio** | dayl foar**mahd**joa |
| chips (Am.) | **delle patatine fritte** | **dayl**lay pahtah**tee**nay **freet**tay |
| chocolate bar | **una stecca di cioccolato** | **oo**nah **stayk**kah dee chokkoa**laa**toa |
| coffee | **del caffè** | dayl kah**ffai** |
| instant | **solubile** | soa**loo**beelay |
| cold cuts | **degli affettati** | **dayl**yee ahffeht**taa**tee |
| cookies | **dei biscotti** | **dai**ee bee**skoat**tee |
| crackers | **dei cracker** | **dai**ee "cracker" |
| crisps | **delle patatine fritte** | **dayl**lay pahtahteenay **freet**tay |
| eggs | **delle uova** | **dayl**lay **waw**vah |
| frankfurters | **dei Würstel** | **dai**ee "würstel" |
| gherkins (pickles) | **dei cetriolini** | **dai**ee chaytreeoa**lee**nee |
| grapes | **dell'uva** | dayl**loo**vah |
| ham | **del prosciutto** | dayl proa**shoot**toa |
| ice-cream | **del gelato** | dayl jay**laa**toa |
| lemon | **un limone** | oon lee**moa**nay |
| milk | **del latte** | dayl **laht**tay |
| mustard | **della senape** | **dayl**lah **say**nahpay |
| (olive) oil | **dell'olio (d'oliva)** | dayl**lol**yoa (do**lee**vah) |
| oranges | **delle arance** | **dayl**lay ah**rahn**chay |
| pastries | **dei pasticcini** | **dai**ee pahsteet**chee**nee |
| peaches | **delle pesche** | **dayl**lay **pay**skay |
| peppers | **dei peperoni** | **dai**ee paypay**roa**nee |
| pickles | **dei sottaceti** | **dai**ee soattah**chay**tee |
| plums | **delle prugne** | **dayl**lay **proo**ñay |
| rolls | **dei panini** | **dai**ee pah**nee**nee |
| salad | **dell'insalata** | daylleensah**laa**tah |
| salami | **del salame** | dayl sah**laa**may |
| salt | **del sale** | dayl **saa**lay |
| sausages | **delle salsicce** | **dayl**lay sahl**seet**chay |
| soft drink | **una bibita** | **oo**nah **bee**beetah |
| sugar | **dello zucchero** | **dayl**loa **tsook**kayroa |
| tea | **del tè** | dayl tai |
| tomatoes | **dei pomodori** | **dai**ee poamoa**daw**ree |
| vinegar | **dell'aceto** | dayllah**chay**toa |
| (mineral) water | **dell'acqua (minerale)** | dayl**lahk**kwah (meenay**raa**lay) |
| wine | **del vino** | dayl **vee**noa |
| yoghurt | **uno yogurt** | **oo**noa eeoagoort |

# Travelling around

## **Plane** *Aereo*

| | | |
|---|---|---|
| Is there a flight to Naples? | **C'è un volo per Napoli?** | chai oon **voa**loa pair **naa**poalee |
| Is it a direct flight? | **È un volo diretto?** | ai oon **voa**loa dee**ray**ttoa |
| When's the next plane to Palermo? | **A che ora parte il prossimo aereo per Palermo?** | ah kay **oa**rah **pahr**tay eel **pros**seemoa ah**ai**rayoa pair pah**lehr**moa |
| Do I have to change planes? | **Devo cambiare aereo?** | **day**voa kahmbee**aa**ray ah**ai**rayoa |
| Can I make a connection to Venice? | **Posso prendere una coincidenza per Venezia?** | **pos**soa **prehn**dayray oonah koeenchee**dehnt**sah pair vay**nayt**seeah |
| I'd like a ticket to Milan. | **Vorrei un biglietto per Milano.** | vor**rai**ee oon beel**yayt**toa pair mee**laa**noa |
| single (one-way) | **andata** | ahn**daa**tah |
| return (roundtrip) | **andata e ritorno** | ahn**daa**tah ay ree**tor**noa |
| What time does the plane take off? | **A che ora decolla l'aereo?** | ah kay **oa**rah day**kol**lah lah**ai**rayoa |
| What time do I have to check in? | **A che ora devo presentarmi?** | ah kay **oa**rah **day**voa prayzehn**taar**mee |
| Is there a bus to the airport? | **C'è un autobus per l'aeroporto?** | chai oon **ow**toabooss pair lahayro**por**toa |
| What's the flight number? | **Qual è il numero del volo?** | kwahl ai eel **noo**mayroa dayl **voa**loa |
| What time do we arrive? | **A che ora arriveremo?** | ah kay **oa**rah ahrreevay**ray**moa |
| I'd like to ... my reservation on flight no ... | **Vorrei ... la mia prenotazione sul volo ...** | vor**rai**ee ... lah **mee**ah praynoatahtsee**oa**nay sool **voa**loa |
| cancel | **annullare** | ahnnool**laa**ray |
| change | **cambiare** | kahmbee**aa**ray |
| confirm | **confermare** | koanfayr**maa**ray |

| | |
|---|---|
| **ARRIVO**<br>ARRIVAL | **PARTENZA**<br>DEPARTURE |

**Train** *Treno*

Italian trains *try* to run on time as advertised. If you haven't booked, it's wise to arrive at the station at least 20 minutes before departure to be sure of a seat: Italy's trains are often very crowded.

The following list describes the various types of trains:

| | |
|---|---|
| **TEE** (teh-eh-eh) | Trans Europ Express; a luxury, international service with first class only; additional fare and reservation required |
| **Rapido (R)** (raapeedoa) | Long-distance express train stopping at major cities only; first and second class |
| **Intercity (IC)** ("intercity") | Inter-city express with very few stops; a luxury, international service with first and second class |
| **Espresso (EXP)/ Direttissimo** (aysprehssoa/ deerehtteesseemoa) | Long-distance train, stopping at main stations |
| **Diretto (D)** (deerehttoa) | Slower than the *Espresso,* it makes a number of local stops |
| **Locale (L)** (loakaalay) | A local train which stops at almost every station |
| **Accelerato (A)** (ahtchaylayraatoa) | Same as a *Locale* |
| **Littorina** (leettoareenah) | Small diesel used on short runs |

Here are some more useful terms which you may need.

| | |
|---|---|
| **Carrozza ristorante** (kahrrottsah reestorahntay) | Dining-car |
| **Vagone letto** (vahgoanay lehttoa) | Sleeping-car with individual compartments and washing facilities |
| **Carrozza cuccette** (kahrrottsah kootchehttay) | A berth with blankets and pillows |
| **Bagagliaio** (bahgahlyaaeeoa) | Guard's van (baggage car): normally only registered luggage permitted |

## To the railway station *Per andare alla stazione*

| | | |
|---|---|---|
| Where's the railway station? | **Dove si trova la stazione (ferroviaria)?** | **doa**vay see **traw**vah lah stahtsee**oa**nay (fehrrovee**aa**reeah) |
| Taxi, please! | **Taxi, per favore!** | "taxi" pair fah**voa**ray |
| Take me to the railway station. | **Mi porti alla stazione.** | mee **por**tee **ahl**lah staht-see**oa**nay |
| What's the fare? | **Quant'è?** | kwahn**tai** |

| | |
|---|---|
| **ENTRATA** | ENTRANCE |
| **USCITA** | EXIT |
| **AI BINARI** | TO THE PLATFORMS |
| **INFORMAZIONI** | INFORMATION |

## Where's the ...? *Dov'è ...?*

| | | |
|---|---|---|
| Where is/are the ...? | **Dov'è ...?** | doa**vai** |
| bar | **il bar** | eel "bar" |
| booking office | **l'ufficio prenotazioni** | looff**ee**choa praynoa-tahtsee**oa**nee |
| currency-exchange | **l'ufficio cambio** | looff**ee**choa **kahm**beeoa |
| left-luggage office (baggage check) | **il deposito bagagli** | eel day**paw**zeetoa bah**gaa**lyee |
| lost property (lost-and-found) office | **l'ufficio oggetti smarriti** | looff**ee**choa od**jeh**ttee smahr**ree**tee |
| luggage lockers | **la custodia automatica dei bagagli** | lah koo**staw**deeah owtoa-maateekah **daiee** bah**gaa**lyee |
| newsstand | **l'edicola** | lay**dee**koalah |
| platform 7 | **il binario 7** | eel bee**naa**reeoa 7 |
| reservations office | **l'ufficio prenotazioni** | looff**ee**choa praynoatahtsee**oa**nee |
| restaurant | **il ristorante** | eel reestor**ahn**tay |
| snack bar | **lo "snack bar"** | loa "snack bar" |
| ticket office | **la biglietteria** | lah beelyayttay**ree**ah |
| waiting room | **la sala d'aspetto** | lah **saa**lah dah**speh**ttoa |
| Where are the toilets? | **Dove sono i gabinetti?** | **doa**vay **soa**noa ee gahbee**nay**ttee |

TAXI, see page 21

## **Inquiries** *Informazioni*

| | | |
|---|---|---|
| When is the ... train to Rome? | **Quando parte ... treno per Roma?** | **kwahn**doa **pahr**tay ... **tray**noa pair **roa**mah |
| first/last | **il primo/l'ultimo** | eel **pree**moa/**lool**teemoa |
| next | **il prossimo** | eel **pros**seemoa |
| What time does the train for Milan leave? | **A che ora parte il treno per Milano?** | ah kay **oa**rah **pahr**tay eel **tray**noa pair mee**laa**noa |
| What's the fare to Ancona? | **Quanto costa il biglietto per Ancona?** | **kwahn**toa **ko**stah eel bee**lyayt**toa pair ahng**koa**nah |
| Is it a through train? | **È un treno diretto?** | ai oon **tray**noa dee**reht**toa |
| Is there a connection to ...? | **C'è una coincidenza per ...?** | chai **oo**nah koaeenchee**dayn**tsah pair |
| Do I have to change trains? | **Devo cambiare treno?** | **day**voa kahmbee**aa**ray **tray**noa |
| How long will the train stop at ...? | **Quanto tempo si fermerà il treno a ...?** | **kwahn**toa **tehm**poa see fayrmay**rah** eel **tray**noa ah |
| Is there sufficient time to change? | **C'è il tempo per cambiare?** | chai eel **tehm**poa pair kahmbee**aa**ray |
| Will the train leave on time? | **Partirà in orario il treno?** | pahrtee**rah** een oa**raa**reeoa eel **tray**noa |
| What time does the train arrive at Florence? | **A che ora arriverà a Firenze il treno?** | ah kay **oa**rah ahrreevay**rah** ah fee**rehn**tsay eel **tray**noa |
| Is there a dining-car/ sleeping-car on the train? | **C'è una carrozza ristorante/un vagone letto sul treno?** | chai **oo**nah kahr**rot**tsah reesto**rahn**tay/oon vah**goa**nay **leht**toa sool **tray**noa |
| Does the train stop at Lugano? | **Il treno si fermerà a Lugano?** | eel **tray**noa see fayrmay**rah** ah loo**gaa**noa |
| What platform does the train for Verona leave from? | **Da che binario parte il treno per Verona?** | dah kay bee**naa**reeoa **pahr**tay eel **tray**noa pair vay**roa**nah |
| What platform does the train from Bari arrive at? | **A che binario arriva il treno proveniente da Bari?** | ah kay bee**naa**reeoa ahr**ree**vah eel **tray**noa proavaynee**ehn**tay dah **baa**ree |
| I'd like to buy a timetable. | **Vorrei comprare un orario ferroviario.** | vor**rai**ee koam**praa**ray oon oa**raa**reeoa fehrroavee**aa**reeoa |

| | |
|---|---|
| **È un treno diretto.** | It's a through train. |
| **Deve cambiare a ...** | You have to change at ... |
| **Cambi a ... e prenda un treno locale.** | Change at ... and get a local train. |
| **Il binario 7 è ...** | Platform 7 is ... |
| **laggiù/su dalle scale a sinistra/a destra** | over there/upstairs on the left/on the right |
| **C'è un treno per ... alle ...** | There's a train to ... at ... |
| **Il suo treno partirà dal binario 8.** | Your train will leave from platform 8. |
| **Ci sarà un ritardo di ... minuti.** | There'll be a delay of ... minutes. |
| **Prima classe in testa/ nel mezzo/in coda.** | First class at the front/ in the middle/at the end. |

## Tickets *Biglietti*

| | | |
|---|---|---|
| I want a ticket to Rome. | **Desidero un biglietto per Roma.** | day**zee**dayroa oon bee**lyayt**toa pair **roa**mah |
| single (one-way) | **andata** | ahn**daa**tah |
| return (roundtrip) | **andata e ritorno** | ahn**daa**tah ay ree**tor**noa |
| first/second class | **prima/seconda classe** | **pree**mah/say**koan**dah **klahs**say |
| half price | **metà tariffa** | may**tah** tah**reef**fah |

## Reservation *Prenotazione*

| | | |
|---|---|---|
| I want to book a ... | **Vorrei prenotare ...** | vor**rai**ee praynoa**taa**ray |
| seat (by the window) | **un posto (vicino al finestrino)** | oon **pos**toa (vee**chee**noa ahl feenay**stree**noa) |
| berth | **una cuccetta** | **oo**nah koot**cheht**tah |
| upper | **superiore** | soopayree**oa**ray |
| middle | **nel mezzo** | nayl **mehd**zoa |
| lower | **inferiore** | eenfayree**oa**ray |
| berth in the sleeping car | **un posto nel vagone letto** | oon **pos**toa nayl vah**goa**nay **leht**toa |

## All aboard *In vettura!*

| | | |
|---|---|---|
| Is this the right platform for the train to Bellinzona? | **È il binario giusto per il treno che va a Bellinzona?** | ai eel bee**naa**reeo **joo**stoa pair eel **tray**noa kay vah ah behlleen**dzoa**nah |
| Is this the right train to Genoa? | **È il treno giusto per Genova?** | ai eel **tray**noa **joo**stoa pair **jai**noavah |
| Excuse me. May I get by? | **Mi scusi. Posso passare?** | mee **skoo**zee. **pos**soa pahs**saa**ray |
| Is this seat taken? | **È occupato questo posto?** | ai oakkoo**paa**toa koo**ay**stoa **pos**toa |

| FUMATORI | NON FUMATORI |
|---|---|
| SMOKER | NONSMOKER |

| | | |
|---|---|---|
| I think that's my seat. | **Penso che questo sia il mio posto.** | **payn**soa kay koo**ay**stoa **see**ah eel **mee**oa **pos**toa |
| Would you let me know before we get to Milan? | **Può avvisarmi prima di arrivare a Milano?** | pwo ahvvee**zaar**mee **pree**mah dee ahrree**vaa**ray ah mee**laa**noa |
| What station is this? | **Che stazione è?** | kay stahtsee**oa**nay ai |
| How long does the train stop here? | **Quanto tempo si ferma qui il treno?** | **kwahn**toa **tehm**poa see **fayr**mah koo**ee** eel **tray**noa |
| When do we get to Pisa? | **Quando arriveremo a Pisa?** | **kwahn**doa ahrreevay**ray**moa ah **pee**zah |

## Sleeping *Nel vagone letto*

| | | |
|---|---|---|
| Are there any free compartments in the sleeping-car? | **Ci sono degli scompartimenti liberi nel vagone letto?** | chee **soa**noa **dai**lyee skoampahrtee**mayn**tee **lee**bayree nail vah**goa**nay **leh**ttoa |
| Where's the sleeping-car? | **Dov'è il vagone letto** | doa**vai** eel vah**goa**nay **leh**ttoa |
| Where's my berth? | **Dov'è la mia cuccetta?** | doa**vai** lah **mee**ah koot**cheh**ttah |
| I'd like a lower berth. | **Vorrei la cuccetta inferiore.** | vor**rai**ee lah koot**cheh**ttah eenfayree**oa**ray |

| | | |
|---|---|---|
| Would you make up our berths? | **Può preparare le nostre cuccette?** | pwo praypah**raa**ray lay **nos**tray koot**cheht**tay |
| Would you call me at 7 o'clock? | **Può svegliarmi alle 7?** | pwo svay**lyahr**mee **ahl**lay 7 |
| Would you bring me some coffee in the morning? | **Può portarmi un caffè domani mattina?** | pwo por**tahr**mee oon kahf**fai** doa**maa**nee maht**tee**nah |

## Eating *Nella carrozza ristorante*

You can get snacks and drinks in the buffet-car and in the dining-car when it isn't being used for main meals. On some trains an attendant comes around with snacks, tea, coffee and soft drinks.

| | | |
|---|---|---|
| Where's the dining-car? | **Dov'è la carrozza ristorante?** | doa**vai** lah kahr**rott**sah reesto**rahn**tay |

## Baggage and porters *Bagagli e facchini*

| | | |
|---|---|---|
| Porter! | **Facchino!** | fahk**kee**noa |
| Can you help me with my luggage? | **Può prendere il mio bagaglio?** | pwo **prehn**dayray eel **mee**oa bah**gaa**lyoa |
| Where are the luggage trolleys (carts)? | **Dove sono i carrelli portabagagli?** | **doa**vay **soa**noa ee kahr**rehl**lee portahbah**gaa**lyee |
| Where are the luggage lockers? | **Dove sono le custodie automatiche dei bagagli?** | **doa**vay **soa**noa lay koos**taw**deeay owtoa**maa**teekay **dai**ee bah**gaa**lyee |
| Where's the left-luggage office (baggage check)? | **Dov'è il deposito bagagli?** | doa**vai** eel day**paw**zeetoa bah**gaa**lyee |
| I'd like to leave my luggage, please. | **Vorrei depositare i miei bagagli, per favore.** | vor**rai**ee daypozee**taa**ray ee mee**ai**ee bah**gaa**lyee pair fah**voa**ray |
| I'd like to register (check) my luggage. | **Vorrei far registrare i miei bagagli.** | vor**rai**ee fahr rayjee**straa**ray ee mee**ai**ee bah**gaa**lyee |

**REGISTRAZIONE BAGAGLI**
REGISTERING (CHECKING) BAGGAGE

PORTERS, see also page 18

**Coach (long-distance bus)** *Pullman/Corriera*

You'll find information on destinations and timetables at the coach terminals, usually situated near railway stations. Many travel agencies offer coach tours.

| | | |
|---|---|---|
| When's the next coach to ...? | **A che ora parte il prossimo pullman per ...?** | ah kay **oa**rah **pahr**tay eel **pros**seemoa **pool**mahn pair |
| Does this coach stop at ...? | **Questa corriera si ferma a ...?** | koo**ay**stah korree**ay**rah see **fayr**mah ah |
| How long does the journey (trip) take? | **Quanto tempo dura il percorso?** | **kwahn**toa **tehm**poa **doo**rah eel payr**koar**soa |

*Note:* Most of the phrases on the previous pages can be used or adapted for travelling on local transport.

**Bus—Tram (streetcar)** *Autobus—Tram*

Many cities have introduced an automatic system of fare-paying: either you insert the exact change into a ticket dispenser at the bus or tram stop or you punch your ticket in the machine.

If you're planning to get around a lot in one city by bus, tram, or *metropolitana* (see next page), enquire about a booklet of tickets or special runabout tickets, such as *biglietto giornaliero* (one-day ticket).

| | | |
|---|---|---|
| I'd like a booklet of tickets. | **Vorrei un blocchetto di biglietti.** | vor**rai**ee oon blok**keht**toa dee bee**lyayt**tee |
| Where can I get a bus to the Vatican? | **Dove posso prendere l'autobus per il Vaticano?** | **doa**vay **pos**soa **prehn**dayray **low**toabooss pair eel vahtee**kaa**noa |
| What bus do I take for the Colosseum? | **Quale autobus devo prendere per andare al Colosseo?** | **kwaa**lay **ow**toabooss **day**voa **prehn**dayray pair ahn**daa**ray ahl koaloas**sai**oa |
| Where's the bus stop? | **Dove si trova la fermata dell'autobus?** | **doa**vay see **traw**vah lah fehr**maa**tah dayl**low**toabooss |

| | | |
|---|---|---|
| When is the ... bus to the Lido? | **A che ora parte ... autobus per il Lido?** | ah kay **oa**rah **pahr**tay ... **ow**toabooss pair eel **lee**doa |
| first/last | **il primo/l'ultimo** | eel **pree**moa/**lool**teemoa |
| next | **il prossimo** | eel **pros**seemoa |
| How much is the fare to ...? | **Quanto costa il biglietto per ...?** | **kwahn**toa **kos**tah eel beel**yayt**toa pair |
| Do I have to change buses? | **Devo cambiare autobus?** | **day**voa kahmbee**aa**ray **ow**toabooss |
| How many bus stops are there to ...? | **Quante fermate ci sono fino a ...?** | **kwahn**tay fayr**maa**tay chee **soa**noa **fee**noa ah |
| Will you tell me when to get off? | **Può dirmi quando devo scendere?** | pwo **deer**mee **kwahn**doa **day**voa **shayn**dayray |
| I want to get off at Piazza di Spagna. | **Voglio scendere a Piazza di Spagna.** | **vol**yoa **shayn**dayray ah pee**ah**tsah dee **spah**ñah |

| | |
|---|---|
| **FERMATA D'AUTOBUS** | REGULAR BUS STOP |
| **FERMATA A RICHIESTA** | STOPS ON REQUEST |

**Underground (subway)** *Metropolitana*

The *metropolitana* in Rome and Milan corresponds to the London underground or the New York subway. In both cities, the fare is always the same, irrespective of the distance you travel. Big maps in every *Metro* station make the system easy to use.

| | | |
|---|---|---|
| Where's the nearest underground station? | **Dove si trova la più vicina stazione della metropolitana?** | **doa**vay see **traw**vah lah pee**oo** vee**chee**nah stahtsee**oa**nay **dayl**lah maytroapoalee**taa**nah |
| Does this train go to ...? | **Questo treno va a ...?** | koo**ay**stoa **tray**noa vah ah |
| Where do I change for ...? | **Dove cambio per andare a ...?** | **doa**vay **kahm**beeoa pair ahn**daa**ray ah |
| Is the next station ...? | **La prossima stazione è ...?** | lah **pros**seemah stahtsee**oa**nay ai |
| Which line should I take for ...? | **Che linea devo prendere per ...?** | kay **lee**nayah **day**voa **prehn**dayray pair |

**Boat service** *Battello*

| | | |
|---|---|---|
| When does the next boat for ... leave? | **A che ora parte il prossimo battello per ...?** | ah kay **oa**rah **pahr**tay eel pros**see**moa baht**tehl**loa pair |
| Where's the embarkation point? | **Dove ci si imbarca?** | **doa**vay chee see eem**bahr**kah |
| How long does the crossing take? | **Quanto tempo dura la traversata?** | **kwahn**toa **tehm**poa **doo**rah lah trahvayr**saa**tah |
| At which ports do we stop? | **A che porti si ferma?** | ah kay **por**tee see **fayr**mah |
| I'd like to take a cruise. | **Vorrei fare una crociera.** | vor**rai**ee **faa**ray **oo**nah kroa**chay**rah |
| boat | **il battello/la nave** | eel baht**tehl**loa/lah **naa**vay |
| cabin | **la cabina** | lah kah**bee**nah |
| single/double | **a un letto/a due letti** | ah oon **leht**toa/ah **doo**ay **leht**tee |
| deck | **il ponte** | eel **poan**tay |
| ferry | **il traghetto** | eel trah**geht**toa |
| hydrofoil | **l'aliscafo** | lahlee**skaa**foa |
| life belt/boat | **la cintura/il canotto di salvataggio** | lah cheen**too**rah/eel kah**not**toa dee sahlvah**tahd**joa |
| ship | **la nave** | lah **naa**vay |

**Bicycle hire** *Noleggio biciclette*

In many cities of Italy there is the possibility to hire a bicycle. Ask any tourist office for the address of a rental firm.

| | | |
|---|---|---|
| I'd like to hire a bicycle. | **Vorrei noleggiare una bicicletta.** | vor**rai**ee noalay**djaa**ray **oo**nah beechee**kleht**tah |

**Other means of transport** *Altri mezzi di trasporto*

| | | |
|---|---|---|
| cable car | **la funivia** | lah fooneé**vee**ah |
| helicopter | **l'elicottero** | laylee**kot**tayroa |
| moped | **il motorino** | eel moatoa**ree**noa |
| motorbike/scooter | **la moto/la motoretta** | lah **mo**toa/lah moatoa**reh**ttah |

Or perhaps you prefer:

| | | |
|---|---|---|
| to hitchhike | **fare l'autostop** | **faa**ray lowtoa**stop** |
| to walk | **camminare** | kahmmee**naa**ray |

## Car *Macchina*

In general roads are good in Italy and Switzerland. Motorways (expressways) are subject to tolls *(il pedaggio)* in Italy. If you use the motorways in Switzerland you must purchase a sticker (valid for one year) to be displayed on the windscreen.

A red reflector warning triangle must be carried for use in case of a breakdown, and seat-belts *(le cinture di sicurezza)* are obligatory in Switzerland.

| | | |
|---|---|---|
| Where's the nearest filling station? | **Dov'è la stazione di rifornimento più vicina?** | doa**vai** lah stahtsee**oa**nay dee reeforneemayntoa peeoo vee**chee**nah |
| Full tank, please. | **Il pieno, per favore.** | eel peeainoa pair fahvoaray |
| Give me ... litres of petrol (gasoline). | **Mi dia ... litri di benzina.** | mee **dee**ah ... **lee**tree dee bayn**dzee**nah |
| super (premium)/ regular/lead-free/ diesel | **super/normale/ senza piombo/ gasolio** | **soo**payr/noar**maa**lay/ **sayn**tsah peeo**am**boa/ gah**zo**lyoa |
| Please check the ... | **Per favore, controlli ...** | pair fah**voa**ray koan**troa**llee |
| battery | **la batteria** | lah bahttay**ree**ah |
| brake fluid | **l'olio dei freni** | **lo**lyoa **dai**ee **fray**nee |
| oil/water | **l'olio/l'acqua** | **lo**lyoa/**lahk**kwah |
| Would you check the tyre pressure? | **Può controllare la pressione delle gomme?** | pwo koantroal**laa**ray lah praysseeoanay **dayl**lay **goam**may |
| 1.6 front, 1.8 rear. | **1,6 davanti, 1,8 dietro.** | **oo**noa ay **se**hee dah**vahn**tee **oo**noa ay **o**ttoa dee**eh**troa |
| Please check the spare tyre, too. | **Per favore, controlli anche la ruota di scorta.** | pair fah**voa**ray koan**troa**llee **ahng**kay lah **rwaw**tah dee **skor**tah |
| Can you mend this puncture (fix this flat)? | **Può riparare questa foratura?** | pwo reepah**raa**ray **kooay**stah forah**too**rah |
| Would you please change the ...? | **Potrebbe cambiare ...** | poa**trehb**bay kahmbee**aa**ray |
| bulb | **la lampadina** | lah lahmpah**dee**nah |
| fan belt | **la cinghia del ventilatore** | lah **cheeng**geeah dayl vaynteelah**toa**ray |

CAR HIRE, see page 20

| | | |
|---|---|---|
| spark(ing) plugs | **le candele** | lay kahn**day**lay |
| tyre | **la gomma** | lah **goam**mah |
| wipers | **i tergicristalli** | ee tayrjeekree**stahl**lee |
| Would you clean the windscreen (windshield)? | **Mi pulisca il parabrezza, per favore.** | mee poo**lee**skah eel pahrah**braydzah** pair fah**voa**ray |

## Asking the way *Per chiedere la strada*

| | | |
|---|---|---|
| Can you tell me the way to ...? | **Può dirmi qual è la strada per ...?** | pwo **deer**mee kwahl ai lah **straa**dah pair |
| How do I get to ...? | **Come si va a ...?** | **koa**may see vah ah |
| Are we on the right road for ...? | **Siamo sulla strada giusta per ...?** | see**aa**moa **sool**lah **straa**dah **joo**stah pair |
| How far is the next village? | **Quanto dista il prossimo villaggio?** | **kwahn**toa **dee**stah eel **pros**seemoa veel**lahd**joa |
| How far is it to ... from here? | **Quanto dista ... da qui?** | **kwahn**toa **dee**stah ... dah koo**ee** |
| Is there a motorway (expressway)? | **C'è un'autostrada?** | chai oonowtoa**straa**dah |
| Is there a road with little traffic? | **C'è una strada con poco traffico?** | chai **oo**nah **straa**dah kon **po**koa **trahf**feekoa |
| How long does it take by car/on foot? | **Quanto tempo ci vuole in macchina/ a piedi?** | **kwahn**toa **tehm**poa chee **vwo**lay een **mahk**keenah/ ah pee**ay**dee |
| Can I drive to the centre of town? | **Si può andare in macchina nel centro città?** | see pwo ahn**daa**ray een **mahk**keenah nayl **chayn**troa cheet**tah** |
| Can you tell me, where ... is? | **Può dirmi dove si trova ...?** | pwo **deer**mee **doa**vay see **traw**vah |
| How can I find this place? | **Come posso trovare questo posto?** | **koa**may **pos**soa tro**vaa**ray koo**ay**stoa **po**stoa |
| Where can I find this address? | **Dove posso trovare questo indirizzo?** | **doa**vay **pos**soa tro**vaa**ray koo**ay**stoa eendee**reet**tsoa |
| Where's this? | **Dov'è questo?** | doa**vai** koo**ay**stoa |
| Can you show me on the map where I am? | **Può indicarmi sulla carta dove mi trovo?** | pwo eendee**kaar**mee **sool**lah **kahr**tah **doa**vay mee **traw**voa |

| | |
|---|---|
| **Lei è sulla strada sbagliata.** | You're on the wrong road. |
| **Vada diritto.** | Go straight ahead. |
| **È laggiù a ...** | It's down there on the ... |
| **sinistra/destra**<br>**di fronte/dietro ...**<br>**accanto a/dopo ...** | left/right<br>opposite/behind ...<br>next to/after ... |
| **nord/sud**<br>**est/ovest** | north/south<br>east/west |
| **Vada fino al primo/ secondo incrocio.** | Go to the first/second crossroad (intersection). |
| **Al semaforo, giri a sinistra.** | Turn left at the traffic lights. |
| **Giri a destra al prossimo angolo.** | Turn right at the next corner. |
| **Prenda la strada per ...** | Take the road for ... |
| **Segua la direzione per Stresa.** | Follow the sign for "Stresa". |
| **Deve tornare indietro ...** | You have to go back to ... |

**Parking** *Parcheggio*

In town centres, most street parking is limited. The blue zones require the *disco di sosta* or parking disc (obtainable from petrol stations), which you set to show when you arrived and when you must leave.

| | | |
|---|---|---|
| Where can I park? | **Dove posso parcheggiare?** | **doa**vay **pos**soa pahrkayd**jaa**ray |
| Is there a car park nearby? | **C'è un parcheggio qui vicino?** | chai oon pahr**kayd**joa koo**ee** vee**chee**noa |
| May I park here? | **Posso parcheggiare qui?** | **pos**soa pahrkayd**jaa**ray koo**ee** |
| How long can I park here? | **Quanto tempo posso restare qui?** | **kwahn**toa **tehm**poa **pos**soa ray**staa**ray koo**ee** |
| What's the charge per hour? | **Quanto si paga all'ora?** | **kwahn**toa see **paa**gah ahl**loa**rah |
| Do you have some change for the parking meter? | **Ha della moneta per il parchimetro?** | ah **dayl**lah moa**nay**tah pair eel pahr**kee**maytroa |

## Breakdown—Road assistance *Guasti—Assistenza stradale*

| | | |
|---|---|---|
| Where's the nearest garage? | **Dov'è il garage più vicino?** | doa**vai** eel gah**raazh** pee**oo** vee**chee**noa |
| Excuse me. My car has broken down. | **Mi scusi. Ho un guasto all'automobile.** | mee **skoo**zee. oa oon **gwaa**stoa ahllowtoa**maw**beelay |
| May I use your phone? | **Posso usare il suo telefono?** | **pos**soa oo**zaa**ray eel **soo**a tay**lay**foanoa |
| I've had a breakdown at ... | **Ho avuto un guasto a ...** | oa ah**voo**toa oon **gwaa**stoa ah |
| Can you send a mechanic? | **Può mandare un meccanico?** | pwo mahn**daa**ray oon mayk**kaa**neekoa |
| My car won't start. | **La mia macchina non parte.** | lah **mee**ah **mahk**keenah noan **pahr**tay |
| The battery is dead. | **La batteria è scarica.** | lah bahttay**ree**ah ai **skaa**reekah |
| I've run out of petrol (gasoline). | **Sono rimasto(a) senza benzina.** | **soa**noa ree**mah**stoa(ah) **sayn**tsah bayn**dzee**nah |
| I have a flat tyre. | **Ho una gomma sgonfia.** | oa **oo**nah **goam**mah **sgoan**feeah |
| The engine is overheating. | **Il motore è surriscaldato.** | eel moa**toa**ray ai soorreeskahl**daa**toa |
| There is something wrong with ... | **Qualcosa non va con ...** | kwahl**kaw**sah noan vah kon |
| brakes | **i freni** | ee **fray**nee |
| carburettor | **il carburatore** | eel kahrboorah**toa**ray |
| exhaust pipe | **il tubo di scappamento** | eel **too**boa dee skahppah**mayn**toa |
| radiator | **il radiatore** | eel rahdeeah**toa**ray |
| wheel | **la ruota** | lah **rwaw**tah |
| Can you send a breakdown van (tow truck)? | **Può mandare un carro attrezzi?** | pwo mahn**daa**ray oon **kahr**roa at**treht**tsee |
| How long will you be? | **Quanto tempo impiegherete?** | **kwahn**toa **tehm**poa eempeeaygay**ray**tay |

## Accident—Police *Incidenti—Polizia*

| | | |
|---|---|---|
| Please call the police. | **Per favore, chiami la polizia.** | pair fah**voa**ray kee**aa**mee lah poalee**tsee**ah |

| | | |
|---|---|---|
| There's been an accident. | **C'è stato un incidente.** | chai **staa**toa oon eencheedayntay |
| Where's the nearest telephone? | **Dov'è il telefono più vicino?** | doa**vai** eel tay**lay**foanoa peeoo vee**chee**noa |
| Call a doctor/an ambulance quickly. | **Chiami un medico/ un'ambulanza, presto.** | kee**aa**mee oon **mai**deekoa/ oonahmboo**lahn**tsah **preh**stoa |
| There are people injured. | **Ci sono dei feriti.** | chee **soa**noa **dai**ee fay**ree**tee |
| What's your name and address? | **Qual è il suo nome e indirizzo?** | kwahl ai eel **soo**oa **noa**may ay eendee**reet**soa |
| What's your insurance company? | **Qual è la sua assicurazione?** | kwahl ai lah **soo**ah ahsseekoorahtsee**oa**nay |

**Road signs** *Segnali stradali*

| | |
|---|---|
| **ACCENDERE I FARI IN GALLERIA** | Switch on headlights before entering tunnel |
| **ACCOSTARE A DESTRA (SINISTRA)** | Keep right (left) |
| **ALT** | Stop |
| **AREA DI SERVIZIO** | Service area |
| **CADUTA MASSI** | Falling rocks |
| **CARABINIERI** | Police |
| **CIRCONVALLAZIONE** | Ring road (belt highway) |
| **CORSIA D'EMERGENZA** | Emergency parking zone |
| **CURVE PER 5 KM.** | Bends (curves) for 5 km. |
| **DEVIAZIONE** | Diversion/detour |
| **DIVIETO DI SOSTA** | No parking |
| **DIVIETO DI SORPASSO** | No overtaking (passing) |
| **LAVORI IN CORSO** | Road works ahead (men working) |
| **PASSAGGIO A LIVELLO** | Level (railroad) crossing |
| **PERICOLO** | Danger |
| **POLIZIA STRADALE** | Highway police |
| **RALLENTARE** | Reduce speed |
| **SENSO UNICO** | One way |
| **SOCCORSO A.C.I.** | A.C.I. emergency road service |
| **STRADA DISSESTATA** | Poor road surface |
| **TRANSITO CON CATENE** | Chains required |
| **VICOLO CIECO** | Dead end |
| **VIETATO L'ACCESSO** | No entry |
| **VIGILI URBANI** | City police |
| **ZONA PEDONALE** | Pedestrian zone |

# Sightseeing

| | | |
|---|---|---|
| Where's the tourist office? | **Dov'è l'azienda di soggiorno e turismo (l'ufficio turistico)?** | doa**vai** lahdzee**ayn**dah dee soad**joar**noa ay too**reez**moa (looff**ee**choa too**ree**steekoa) |
| What are the main points of interest? | **Quali sono i principali punti di interesse?** | **kwaa**lee **soa**noa ee preenchee**paa**lee **poon**tee dee eentay**rays**say |
| We're here for ... | **Siamo qui per ...** | see**aa**moa koo**ee** pair |
| only a few hours | **alcune ore soltanto** | ahl**koo**nay **oa**ray sol**tahn**toa |
| a day | **un giorno** | oon **joar**noa |
| a week | **una settimana** | **oo**nah saytteemaanah |
| Can you recommend a sightseeing tour/an excursion? | **Può consigliare un giro turistico/una gita?** | pwo konsee**lyaa**ray oon **jee**roa too**ree**steekoa/ oonah **jee**tah |
| What's the point of departure? | **Da dove si parte?** | dah **doa**vay see **pahr**tay |
| Will the bus pick us up at the hotel? | **Il pullman passerà a prenderci all'hotel?** | eel **pool**mahn pahssay**rah** ah **prehn**dehrchee ahllo**tehl** |
| How much does the tour cost? | **Quanto costa il giro?** | **kwahn**toa **koa**stah eel **jee**roa |
| What time does the tour start? | **A che ora inizia il giro?** | ah kay **oa**rah ee**nee**tseeah eel **jee**roa |
| Is lunch included? | **Il pranzo è compreso?** | eel **prahn**dzoa ai koam**pray**soa |
| What time do we get back? | **A che ora si ritorna?** | ah kay **oa**rah see ree**toar**nah |
| Do we have free time in ...? | **Avremo del tempo libero a ...?** | ah**vray**moa dayl **tehm**poa **lee**bayroa ah |
| Is there an English-speaking guide? | **C'è una guida che parla inglese?** | chai **oo**nah goo**ee**dah kay **pahr**lah eeng**glay**say |
| I'd like to hire a private guide for ... | **Vorrei avere una guida privata per ...** | vor**raiee** ah**vay**ray **oo**nah goo**ee**dah pree**vaa**tah pair |
| half a day | **mezza giornata** | **mehd**dzah joar**naa**tah |
| a full day | **una giornata intera** | **oo**nah joar**naa**tah een**tay**rah |

| | | |
|---|---|---|
| Where is/Where are the ...? | **Dove si trova/Dove si trovano ...?** | **doa**vay see **traw**vah/ **doa**vay see **traw**vahnoa |
| abbey | **l'abbazia** | lahbbah**tsee**ah |
| art gallery | **la galleria d'arte** | lah gahllay**ree**ah **dahr**tay |
| artists' quarter | **il quartiere degli artisti** | eel kwahrteeayray **day**lyee ahr**tee**stee |
| botanical gardens | **i giardini botanici** | ee jahr**dee**nee bota**a**neechee |
| building | **l'edificio** | laydee**fee**choa |
| business district | **il quartiere degli affari** | eel kwahrtee**ay**ray **day**lyee ahf**faa**ree |
| castle | **il castello** | eel kah**stehl**loa |
| catacombs | **le catacombe** | lay kahtah**kom**bay |
| cathedral | **la cattedrale** | lah kahttay**draa**lay |
| cave | **la grotta** | lah **grot**tah |
| cemetery | **il cimitero** | eel cheemee**tai**roa |
| city centre | **il centro città** | eel **chayn**troa cheet**tah** |
| chapel | **la cappella** | lah kahp**pehl**lah |
| church | **la chiesa** | lah kee**ay**zah |
| concert hall | **la sala dei concerti** | lah **saa**lah **dai**ee kon**chehr**tee |
| convent | **il convento** | eel kon**vayn**toa |
| court house | **il palazzo di giustizia** | eel pah**lahtt**soa dee joo**stee**tseeah |
| downtown area | **il centro (città)** | eel **chayn**troa (cheet**tah**) |
| exhibition | **l'esposizione** | layspozeetsee**oa**nay |
| factory | **la fabbrica** | lah **fahb**breekah |
| fair | **la fiera** | lah fee**ay**rah |
| flea market | **il mercato delle pulci** | eel mehr**kaa**toa **dayl**lay **pool**chee |
| fortress | **la fortezza** | lah for**teht**tsah |
| fountain | **la fontana** | lah foan**taa**nah |
| gardens | **i giardini** | ee jahr**dee**nee |
| harbour | **il porto** | eel **por**toa |
| lake | **il lago** | eel **laa**goa |
| library | **la biblioteca** | lah beebleeo**tai**kah |
| market | **il mercato** | eel mayr**kaa**toa |
| memorial | **il memoriale** | eel maymoaree**aa**lay |
| monastery | **il monastero** | eel moanah**stai**roa |
| monument | **il monumento** | eel moanoo**mayn**toa |
| museum | **il museo** | eel moo**zai**oa |
| old town | **la città vecchia** | lah cheet**tah vehk**keeah |
| opera house | **il teatro dell'opera** | eel tay**aa**troa dayl**lo**payrah |
| palace | **il palazzo** | eel pah**laht**tsoa |
| park | **il parco** | eel **pahr**koa |
| parliament building | **il Parlamento** | eel pahrlah**mayn**toa |

| | | |
|---|---|---|
| planetarium | **il planetario** | eel plahnay**taa**reeoa |
| royal palace | **il palazzo reale** | eel pah**laht**tsoa ray**aa**lay |
| ruins | **le rovine** | lay ro**vee**nay |
| shopping area | **la zona dei negozi** | lah **dzo**nah **dai**ee nay**go**tsee |
| square | **la piazza** | lah pee**aht**sah |
| stadium | **lo stadio** | loa **staa**deeoa |
| statue | **la statua** | lah **staa**tooah |
| stock exchange | **la borsa valori** | lah **bor**sah vah**loa**ree |
| theatre | **il teatro** | eel tay**aa**troa |
| tomb | **la tomba** | lah **toam**bah |
| tower | **la torre** | lah **toar**ray |
| town hall | **il municipio** | eel moonee**chee**peeoa |
| university | **l'università** | looneevayrsee**tah** |
| zoo | **lo zoo** | loa dzoo |

## Admission *All'entrata*

| | | |
|---|---|---|
| Is ... open on Sundays? | **È aperto la domenica il ...?** | ai ah**pehr**toa lah doa**may**neekah eel |
| When does it open? | **Quando apre?** | **kwahn**doa **aa**pray |
| When does it close? | **Quando chiude?** | **kwahn**doa kee**oo**day |
| How much is the entrance fee? | **Quanto costa l'entrata?** | **kwahn**toa **ko**stah layn**traa**tah |
| Is there any reduction for ...? | **C'è una riduzione per ...?** | chai **oo**nah reedootsee**oa**nay pair |
| children | **i bambini** | ee bahm**bee**nee |
| disabled | **gli andicappati** | lyee ahndeekahp**paa**tee |
| groups | **i gruppi** | ee **groop**pee |
| pensioners | **i pensionati** | ee paynseeoa**naa**tee |
| students | **gli studenti** | lyee stoo**dayn**tee |
| Have you a guidebook (in English)? | **Avete una guida turistica (in inglese)?** | ah**vay**tay **oo**nah goo**ee**dah too**ree**steekah (een eeng**glay**say) |
| Can I buy a catalogue? | **Posso comprare un catalogo?** | **pos**soa koam**praa**ray oon kah**taa**loagoa |
| Is it all right to take pictures? | **È permesso fare delle fotografie?** | ai pehr**mays**soa **faa**ray **dayl**lay foatoagrah**fee**ay |

| | |
|---|---|
| **ENTRATA LIBERA** | ADMISSION FREE |
| **VIETATO FOTOGRAFARE** | NO CAMERAS ALLOWED |

## Who—What—When? *Chi—Cosa—Quando?*

| | | |
|---|---|---|
| What's that building? | **Che cos'è quest'edificio?** | kay ko**sai** koo**ay**staydeefeechoa |
| Who was the ...? | **Chi è stato ...?** | kee ai **staa**toa |
| architect | **l'architetto** | lahrkee**teht**toa |
| artist | **l'artista** | lahr**tee**stah |
| painter | **il pittore** | eel peet**toa**ray |
| sculptor | **lo scultore** | loa skool**toa**ray |
| Who built it? | **Chi lo costruì?** | kee loa koastroo**ee** |
| Who painted that picture? | **Chi dipinse questo quadro?** | kee dee**peen**say koo**ay**stoa **kwaa**droa |
| When did he live? | **Quando è vissuto?** | **kwahn**doa ai vees**soo**toa |
| When was it built? | **Quando fu costruito?** | **kwahn**doa foo koastroo**ee**toa |
| Where's the house where ... lived? | **Dove si trova la casa in cui visse ...?** | **doa**vay see **traw**vah lah **kaa**sah een **koo**ee **vees**say |
| We're interested in ... | **Ci interessiamo di ...** | chee eentayrays**see**aamoa dee |
| antiques | **antichità** | ahnteekee**tah** |
| archaeology | **archeologia** | ahrkayoaloa**jee**ah |
| art | **arte** | **ahr**tay |
| botany | **botanica** | bo**taa**neekah |
| ceramics | **ceramiche** | chay**raa**meekay |
| coins | **monete** | mo**nai**tay |
| fine arts | **belle arti** | **behl**lay **ahr**tee |
| furniture | **mobilio** | mo**bee**lyoa |
| geology | **geologia** | jayoaloa**jee**ah |
| handicrafts | **artigianato** | ahrteejah**naa**toa |
| history | **storia** | **sto**reeah |
| medicine | **medicina** | maydee**chee**nah |
| music | **musica** | **moo**zeekah |
| natural history | **storia naturale** | **sto**reeah nahtoo**raa**lay |
| ornithology | **ornitologia** | oarneetoaloa**jee**ah |
| painting | **pittura** | peet**too**rah |
| pottery | **terrecotte** | tehrray**kot**tay |
| prehistory | **preistoria** | prayee**sto**reeah |
| religion | **religione** | raylee**joa**nay |
| sculpture | **scultura** | skool**too**rah |
| zoology | **zoologia** | dzoaoaloa**jee**ah |
| Where's the ... department? | **Dov'è il reparto di/del ...?** | doa**vai** eel ray**pahr**toa dee/dayl |

| It's ... | **È ...** | ai |
|---|---|---|
| amazing | **sorprendente** | soarprayn**dehn**tay |
| awful | **orribile** | or**ree**beelay |
| beautiful | **bello** | **behl**loa |
| excellent | **eccellente** | ehtchehl**layn**tay |
| gloomy | **malinconico** | mahleeng**kaw**neekoa |
| impressive | **impressionante** | eempraysseeoa**nahn**tay |
| interesting | **interessante** | eentayrays**sahn**tay |
| magnificent | **magnifico** | mah**ñee**feekoa |
| nice | **bello** | **behl**loa |
| overwhelming | **sbalorditivo** | sbahloardee**tee**voa |
| strange | **strano** | **straa**noa |
| superb | **superbo** | soo**pehr**boa |
| terrifying | **terrificante** | tayrreefee**kahn**tay |
| tremendous | **fantastico** | fahn**tah**steekoa |
| ugly | **brutto** | **broot**toa |

## Religious services *Funzioni religiose*

Most churches and cathedrals are open to the public, except, of course, during mass.

If you are interested in taking pictures, you should obtain permission first. Shorts and backless dresses are definitely out when visiting churches.

| | | |
|---|---|---|
| Is there a/an ... near here? | **C'è una ... qui vicino?** | chai **oo**nah ... koo**ee** vee**chee**noa |
| Catholic church | **chiesa cattolica** | kee**ay**zah kaht**toa**leekah |
| Protestant church | **chiesa protestante** | kee**ay**zah proatay**stahn**tay |
| synagogue | **sinagoga** | seenah**gaw**gah |
| mosque | **moschea** | moa**skai**ah |
| At what time is ...? | **A che ora è ...?** | ah kay **oa**rah ai |
| mass | **la messa** | lah **may**ssah |
| the service | **la funzione** | lah foontsee**oa**nay |
| Where can I find a ... who speaks English? | **Dove posso trovare un ... che parla inglese?** | **doa**vay **pos**soa tro**vaa**ray oon ... kay **pahr**lah een**glay**say |
| priest/minister | **prete/pastore** | **prai**tay/pah**stoa**ray |
| rabbi | **rabbino** | rahb**bee**noa |
| I'd like to visit the church. | **Vorrei visitare la chiesa.** | vor**rai**ee veezee**taa**ray lah kee**ay**zah |

### In the countryside *In campagna*

| | | |
|---|---|---|
| Is there a scenic route to ...? | **C'è una strada panoramica per ...?** | chai **oo**nah **straa**dah pahnoa**raa**meekah pair |
| How far is it to ...? | **Quanto dista ...?** | **kwahn**toa **dee**stah |
| Can we walk? | **Possiamo andare a piedi?** | posseea**a**moa ahn**daa**ray ah peeaydee |
| How high is that mountain? | **Quanto è alta quella montagna?** | **kwahn**toa ai **ahl**tah kooa**yl**lah moan**taa**ñah |
| What's the name of that ...? | **Come si chiama questo ...?** | **koa**may see kee**aa**mah koo**ay**stoa |
| animal/bird | **animale/uccello** | ahnee**maa**lay/oot**chehl**loa |
| flower/tree | **fiore/albero** | fee**oa**ray/**ahl**bayroa |

### Landmarks *Punti di riferimento*

| | | |
|---|---|---|
| bridge | **il ponte** | eel **poan**tay |
| cliff | **la scogliera** | lah skoa**lyay**rah |
| farm | **la fattoria** | lah fahttoa**ree**ah |
| field | **il campo** | eel **kahm**poa |
| footpath | **il sentiero** | eel saynteeayroa |
| forest | **la foresta** | lah faw**reh**stah |
| garden | **il giardino** | eel jahr**dee**noa |
| hamlet | **il gruppo di casolari** | eel **groop**poa dee kahsoa**laa**ree |
| hill | **la collina** | lah koal**lee**nah |
| house | **la casa** | lah **kaa**sah |
| lake | **il lago** | eel **laa**goa |
| meadow | **il prato** | eel **praa**toa |
| mountain | **la montagna** | lah moan**taa**ñah |
| (mountain) pass | **il passo** | eel **pahs**soa |
| peak | **il picco** | eel **peek**koa |
| pond | **lo stagno** | loa **staa**ñoa |
| river | **il fiume** | eel fee**oo**may |
| road | **la strada** | lah **straa**dah |
| sea | **il mare** | eel **maa**ray |
| spring | **la sorgente** | lah soar**jayn**tay |
| valley | **la valle** | lah **vahl**lay |
| village | **il villaggio/il paese** | eel veel**lahd**joa/eel pah**ay**zay |
| vineyard | **la vigna** | lah **vee**ñah |
| wall | **il muro** | eel **moo**roa |
| waterfall | **la cascata** | lah kah**skaa**tah |
| well | **il pozzo** | eel **poat**soa |
| wood | **il bosco** | eel **boa**skoa |

ASKING THE WAY, see page 76

# Relaxing

## **Cinema (movies)—Theatre** *Cinema—Teatro*

You can find out what's playing from newspapers and billboards. In Rome and in the main towns in Italy look for the weekly entertainment guides available at major newsstands, at the tourist office and the hotel reception.

| | | |
|---|---|---|
| What's showing at the cinema tonight? | **Cosa danno al cinema questa sera?** | kawsah dahnnoa ahl cheenaymah kooaystah sayrah |
| What's playing at the ... theatre? | **Che spettacolo c'è al teatro ...?** | kay spayttaakoaloa chai ahl tayaatroa |
| What sort of play is it? | **Che genere di commedia è?** | kay jainayray dee koammaideeah ai |
| Who's it by? | **Di chi è?** | dee kee ai |
| Can you recommend (a) ...? | **Può consigliarmi ...?** | pwo konseelyaarmee |
| good film | **un buon film** | oon bwawn "film" |
| comedy | **una commedia** | oonah koammaideeah |
| musical | **una commedia musicale** | oonah koammaideeah moozeekaalay |
| Where's that new film by ... being shown? | **In che cinema danno il nuovo film di ...?** | een kay cheenaymah dahnnoa eel nwovoa "film" dee |
| Who's in it? | **Chi sono gli attori?** | kee soanoa lyee ahttoaree |
| Who's playing the lead? | **Chi interpreta il ruolo principale?** | kee eentehrprehtah eel rwoloa preencheepaalay |
| Who's the director? | **Chi è il regista?** | kee ai eel rayjeestah |
| At what theatre is that new play by ... being performed? | **In quale teatro viene rappresentata la nuova commedia di ...?** | een kwaalay tayaatroa veeaynay rahppraysayntaatah lah nwovah koammaideeah dee |
| Is there a sound-and-light show on somewhere? | **C'è uno spettacolo suoni e luci da qualche parte?** | chai oonoa spayttaakoaloa swonee ay loochee dah kwahlkay paartay |

| | | |
|---|---|---|
| What time does it begin? | **A che ora incomincia?** | ah kay **oa**rah eengkoa**meen**chah |
| Are there any seats for tonight? | **Ci sono posti per questa sera?** | chee **soa**noa **pos**tee pair koo**ay**stah **say**rah |
| How much are the seats? | **Quanto costano i posti?** | **kwahn**toa **kos**tahnoa ee **pos**tee |
| I want to reserve 2 seats for the show on Friday evening. | **Desidero prenotare 2 posti per lo spettacolo di venerdì sera.** | day**zee**dayroa praynoa**taa**ray 2 **pos**tee pair loa spayt**taa**koaloa dee vaynayr**dee say**rah |
| Can I have a ticket for the matinée on Tuesday? | **Posso avere un biglietto per lo spettacolo del pomeriggio di martedì?** | **pos**soa ah**vay**ray oon bee**lyayt**toa pair loa spayt**taa**koaloa dayl poamay**ree**djoa dee mahrtay**dee** |
| I want a seat in the stalls (orchestra). | **Desidero una poltrona.** | day**zee**dayroa **oo**nah poal**troa**nah |
| Not too far back. | **Non troppo indietro.** | noan **trop**poa eendee**ay**troa |
| Somewhere in the middle. | **A metà circa.** | ah may**tah cheer**kah |
| How much are the seats in the circle (mezzanine)? | **Quanto costano i posti in galleria?** | **kwahn**toa **kos**tahnoa ee **pos**tee een gahllay**ree**ah |
| May I please have a programme? | **Per favore, posso avere un programma?** | pair fah**voa**ray **pos**soa ah**vay**ray oon pro**grahm**mah |
| Where's the cloakroom? | **Dov'è il guardaroba?** | doa**vai** eel gwahrdah**ro**bah |

| | |
|---|---|
| **Sono spiacente, è tutto esaurito.** | I'm sorry, we're sold out. |
| **Vi sono solo alcuni posti in galleria.** | There are only a few seats left in the circle (mezzanine). |
| **Posso vedere il suo biglietto?** | May I see your ticket?* |
| **Questo è il suo posto.** | This is your seat. |

* It's customary to tip usherettes *(la maschera)* in most Italian theatres.

DAYS OF THE WEEK, see page 151

## Opera—Ballet—Concert *Opera—Balletto–Concerto*

| | | |
|---|---|---|
| Can you recommend a ...? | **Può consigliarmi ...?** | pwo konsee**lyahr**mee |
| ballet | **un balletto** | oon bahl**leht**toa |
| concert | **un concerto** | oon koan**chehr**toa |
| opera | **un'opera** | oonopayrah |
| operetta | **un'operetta** | oonopay**ray**ttah |
| Where's the opera house/the concert hall? | **Dov'è il teatro dell'opera/la sala dei concerti?** | doa**vai** eel tay**aa**troa dayl**lo**payrah/lah **saa**lah **dai**ee koan**chehr**tee |
| What's on at the opera tonight? | **Cosa danno all'Opera questa sera?** | **kaw**sah **dahn**noa ahllopay-rah koo**ay**stah **say**rah |
| Who's singing/ dancing? | **Chi canta/balla?** | kee **kahn**tah/**bahl**lah |
| What orchestra is playing? | **Che orchestra suona?** | kay oar**kay**strah **swo**nah |
| What are they playing? | **Cosa suonano?** | **kaw**sah **swo**nahnoa |
| Who's the conductor/ soloist? | **Chi è il maestro/ il solista?** | kee ai eel mah**eh**stroa/ eel so**lee**stah |

## Nightclub *Night-club*

| | | |
|---|---|---|
| Can you recommend a good nightclub? | **Può consigliarmi un buon night-club?** | pwo konsee**lyahr**mee oon bwon "night-club" |
| Is there a floor show? | **C'è il varietà?** | chai eel vahreeay**tah** |
| What time does the floor show start? | **A che ora inizia il varietà?** | ah kay **oa**rah ee**neet**seeah eel vahreeay**tah** |
| Is evening dress necessary? | **È necessario l'abito da sera?** | ai naychays**saa**reeoa **laa**beetoa dah **say**rah |

## Discos *Discoteche*

| | | |
|---|---|---|
| Where can we go dancing? | **Dove possiamo andare a ballare?** | **doa**vay possee**aa**moa ahn**daa**ray ah bahl**laa**ray |
| Is there a disco-theque in town? | **C'è una discoteca in città?** | chai **oo**nah deeskoa**tay**kah een cheet**tah** |
| Would you like to dance? | **Vuole ballare?** | **vwo**lay bahl**laa**ray |

## Sports *Sport*

Football (soccer), tennis, boxing, wrestling and bicycle, car and horse racing are among popular spectator sports. If you like sailing, fishing, horseback riding, golf, tennis, hiking, cycling, swimming, golf or trap shooting, you'll find plenty of opportunity to satisfy your recreational bent.

| | | |
|---|---|---|
| Is there a football (soccer) match anywhere this Saturday? | **C'è una partita di calcio da qualche parte, sabato?** | chai **oo**nah pahr**tee**tah dee **kahl**choa dah **kwahl**kay **pahr**tay **saa**bahtoa |
| Which teams are playing? | **Che squadre giocano?** | kay **skwaa**dray **joa**kahnoa |
| Can you get me a ticket? | **Mi può procurare un biglietto?** | mee pwo proakoo**raa**ray oon bee**lyayt**toa |

| | | |
|---|---|---|
| basketball | **la pallacanestro** | lah pahllahkah**neh**stroa |
| boxing | **il pugilato** | eel poojee**laa**toa |
| car racing | **la corsa automobilistica** | lah **koar**sah owtoamoabee**lee**steeka |
| cycling | **il ciclismo** | eel chee**kleez**moa |
| football (soccer) | **il calcio** | eel **kahl**choa |
| horse racing | **la corsa di cavalli** | lah **koar**sah dee kah**vahl**lee |
| skiing | **lo sci** | loa shee |
| swimming | **il nuoto** | eel **nwo**toa |
| tennis | **il tennis** | eel "tennis" |
| volleyball | **la pallavolo** | lah pahllah**voa**loa |

| | | |
|---|---|---|
| I'd like to see a boxing match. | **Vorrei vedere un incontro di pugilato.** | vor**raiee** vay**day**ray oon eeng**koan**troa dee poojee**laa**toa |
| What's the admission charge? | **Quanto costa l'entrata?** | **kwahn**toa **kos**tah layn**traa**tah |
| Where's the nearest golf course? | **Dove si trova il campo da golf più vicino?** | **doa**vay see **traw**vah eel **kahm**poa dah golf pee**oo** vee**chee**noa |
| Where are the tennis courts? | **Dove sono i campi da tennis?** | **doa**vay **soa**noa ee **kahm**pee dah "tennis" |
| What's the charge per ...? | **Qual è il prezzo per ...?** | kwahl ai eel **preht**tsoa pair |
| day/round/hour | **un giorno/una partita/un'ora** | oon **joar**noa/**oo**nah pahr**tee**tah/oo**noa**rah |

| | | |
|---|---|---|
| Can I hire (rent) rackets? | **Posso noleggiare le racchette?** | **pos**soa noalay**djaa**ray lay rahk**keht**tay |
| Where is the race course (track)? | **Dov'è l'ippodromo?** | doa**vai** leeppoa**drawm**oa |
| Is there any good fishing around here? | **Ci sono buone possibilità di pesca in questa zona?** | chee **so**anoa **bwaw**nay posseebeelee**tah** dee **pay**skah een koo**ay**stah **dzo**anah |
| Do I need a permit? | **È necessario il permesso?** | ai naychays**saa**reeoa eel payr**mays**soa |
| Where can I get one? | **Dove posso procurarmene uno?** | **doa**vay **pos**soa proakoo**rahr**maynay **oo**noa |
| Can one swim in the lake/river? | **Si può nuotare nel lago/fiume?** | see pwo nwaw**taa**ray nayl **laa**goa/fee**oo**may |
| Is there a swimming pool here? | **C'è una piscina qui?** | chai **oo**nah pee**shee**nah koo**ee** |
| Is it open-air or indoors? | **È una piscina all'aperto o coperta?** | ai **oo**nah pee**shee**nah ahllah**pehr**toa oa koa**pehr**tah |
| Is it heated? | **È riscaldata?** | ai reeskahl**daa**tah |
| What's the temperature of the water? | **Qual è la temperatura dell'acqua?** | kwahl ai lah taympayrah**too**rah day**llahk**kwah |
| Is there a sand beach? | **C'è una spiaggia di sabbia?** | chai **oo**nah spee**ahd**jah dee **sahb**beeah |

## On the beach *In spiaggia*

| | | |
|---|---|---|
| Is it safe for swimming? | **Si può nuotare senza pericolo?** | see pwo nwaw**taa**ray **saynt**sah payr**ree**koaloa |
| Is there a lifeguard? | **C'è un bagnino?** | chai oon bah**ñee**noa |
| There are some big waves. | **Ci sono cavalloni.** | chee **so**anoa kahvahl**loa**nee |
| Is it safe for children? | **È sicuro per i bambini?** | ai see**koo**roa pair ee bahm**bee**nee |
| Are there any dangerous currents? | **Vi sono correnti pericolose?** | vee **so**anoa koar**rayn**tee payreekoa**loa**sah |
| What time is high tide/low tide? | **A che ora è l'alta marea/la bassa marea?** | ah kay **oa**rah ai **lahl**tah mah**ray**ah/lah **bahs**sah mah**ray**ah |

| | | |
|---|---|---|
| I want to hire a/an/ some ... | **Vorrei noleggiare ...** | vorr**aiee** noalayd**jaa**ray |
| bathing hut (cabana) | **una cabina** | **oo**nah kah**bee**nah |
| deck-chair | **una sedia a sdraio** | **oo**nah **say**deeah ah sdraaeeoa |
| motorboat | **una barca a motore** | **oo**nah **bahr**kah ah mo**toa**ray |
| rowing-boat | **una barca a remi** | **oo**nah **bahr**kah ah **ray**mee |
| sailboard | **una tavola a vela** | **oo**nah **taa**volah ah **vai**lah |
| sailing-boat | **una barca a vela** | **oo**nah **bahr**kah ah **vai**lah |
| sunshade (umbrella) | **un ombrellone** | oon oambrayl**loa**nay |
| surfboard | **un sandolino** | oon sahndoa**lee**noa |
| water-skis | **degli sci nautici** | **day**lyee shee **now**teechee |

| | |
|---|---|
| **SPIAGGIA PRIVATA** | PRIVATE BEACH |
| **DIVIETO DI BALNEAZIONE** | NO SWIMMING |

## Winter sports *Sport invernali*

| | | |
|---|---|---|
| Is there a skating rink near here? | **C'è una pista di pattinaggio qui vicino?** | chai **oo**nah **pee**stah dee pahttee**na**djoa koo**ee** vee**chee**noa |
| I'd like to ski. | **Vorrei sciare.** | vorr**aiee** shee**aa**ray |
| downhill/cross-country skiing | **sci di pista/sci di fondo** | shee dee **pee**stah/shee dee **foan**doa |
| Are there any ski runs for ...? | **Vi sono delle piste per ...?** | vee **soa**noa **dayl**lay **pee**stay pair |
| beginners | **principianti** | preencheepee**ahn**tee |
| average skiers | **sciatori medi** | sheeah**toa**ree **may**dee |
| good skiers | **buoni sciatori** | **bwaw**nee sheeah**toa**ree |
| Can I take skiing lesson there? | **Posso prendere delle lezioni di sci?** | **pos**soa **prehn**dayray **dayl**lay laytsee**oa**nee dee shee |
| Are there ski lifts? | **Ci sono delle sciovie?** | chee **soa**noa **dayl**lay sheeo**vee**ai |
| I want to hire a/ some ... | **Vorrei noleggiare ...** | vorr**aiee** noalayd**jaa**ray |
| poles | **dei bastoni** | **dai**ee bah**stoa**nee |
| skates | **dei pattini** | **dai**ee **paht**teenee |
| ski boots | **degli scarponi da sci** | **day**lyee skahr**poa**nee dah shee |
| skiing equipment | **una tenuta da sci** | **oo**nah tay**noo**tah dah shee |
| skis | **degli sci** | **day**lyee shee |

# Making friends

## Introductions *Presentazioni*

| | | |
|---|---|---|
| May I introduce ...? | **Posso presentarle ...?** | possoa prayzayn**taar**lay |
| John, this is ... | **Giovanni, ti presento ...** | jo**vahn**nee tee prayz**ayn**toa |
| My name is ... | **Mi chiamo ...** | mee kee**aa**moa |
| Glad to know you. | **Piacere.** | peeah**chay**ray |
| What's your name? | **Come si chiama?** | koamay see kee**aa**mah |
| How are you? | **Come sta?** | **koa**may stah |
| Fine, thanks. And you? | **Bene, grazie. E lei?** | **bai**nay **graat**seeay. ay **lai**ee |

## Follow-up *Per rompere il ghiaccio*

| | | |
|---|---|---|
| How long have you been here? | **Da quanto tempo è qui?** | dah **kwahn**toa **tehm**poa ai kooee |
| We've been here a week. | **Siamo qui da una settimana.** | see**aa**moa koo**ee** dah **oo**nah saytteem**aa**nah |
| Is this your first visit? | **È la prima volta che viene?** | ai lah **pree**mah **vol**tah kay vee**ay**nay |
| No, we came here last year. | **No, siamo già venuti l'anno scorso.** | noa see**aa**moa jah vaynootee **lahn**noa **skoar**soa |
| Are you enjoying your stay? | **Le piace il suo soggiorno?** | lay pee**aa**chay eel **soo**o soad**joar**noa |
| Yes, I like it very much. | **Sì, mi piace molto.** | see mee pee**aa**chay **moal**toa |
| I like the landscape a lot. | **Mi piace molto il paesaggio.** | mee peeaachay **moal**toa eel pahay**zahd**joa |
| Do you travel a lot? | **Viaggia molto?** | vee**ahd**jah **moal**toa |
| Where do you come from? | **Da dove viene?** | dah **doa**vay vee**ay**nay |
| I'm from ... | **Sono di ...** | **soa**noa dee |
| What's your nationality? | **Di che nazionalità è?** | dee kai nahtseeoanahlee**tah** ai |

COUNTRIES, see page 146

| | | |
|---|---|---|
| I'm ... | **Sono ...** | **soa**noa |
| American<br>British<br>Canadian<br>English<br>Irish<br>Scottish | **americano(a)**<br>**britannico(a)**<br>**canadese**<br>**inglese**<br>**irlandese**<br>**scozzese** | ahmayree**kaa**noa(ah)<br>bree**tahn**neekoa(ah)<br>kahnah**day**say<br>eeng**glay**say<br>eerlahn**day**say<br>skot**say**say |
| Where are you staying? | **Dove soggiorna?** | **doa**vay soad**joar**nah |
| Are you on your own? | **È solo(a)?** | ai **soa**loa(ah) |
| I'm with my ... | **Sono con ...** | **soa**noa kon |
| wife<br>husband<br>family<br>parents<br>boyfriend<br>girlfriend | **mia moglie**<br>**mio marito**<br>**la mia famiglia**<br>**i miei genitori**<br>**il mio ragazzo**<br>**la mia ragazza** | **mee**ah **moa**lyay<br>**mee**oa mah**ree**toa<br>lah **mee**ah fah**mee**lyah<br>ee mee**aiee** jaynee**toa**ree<br>eel **mee**oa rah**gaht**tsoa<br>lah **mee**ah rah**gaht**tsah |

| | | |
|---|---|---|
| father/mother | **il padre/la madre** | eel **paa**dray/lah **maa**dray |
| son/daughter | **il figlio/la figlia** | eel **fee**lyoa/lah **fee**lyah |
| brother/sister | **il fratello/la sorella** | eel frah**tehl**loa/lah so**rehl**lah |
| uncle/aunt | **lo zio/la zia** | loa **dzee**oa/lah **dzee**ah |
| nephew/niece | **il nipote/la nipote** | eel nee**poa**tay/lah nee**poa**tay |
| cousin | **il cugino/la cugina** | eel koo**jee**noa/lah koo**jee**nah |

| | | |
|---|---|---|
| Are you married/ single? | **È sposato(a)/scapolo (nubile)?** | ai spoz**aa**toa(ah)/**skaa**poaloa (**noo**beelay) |
| Do you have children? | **Ha dei bambini?** | ah **dai**ee bahm**bee**nee |
| What do you think of the country/people? | **Cosa pensa del paese/della gente?** | **kaw**sah **payn**sah dayl pah**ay**say/**dayl**lah **jayn**tay |
| What's your occupation? | **Qual è la sua occupazione?** | kwahl ai lah **soo**ah okkoopahtsee**oa**nay |
| I'm a student. | **Sono studente.** | **soa**noa stoo**dehn**tay |
| I'm here on a business trip. | **Sono qui in viaggio d'affari.** | **soa**noa koo**ee** een vee**ahd**joa dah**ffaa**ree |
| Do you play cards/ chess? | **Gioca a carte/a scacchi?** | **joa**kah ah **kahr**tay/ah **skahk**kee |

## The weather *Il tempo*

| | | |
|---|---|---|
| What a lovely day! | **Che bella giornata!** | kay **behl**lah joar**naa**tah |
| What awful weather! | **Che tempo orribile!** | kay **tehm**poa or**ree**beelay |
| Isn't it cold/hot today? | **Che freddo/caldo fa oggi!** | kay **frehd**doa/**kahl**doa fah **od**jee |
| Is it usually as warm as this? | **Fa sempre caldo così?** | fah **sehm**pray **kahl**doa kaw**see** |
| Do you think it's going to ... tomorrow? | **Pensa che domani ...?** | **payn**sah kay doa**maa**nee |
| be a nice day | **sarà una bella giornata** | sah**rah oo**nah **behl**lah joar**naa**tah |
| rain | **pioverà** | peeoavay**rah** |
| snow | **nevicherà** | nayveekay**rah** |
| What is the weather forecast? | **Come sono le previsioni del tempo?** | **koa**may **soa**noa lay prehveezee**oa**nee dayl **tehm**poa |

| | | |
|---|---|---|
| cloud | **la nuvola** | lah **noo**volah |
| fog | **la nebbia** | lah **nehb**beeah |
| frost | **il gelo** | eel **jay**loa |
| ice | **il ghiaccio** | eel gee**aht**choa |
| lightning | **il lampo** | eel **lahm**poa |
| moon | **la luna** | lah **loo**nah |
| rain | **la pioggia** | lah pee**odj**ah |
| sky | **il cielo** | eel **chay**loa |
| snow | **la neve** | lah **nay**vay |
| star | **la stella** | lah **stayl**lah |
| sun | **il sole** | eel **soa**lay |
| thunder | **il tuono** | eel **twon**oa |
| thunderstorm | **il temporale** | eel tehmpoa**raa**lay |
| wind | **il vento** | eel **vayn**toa |

## Invitations *Inviti*

| | | |
|---|---|---|
| Would you like to have dinner with us on ...? | **Vorrebbe cenare con noi ...?** | vor**rehb**bay chay**naa**ray kon **no**aee |
| May I invite you for lunch? | **Posso invitarla a pranzo?** | **pos**soa-eenvee**taar**lah ah **prahn**dzoa |

DAYS OF THE WEEK, see page 151

| | | |
|---|---|---|
| Can you come over for a drink this evening? | **Può venire a bere un bicchiere da me questa sera?** | pwo vay**nee**ray ah **bay**ray oon beekkee**ay**ray dah mai kooaystah **say**rah |
| There's a party. Are you coming? | **C'è un ricevimento. Viene?** | chai oon reechayvee-**mayn**toa. vee**ay**nay |
| That's very kind of you. | **È molto gentile da parte sua.** | ai **moal**toa jayn**tee**lay dah **pahr**tay **soo**ah |
| I'd love to come. | **Verrò con piacere.** | vayr**ro** kon peeah**chay**ray |
| What time shall we come? | **A che ora dobbiamo venire?** | ah kay **oa**rah doab-bee**aa**moa vay**nee**ray |
| May I bring a friend? | **Posso portare un amico (un'amica)?** | **pos**soa por**taa**ray oon ah**mee**koa (oonah**mee**kah) |
| I'm afraid we've got to go now. | **Mi dispiace, ma adesso dobbiamo andare.** | mee deespee**aa**chay mah ah**dehs**soa doabbee**aa**moa ahn**daa**ray |
| Next time you must come to visit us. | **La prossima volta dovete venire da noi.** | lah **pros**seemah **vol**tah doa**vay**tay vay**nee**ray dah **noa**ee |
| Thanks for the evening. It was great. | **Grazie per la serata. È stata splendida.** | **graa**tseeay pair la say-**raa**tah. ai **staa**tah **splehn**deedah |

## Dating *Appuntamento*

| | | |
|---|---|---|
| Do you mind if I smoke? | **La disturbo se fumo?** | lah dee**stoor**boa say **foo**moa |
| Would you like a cigarette? | **Posso offrirle una sigaretta?** | **pos**soa off**reer**lay **oo**nah seegah**rayt**tah |
| Do you have a light, please? | **Ha un fiammifero, per favore?** | ah oon feeahm**mee**fayroa pair fah**voa**ray |
| Why are you laughing? | **Perchè ride?** | payr**kai** **ree**day |
| Is my Italian that bad? | **È così cattivo il mio italiano?** | ai ko**see** kaht**tee**voa eel **mee**oa eetahlee**aa**noa |
| Do you mind if I sit down here? | **Permette che mi sieda qui?** | pehr**mayt**tay kay mee see**ay**dah koo**ee** |
| Can I get you a drink? | **Posso offrirle qualcosa da bere?** | **pos**soa off**reer**lay kwahl**kaw**sah dah **bay**ray |
| Are you waiting for someone? | **Aspetta qualcuno?** | ah**spayt**tah kwahl**koo**noa |

| | | |
|---|---|---|
| Are you free this evening? | **È libera stasera?** | ai **lee**bayrah stah**say**rah |
| Would you like to go out with me tonight? | **Uscirebbe con me stasera?** | oosheer**ehb**bay kon mai stah**say**rah |
| Would you like to go dancing? | **Le piacerebbe andare a ballare?** | lay peeahchay**rehb**bay ahn**daa**ray ah bahl**laa**ray |
| I know a good discotheque. | **Conosco una buona discoteca.** | koa**noa**skoa **oo**nah **bwaw**nah deeskoa**tay**kah |
| Shall we go to the cinema (movies)? | **Andiamo al cinema?** | ahndee**aa**moa ahl **chee**naymah |
| Would you like to go for a drive? | **Andiamo a fare un giro in macchina?** | ahndee**aa**moa ah **faa**ray oon **jee**roa een **mahk**keenah |
| Where shall we meet? | **Dove possiamo incontrarci?** | **doa**vay possee**aa**moa eengkon**traar**chee |
| I'll pick you up at your hotel. | **Passerò a prenderla all'albergo.** | pahssay**roa** ah **prayn**dayrlah ahllahl**behr**goa |
| I'll call for you at 8. | **Passerò da lei alle 8.** | pahssay**roa** dah **lai**ee **ahl**lay 8 |
| May I take you home? | **Posso accompagnarla a casa?** | **pos**soa ahkkoampah**ñaar**lah ah **kaa**sah |
| Can I see you again tomorrow? | **Posso rivederla domani?** | **pos**soa reevay**dayr**lah doa**maa**nee |
| What's your telephone number? | **Qual è il suo numero di telefono?** | kwahl ai eel **soo**oa **noo**mayroa dee tay**lai**foanoa |

## ... and you might answer:

| | | |
|---|---|---|
| I'd love to, thank you. | **Con piacere, grazie.** | kon peeah**chay**ray **graa**tseeay |
| Thank you, but I'm busy. | **Grazie, ma sono impegnato(a).** | **graa**tseeay mah **soa**noa eempay**ñaa**toa(ah) |
| No, I'm not interested, thank you. | **No, non mi interessa, grazie.** | no noan mee eentay**rehs**sah **graa**tseeay |
| Leave me alone! | **Mi lasci in pace!** | mee **lah**shee een **paa**chay |
| Thank you, it's been a wonderful evening. | **Grazie, è stata una magnifica serata.** | **graa**tseeay ai **staa**tah oonah mah**ñee**feekah sayr**aa**tah |
| I've enjoyed myself. | **Mi sono divertito(a) molto.** | mee **soa**noa deevayr**tee**toa(ah) **moal**toa |

# Shopping guide

This shopping guide is designed to help you find what you want with ease, accuracy and speed. It features:

1. A list of all major shops, stores and services (p. 98);
2. Some general expressions required when shopping to allow you to be specific and selective (p. 100);
3. Full details of the shops and services most likely to concern you. Here you'll find advice, alphabetical lists of items and conversion charts listed under the headings below.



LAUNDRY, see page 29/HAIRDRESSER, see page 30

### Shops, stores and services *Negozi e servizi*

Shop hours in Italy differ from summer to winter. In winter the shops are generally open from 8 a.m. to 7 p.m. with a lunch break between 1 and 3 p.m. During the tourist season, shops open and close later in the afternoon (4 to 8 p.m.). Some remain open on Sundays but most close a half day during the week—often Monday morning or Thursday afternoon.

Swiss shops are open from 8 a.m. to noon or 12.30 p.m. and from 1.30 to 6.30 or 7 p.m. (Saturdays until 5 p.m.) with half-day closings similar to Italy.

| | | |
|---|---|---|
| Where's the nearest ...? | **Dove si trova ... più vicino(a)?** | **doa**vay see **traw**vah ... pee**oo** vee**chee**noa(ah) |
| antique shop | **l'antiquario** | lahnteek**waa**reeoa |
| art gallery | **la galleria d'arte** | lah gahllay**ree**ah **dahr**tay |
| baker's | **la panetteria** | lah pahnehttay**ree**ah |
| bank | **la banca** | lah **bahng**kah |
| barber's | **il barbiere** | eel bahrbee**ay**ray |
| beauty salon | **l'istituto di bellezza** | leesteet**oo**toa dee behl**leht**tsah |
| bookshop | **la libreria** | lah leebray**ree**ah |
| butcher's | **la macelleria** | lah mahchayllay**ree**ah |
| cake shop | **la pasticceria** | lah pahsteetchay**ree**ah |
| camera shop | **il negozio d'apparecchi fotografici** | eel nay**go**tseeoa dahppah**rehk**kee foatoa**graa**feechee |
| chemist's | **la farmacia** | lah fahrmah**chee**ah |
| confectioner's | **la pasticceria** | lah pahsteetchay**ree**ah |
| dairy | **la latteria** | lah lahttay**ree**ah |
| delicatessen | **la salumeria** | lah sahloomay**ree**ah |
| department store | **il grande magazzino** | eel **grahn**day mahgah**dzee**noa |
| drugstore | **la farmacia** | lah fahrmah**chee**ah |
| dry cleaner's | **la lavanderia a secco** | lah lahvahndayr**ee**ah ah **sayk**koa |
| electrician | **l'elettricista** | laylehttree**chee**stah |
| fishmonger's | **la pescheria** | lah payskay**ree**ah |
| flower shop | **il fiorista** | eel feeoa**ree**stah |
| furrier's | **la pellicceria** | lah paylleetchay**ree**ah |
| greengrocer's | **il negozio di frutta e verdura** | eel nay**go**tseeoa dee **froot**tah ay vehr**doo**rah |
| grocery | **il negozio di alimentari** | eel nay**go**tseeoa dee ahleemayn**taa**ree |
| hairdresser's | **il parrucchiere** | eel pahrrookkee**ay**ray |

| | | |
|---|---|---|
| hardware store | **il negozio di ferramenta** | eel nay**go**tseeoa dee fehrrah**mayn**tah |
| health food shop | **il negozio di cibi dietetici** | eel nay**go**tseeoa dee **chee**-beeh deeay**tay**teechee |
| ironmonger's | **il negozio di ferramenta** | eel nay**go**tseeoa dee fehrrah**mayn**tah |
| jeweller's | **la gioielleria** | lah joeeayllay**ree**ah |
| launderette | **la lavanderia automatica** | lah lahvahnday**ree**ah owtoa**maa**teekah |
| laundry | **la lavanderia** | la lahvahnday**ree**ah |
| library | **la biblioteca** | lah beebleeoa**tay**kah |
| market | **il mercato** | eel mayr**kaa**toa |
| newsagent's | **il giornalaio** | eel joarnah**laa**eeoa |
| newsstand | **l'edicola** | lay**dee**koalah |
| optician | **l'ottico** | **lot**teekoa |
| pastry shop | **la pasticceria** | lah pahsteetchay**ree**ah |
| photographer | **il fotografo** | eel foa**toa**grahfoa |
| police station | **il posto di polizia** | eel **poa**stoa dee poalee-**tsee**ah |
| post office | **l'ufficio postale** | looff**fee**choa poa**staa**lay |
| shoemaker's (repairs) | **il calzolaio** | eel kahltsoa**laa**eeoa |
| shoe shop | **il negozio di scarpe** | eel nay**go**tseeoa dee **skahr**pay |
| souvenir shop | **il negozio di ricordi** | eel nay**go**tseeoa dee ree**kor**dee |
| sporting goods shop | **il negozio di articoli sportivi** | eel nay**go**tseeoa dee ahr-**tee**koalee spor**tee**vee |
| stationer's | **la cartoleria** | lah kahrtoalay**ree**ah |
| supermarket | **il supermercato** | eel soopairmayr**kaa**toa |
| tailor's | **la sartoria** | lah sahrto**ree**ah |
| tobacconist's | **la tabaccheria** | lah tahbahkkay**ree**ah |
| toy shop | **il negozio di giocattoli** | eel nay**go**tseeoa dee joa**kaht**toalee |
| travel agency | **l'agenzia di viaggi** | lahjayn**tsee**ah dee vee**ahd**jee |
| vegetable store | **il negozio di frutta e verdura** | eel nay**go**tseeoa dee **froot**tah ay vehr**doo**rah |
| watchmaker's | **l'orologiaio** | loaroaloa**jaa**eeoa |
| wine merchant | **il vinaio** | eel vee**naa**eeoa |

| | |
|---|---|
| **ENTRATA** | ENTRANCE |
| **USCITA** | EXIT |
| **USCITA DI SICUREZZA** | EMERGENCY EXIT |

## General expressions *Espressioni generali*

### Where? *Dove?*

| | | |
|---|---|---|
| Where's a good ...? | **Dov'è un buon ...?** | doa**vai** oon bwawn |
| Where can I find ...? | **Dove posso trovare ...?** | **doa**vay **poss**oa tro**vaa**ray |
| Where's the main shopping area? | **Dov'è la zona principale dei negozi?** | doa**vai** lah **dzoa**nah preencheepaalay **dai**ee nay**go**tsee |
| How far is from here? | **Quanto dista da qui?** | **kwahn**toa **dee**stah dah koo**ee** |
| How do I get there? | **Come ci si può arrivare?** | **koa**may chee see pwo ahrree**vaa**ray |

**SALDI** SALE

### Service *Servizio*

| | | |
|---|---|---|
| Can you help me? | **Può aiutarmi?** | pwo aheeoo**taar**mee |
| I'm just looking. | **Do soltanto un'occhiata.** | doa soal**tahn**toa oonokkee**aa**tah |
| I want ... | **Desidero ...** | day**zee**dayroa |
| Can you show me some ...? | **Può mostrarmi dei ...?** | pwo moa**straar**mee **dai**ee |
| Do you have any ...? | **Ha dei ...?** | ah **dai**ee |
| Where is the ... department? | **Dove si trova il reparto ...?** | **doa**vay see **traw**vah eel ray**pahr**toa |
| Where is the lift (elevator)/escalator? | **Dov'è l'ascensore/ la scala mobile?** | doa**vai** lahshayn**soa**ray/ lah **skah**lah **mo**beelay |
| Where do I pay? | **Dov'è la cassa?** | doa**vai** lah **kah**ssah |

### That one *Quello là*

| | | |
|---|---|---|
| Can you show me ...? | **Mi può mostrare ...?** | mee pwo moa**straa**ray |
| this/that | **questo/quello** | koo**ay**stoa/koo**ayl**loa |
| the one in the window/on the shelf | **quello in vetrina/ sullo scaffale** | koo**ayl**loa een vay**tree**nah/ **sool**loa skahf**faa**lay |

## Defining the article *Descrizione dell'articolo*

| | | |
|---|---|---|
| I'd like a ... one. | **Ne vorrei un ...** | nay vo**rrai**ee oon |
| big | **grande** | **grahn**day |
| cheap | **economico** | aykoa**naw**meekoa |
| dark | **scuro** | **skoo**roa |
| good | **buono** | **bwaw**noa |
| heavy | **pesante** | pay**sahn**tay |
| large | **grande** | **grahn**day |
| light (weight) | **leggero** | lay**djai**roa |
| light (colour) | **chiaro** | kee**aa**roa |
| oval | **ovale** | o**vaa**lay |
| rectangular | **rettangolare** | rehttahngo**laa**ray |
| round | **rotondo** | ro**toan**doa |
| small | **piccolo** | **peek**koaloa |
| square | **quadrato** | kwah**draa**toa |
| sturdy | **solido** | **soa**leedoa |
| I don't want anything too expensive. | **Non voglio qualcosa di troppo caro.** | noan **vol**yoa kwahl**kaw**sah dee **trop**poa **kaa**roa |

## Preference *Preferenze*

| | | |
|---|---|---|
| Can you show me some more? | **Me ne può mostrare degli altri?** | may nay pwo moa**straa**ray **day**lyee **ahl**tree |
| Haven't you anything ...? | **Non ha qualcosa ...?** | noan ah kwahl**kaw**sah |
| better | **migliore** | mee**lyoa**ray |
| cheaper | **meno caro** | **may**noa **kaa**roa |
| larger | **più grande** | pee**oo** **grahn**day |
| smaller | **più piccolo** | pee**oo** **peek**koaloa |

## How much? *Quanto?*

| | | |
|---|---|---|
| How much is this? | **Quanto costa questo?** | **kwahn**toa **kos**tah koo**ay**stoa |
| How much are they? | **Quanto costano?** | **kwahn**toa **kos**tahnoa |
| I don't understand. | **Non capisco.** | noan kah**pee**skoa |
| Please write it down. | **Per favore, me lo scriva.** | pair fah**voa**ray may loa **skree**vah |
| I don't want to spend more than ... lire. | **Non voglio spendere più di ... lire.** | noan **vol**yoa **spehn**dayray pee**oo** dee ... **lee**ray |

COLOURS, see page 113

## Decision *Decisione*

| | | |
|---|---|---|
| It's not quite what I want. | **Non è ciò che volevo.** | noan ai choa kay voa**lay**voa |
| No, I don't like it. | **No, non mi piace.** | noa noan mee pee**aa**chay |
| I'll take it. | **Lo prendo.** | loa **prayn**doa |

## Ordering *Ordinazione*

| | | |
|---|---|---|
| Can you order it for me? | **Può ordinarmelo?** | pwo oardee**naar**mayloa |
| How long will it take? | **Quanto tempo ci sarà da aspettare?** | **kwahn**toa **tehm**poa chee sah**rah** dah ahspeht**taa**ray |

## Delivery *Consegna*

| | | |
|---|---|---|
| I'll take it with me. | **Lo porto via.** | loa **por**toa **vee**ah |
| Deliver it to the ... Hotel. | **Lo consegni all'Albergo ...** | loa kon**say**ñee ahllahl**bayr**goa |
| Please send it to this address. | **Per favore, lo mandi a questo indirizzo.** | pair fah**voa**ray loa **mahn**dee ah koo**ay**stoa eendee**reet**tsoa |
| Will I have any difficulty with the customs? | **Avrò delle difficoltà alla dogana?** | ah**vroa dayl**lay deeffeekoal**tah ahl**lah doa**gaa**nah |

## Paying *Pagamento*

| | | |
|---|---|---|
| How much is it? | **Quant'è?** | kwahn**tai** |
| Can I pay by traveller's cheque? | **Accettate i traveller's cheque?** | ahtcheht**taa**tay ee "traveller's cheque" |
| Do you accept dollars/pounds? | **Accettate dei dollari/ delle sterline?** | ahtcheht**taa**tay **daiee dol**lahree/**dayl**lay stayr**lee**nay |
| Do you accept credit cards? | **Accettate carte di credito?** | ahtcheht**taa**tay **kahr**tay dee **kray**deetoa |
| Do I have to pay the VAT (sales tax)? | **Devo pagare l'I.V.A.?** | **day**voa pah**gaa**ray **lee**vah |
| Haven't you made a mistake in the bill? | **Non vi siete sbagliati nel fare il conto?** | noan vee see**ay**tay sbah**lyaa**tee nayl **faa**ray eel **koan**toa |

## Anything else? *Qualcos'altro?*

| | | |
|---|---|---|
| No, thanks, that's all. | **No, grazie, è tutto.** | no **graa**tseeay ai **toot**toa |
| Yes. I want ... | **Sì, desidero ...** | see day**zee**dayroa |
| Show me ... | **Mi mostri ...** | mee **moa**stree |
| May I have a bag, please? | **Può darmi un sacchetto, per favore?** | pwo **daar**mee oon sahk**keht**toa pair fah**voa**ray |

## Dissatisfied *Scontento*

| | | |
|---|---|---|
| Can you please exchange this? | **Può cambiare questo, per favore?** | pwo kahmbee**aa**ray koo**ay**stoa pair fah**voa**ray |
| I want to return this. | **Desidero rendere questo.** | day**zee**dayroa **rayn**dayray koo**ay**stoa |
| I'd like a refund. Here's the receipt. | **Desidero essere rimborsato. Ecco la ricevuta.** | day**zee**dayroa **ehs**sayray reemboar**saa**toa. **ehk**koa lah reechay**voo**tah |

| | |
|---|---|
| **Posso aiutarla?** | Can I help you? |
| **Cosa desidera?** | What would you like? |
| **Che ... desidera?** | What ... would you like? |
| **colore/forma qualità/quantità** | colour/shape quality/quantity |
| **Mi dispiace, non ne abbiamo.** | I'm sorry, we haven't any. |
| **L'abbiamo esaurito.** | We're out of stock. |
| **Dobbiamo ordinarglielo?** | Shall we order it for you? |
| **Lo porta via o dobbiamo mandarglielo?** | Will you take it with you or shall we send it? |
| **Qualcos'altro?** | Anything else? |
| **Sono ... lire, per favore.** | That's ... lire, please. |
| **La cassa è laggiù.** | The cashier's over there. |

**Bookshop—Stationer's** *Libreria—Cartoleria*

In Italy, bookshops and stationer's are usually separate shops, though the latter will often sell paperbacks. Newspapers and magazines are sold at newsstands.

| | | |
|---|---|---|
| Where's the nearest ...? | **Dov'è ... più vicina?** | doa**vai** ... pee**oo** vee**chee**nah |
| bookshop | **la libreria** | lah leebray**ree**ah |
| stationer's | **la cartoleria** | lah kahrtoalay**ree**ah |
| newsstand | **l'edicola** | lay**dee**koalah |
| Where can I buy an English-language newspaper? | **Dove posso comprare un giornale in inglese?** | **doa**vay **pos**soa kom**praa**ray oon joar**naa**lay een eeng**glay**say |
| Where's the guide-book section? | **Dov'è il reparto delle guide turistiche?** | doa**vai** eel ray**pahr**toa **dayl**lay goo**ee**day too**ree**steekay |
| Where do you keep the English books? | **Dov'è il reparto dei libri inglesi?** | doa**vai** eel ray**pahr**toa **dai**ee **lee**bree eeng**glay**see |
| Do you have second-hand books? | **Avete libri d'occasione?** | ah**vay**tay **lee**bree dokkahzee**oa**nay |
| I'd like a/an/some ... | **Vorrei ...** | vor**rai**ee |
| address book | **un'agenda per gli indirizzi** | oonah**jayn**dah pair lyee eendee**reet**tsee |
| ball-point pen | **una biro** | **oo**nah **bee**roa |
| book | **un libro** | oon **lee**broa |
| calendar | **un calendario** | oon kahlayn**daa**reeoa |
| carbon paper | **della carta carbone** | **dayl**lah **kahr**tah kahr**boa**nay |
| cellophane tape | **del nastro adesivo** | dayl **nah**stroa ahday**zee**voa |
| crayons | **dei pastelli** | **dai**ee pah**stehl**lee |
| dictionary | **un dizionario** | oon deetseeoa**naa**reeoa |
| Italian-English | **italiano-inglese** | eetahlee**aa**noa/ eeng**glay**say |
| pocket | **tascabile** | tah**skaa**beelay |
| drawing paper | **della carta da disegno** | **dayl**lah **kahr**tah dah dee**say**ñoa |
| drawing pins | **delle puntine** | **dayl**lay poon**tee**nay |
| envelopes | **delle buste** | **dayl**lay **boo**stay |
| eraser | **una gomma** | **oo**nah **goam**mah |
| exercise book | **un quaderno** | oon kwah**dair**noa |
| felt-tip pen | **un pennarello** | oon paynnah**rehl**loa |
| fountain pen | **una penna stilografica** | **oo**nah **payn**nah steeloa**graa**feekah |

| | | |
|---|---|---|
| glue | **della colla** | day**llah kol**lah |
| grammar book | **una grammatica** | oonah grahm**mah**teekah |
| guidebook | **una guida turistica** | **oo**nah goo**ee**dah too**rees**teekah |
| ink | **dell'inchiostro** | daylleengkeeostroa |
| (adhesive) labels | **delle etichette (adesive)** | **day**llay aytee**keht**tay (ahday**zee**vay) |
| magazine | **una rivista** | **oo**nah ree**vee**stah |
| map | **una carta geografica** | **oo**nah **kahr**tah jayoa**graa**feekah |
| map of the town | **una pianta della città** | **oo**nah pee**ahn**tah **day**llah cheet**tah** |
| road map of ... | **una carta stradale di ...** | **oo**nah **kahr**tah strah**daa**lay dee |
| mechanical pencil | **un portamine** | oon poartah**mee**nay |
| newspaper | **un giornale** | oon joar**naa**lay |
| notebook | **un taccuino** | oon tahkkoo**ee**noa |
| note paper | **della carta da lettere** | **day**llah **kahr**tah dah **leht**tayray |
| paintbox | **una scatola di colori** | **oo**nah **skaa**toalah dee koa**loa**ree |
| paper | **della carta** | **day**llah **kahr**tah |
| paperback | **un libro tascabile** | oon **lee**broa tah**skaa**beelay |
| paperclips | **dei fermagli** | **dai**ee fayr**mah**lyee |
| paste | **della colla** | **day**llah **kol**lah |
| pen | **una penna** | **oo**nah **payn**nah |
| pencil | **una matita** | **oo**nah mah**tee**tah |
| pencil sharpener | **un temperamatite** | oon taympayrahmah**tee**tay |
| playing cards | **delle carte da gioco** | **day**llay **kahr**tay dah **jo**koa |
| pocket calculator | **una calcolatrice tascabile** | **oo**nah kahlkoalah**tree**chay tah**skaa**beelay |
| postcard | **una cartolina** | **oo**nah kahrtoa**lee**nah |
| propelling pencil | **un portamine** | oon poartah**mee**nay |
| refill (for a pen) | **un ricambio (per biro)** | oon ree**kahm**beeoa (pair **bee**roa) |
| rubber | **una gomma** | **oo**nah **goam**mah |
| ruler | **una riga** | **oo**nah **ree**gah |
| staples | **delle graffette** | **day**llay grah**ffeht**tay |
| string | **dello spago** | **day**lloa **spaa**goa |
| thumbtacks | **delle puntine** | **day**llay poon**tee**nay |
| tissue paper | **della carta velina** | **day**llah **kahr**tah vay**lee**nah |
| typewriter ribbon | **un nastro per macchina da scrivere** | oon **nah**stroa pair **mahk**keenah dah **skree**vayray |
| typing paper | **della carta per macchina da scrivere** | **day**llah **kahr**tah pair **mahk**keenah dah **skree**vayray |
| writing pad | **un blocco per appunti** | oon **blok**koa pair ap**poon**tee |

COLOURS, see page 113

## Camping equipment *Materiale da campeggio*

| | | |
|---|---|---|
| I'd like a/an/some ... | **Vorrei ...** | vor**rai**ee |
| bottle-opener | **un apribottiglia** | oon ahpreebot**tee**lyah |
| bucket | **un secchio** | oon **sayk**keeoa |
| butane gas | **del gas butano** | dayl gahz boo**taa**noa |
| campbed | **un letto da campo** | oon **leht**toa dah **kahm**poa |
| can opener | **un apriscatole** | oon ahpree**skaa**toalay |
| candles | **delle candele** | **dayl**lay kahn**day**lay |
| (folding) chair | **una sedia (pieghevole)** | **oo**nah **say**deeah (peeay**gay**voalay) |
| charcoal | **della carbonella** | **dayl**lah kahrboa**nayl**lah |
| clothes pegs | **delle mollette da bucato** | **dayl**lay mol**leht**tay dah boo**kaa**toa |
| compass | **una bussola** | **oo**nah **boos**soalah |
| cool box | **una ghiacciaia** | **oo**nah geeaht**chaa**eeah |
| corkscrew | **un cavatappi** | oon kahvah**tahp**pee |
| dishwashing detergent | **del detersivo per lavare i piatti** | dayl dehtehr**see**voa pair lah**vaa**ray ee pee**aht**tee |
| first-aid kit | **una cassetta del pronto soccorso** | **oo**nah kahs**seht**tah dayl **proan**toa soak**koar**soa |
| fishing tackle | **degli arnesi da pesca** | **day**lyee ahr**nay**zee dah **pay**skah |
| flashlight | **una lampadina tascabile** | **oo**nah lahmpah**dee**nah tah**skaa**beelay |
| food box | **un contenitore per il cibo** | oon koantaynee**toa**ray pair eel **chee**boa |
| frying-pan | **una padella** | **oo**nah pah**dehl**lah |
| groundsheet | **un telo per il terreno** | oon **tay**loa pair eel tayr**ray**noa |
| hammer | **un martello** | oon mahr**tehl**loa |
| hammock | **un'amaca** | oo**naa**mahkah |
| ice-pack | **un elemento refrigerante** | oon aylay**mayn**toa rayfreejay**rahn**tay |
| kerosene | **del petrolio** | dayl pay**tro**lyo |
| knapsack | **uno zaino** | **oo**noa **dzaa**eenoa |
| lamp | **una lampada** | **oo**nah **lahm**pahdah |
| lantern | **una lanterna** | **oo**nah lahn**tehr**nah |
| matches | **dei fiammiferi** | **da**iee feeahm**mee**fayree |
| mattress | **un materasso** | oon mahtay**rahs**soa |
| methylated spirits | **dell'alcool metilico** | dayl**lahl**koal may**tee**leekoa |
| mosquito net | **una zanzariera** | **oo**nah dzahndzahree**ay**rah |
| pail | **un secchio** | oon **sayk**keeoa |
| paper napkins | **dei tovagliolo di carta** | **da**iee toavah**lyoa**lee dee **kahr**tah |
| paraffin | **del petrolio** | dayl pay**tro**lyo |

| | | |
|---|---|---|
| penknife | **un temperino** | oon taympay**ree**noa |
| picnic basket | **un cestino da picnic** | oon chay**stee**noa dah "picnic" |
| plastic bag | **un sacchetto di plastica** | oon sahk**keht**toa dee **plah**steekah |
| rope | **della corda** | day**l**lah **koar**dah |
| rucksack | **uno zaino** | **oo**noa **dzaa**eenoa |
| saucepan | **una casseruola** | **oo**nah kahssay**rwoa**lah |
| scissors | **un paio di forbici** | oon **paa**eeoa dee **foar**beechee |
| screwdriver | **un cacciavite** | oon kahtchah**vee**tay |
| sleeping bag | **un sacco a pelo** | oon **sahk**koa ah **pay**loa |
| (folding) table | **una tavola (pieghevole)** | **oo**nah **taa**voalah (peeay**gay**voalay) |
| tent | **una tenda** | **oo**nah **tayn**dah |
| tent pegs | **dei picchetti per tenda** | **dai**ee peek**keht**tee pair **tayn**dah |
| tent pole | **un palo per tenda** | oon **paa**loa pair **tayn**dah |
| tinfoil | **un foglio di alluminio** | oon **foa**lyoa dee ahlloo**mee**neeoa |
| tin opener | **un apriscatole** | oon ahpree**skaa**toalay |
| tongs | **un paio di tenaglie** | oon **paa**eeoa dee tay**naa**lyay |
| torch | **una lampadina tascabile** | **oo**nah lahmpah**dee**nah tah**skaa**beelay |
| vacuum flask | **un thermos** | oon **tair**moas |
| washing powder | **del detersivo** | dayl daytehr**see**voa |
| water flask | **una borraccia** | **oo**nah boar**rat**chah |
| wood alcohol | **dell'alcool metilico** | dayl**lahl**koal may**tee**leekoa |

## Crockery *Stoviglie*

| | | |
|---|---|---|
| cups | **delle tazze** | day**l**lay **taht**tsay |
| mugs | **dei boccali** | **dai**ee boak**kaa**lee |
| plates | **dei piatti** | **dai**ee pee**aht**tee |
| saucers | **dei piattini** | **dai**ee peeaht**tee**nee |
| tumblers | **dei bicchieri** | **dai**ee beekee**ay**ree |

## Cutlery *Posate*

| | | |
|---|---|---|
| forks | **delle forchette** | day**l**lay for**keht**tay |
| knives | **dei coltelli** | **dai**ee koal**tehl**lee |
| spoons | **dei cucchiai** | **dai**ee kookkee**aa**ee |
| teaspoons | **dei cucchiaini** | **dai**ee kookkeeah**ee**nee |
| (made of) plastic | **(di) plastica** | (dee) **plah**steekah |
| (made of) stainless steel | **(di) acciaio inossidabile** | (dee) aht**chaa**eeoa eenossee**daa**beelay |

## Chemist's (drugstore) *Farmacia*

The Italian chemists' normally don't stock the great range of goods that you'll find in England or in the U.S. For example, they don't sell photographic equipment or books. For perfume, make-up, etc., you can also go to a *profumeria* (proafoomay**ree**ah).

You can recognize a chemist's by the sign outside—a green or red cross, illuminated at night. In the window you'll see a notice telling where the nearest all-night chemist's is.

This section is divided into two parts:

1. Pharmaceutical—medicine, first-aid, etc.
2. Toiletry—toilet articles, cosmetics

### General *Generalità*

| | | |
|---|---|---|
| Where's the nearest (all-night) chemist's? | **Dov'è la farmacia (di turno) più vicina?** | doa**vai** lah fahrmah**chee**ah (dee **toor**noa) pee**oo** vee**chee**nah |
| What time does the chemist's open/ close? | **A che ora apre/ chiude la farmacia?** | ah kay **oa**rah **aa**pray/ kee**oo**day lah fahrmah**chee**ah |

### 1—Pharmaceutical *Medicine, primi soccorsi, ecc.*

| | | |
|---|---|---|
| I want something for a ... | **Desidero qualcosa per ...** | day**zee**dayroa kwahl**kaw**sah pair |
| cold | **il raffreddore** | eel rahffrayd**doa**ray |
| cough | **la tosse** | lah **toas**say |
| hay fever | **la febbre del fieno** | lah **fayb**bray dayl fee**ay**noa |
| insect bites | **le punture d'insetti** | lay poon**too**ray deen**seht**tee |
| hangover | **il mal di testa** | eel mahl dee **teh**stah |
| sunburn | **una scottatura solare** | **oo**nah skoattah**too**rah soa**laa**ray |
| travel sickness | **il mal d'auto** | eel mahl **dow**toa |
| upset stomach | **il mal di stomaco** | eel mahl dee **sto**mahkoa |
| Can you make up this prescription for me? | **Può prepararmi questa ricetta?** | pwo praypah**raar**mee koo**ay**stah ree**cheht**tah |
| Can I get it without a prescription? | **Può darmi questa medicina senza ricetta?** | pwo **daar**mee koo**ay**stah maydee**chee**nah **saynt**sah ree**cheht**tah |

DOCTOR, see page 137

| | | |
|---|---|---|
| Can I have a/an/ some ...? | **Mi può dare ...?** | mee pwo **daa**ray |
| analgesic | **un analgesico** | oon ahnahl**jai**zeekoa |
| antiseptic cream | **della crema antisettica** | **day**llah **krai**mah ahntee**seht**teekah |
| aspirin | **delle aspirine** | **day**llay ahspee**ree**nay |
| bandage | **una benda** | **oo**nah **bayn**dah |
| elastic bandage | **una benda elastica** | **oo**nah **bayn**dah ay**lah**steekah |
| Band-Aids | **dei cerotti** | **dai**ee chay**rot**tee |
| contraceptives | **degli antifecondativi** | **day**lyee ahnteefaykoandah**tee**vee |
| corn plasters | **dei cerotti callifughi** | **dai**ee chay**rot**tee kahllee**foo**gee |
| cotton wool (absorbent cotton) | **del cotone idrofilo** | dayl koa**toa**nay **eedroa**feeloa |
| cough drops | **delle pasticche per la tosse** | **day**llay pah**steek**kay pair lah **toa**ssay |
| disinfectant | **del disinfettante** | dayl deeseenfeht**tahn**tay |
| ear drops | **delle gocce per le orecchie** | **day**llay **goat**chay pair lay o**rayk**keeay |
| Elastoplast | **dei cerotti** | **dai**ee chay**rot**tee |
| eye drops | **delle gocce per gli occhi** | **day**llay **goat**chay pair lyee **ok**kee |
| gauze | **della garza** | **day**llah **gahr**dzah |
| insect repellent/ spray | **una crema contro gli insetti/uno spray insetticida** | **oo**nah **krai**mah **koan**troa lyee een**seht**tee/**oo**noa "spray" eensehttee**chee**dah |
| iodine | **della tintura di iodio** | **day**llah teen**too**rah dee ee**o**deeoa |
| laxative | **un lassativo** | oon lahssah**tee**voa |
| mouthwash | **un gargarismo** | oon gahrgah**reez**moa |
| nose drops | **delle gocce nasali** | **day**llay **goat**chay naa**saa**lee |
| sanitary napkins | **degli assorbenti igienici** | **day**lyee ahssoar**bayn**tee ee**jay**neechee |
| sleeping pills | **dei sonniferi** | **dai**ee soan**nee**fayree |
| suppositories | **delle supposte** | **day**llay soop**po**stay |
| ... tablets | **delle pastiglie ...** | **day**llay pah**stee**lyay |
| tampons | **dei tamponi igienici** | **dai**ee tahm**poa**nee ee**jay**neechee |
| thermometer | **un termometro** | oon tayr**moa**maytroa |
| throat lozenges | **delle pasticche per la gola** | **day**llay pah**steek**kay pair lah **goa**lah |
| tranquillizers | **dei tranquillanti** | **dai**ee trahnkooeel**lahn**tee |
| vitamin pills | **delle vitamine** | **day**llay veetah**mee**nay |

## 2—Toiletry *Articoli da toilette*

| | | |
|---|---|---|
| I'd like a/an/some ... | **Desidero ...** | dayzeedayroa |
| after-shave lotion | **una lozione dopobarba** | oonah loatseeoanay dawpoabahrbah |
| bath salts | **dei sali da bagno** | daiee saalee dah baañoa |
| bubble bath | **un bagnoschiuma** | oon baañoaskeeoomah |
| cream | **una crema** | oonah kraimah |
| cleansing cream | **una crema detergente** | oonah kraimah daytehrjayntay |
| foundation cream | **un fondo tinta** | oon foandoa teentah |
| moisturizing cream | **una crema idratante** | oonah kraimah eedrahtahntay |
| night cream | **una crema da notte** | oonah kraimah dah nottay |
| cuticle remover | **un prodotto per togliere le pellicine** | oon proadoattoa pair tolyayray lay pehlleecheenay |
| deodorant | **un deodorante** | oon dayoadoarahntay |
| emery board | **una limetta per unghie** | oonah leemehttah pair oonggeeay |
| eye liner | **un eye-liner** | oon "eye-liner" |
| eye pencil | **una matita per occhi** | oonah mahteetah pair okkee |
| eye shadow | **un ombretto** | oon oambrayttoa |
| face powder | **della cipria** | dayllah cheepreeah |
| foot cream | **una crema per i piedi** | oonah kraimah pair ee peeaydee |
| hand cream | **una crema per le mani** | oonah kraimah pair lay maanee |
| lipsalve | **un burro cacao** | oon boorroa kahkaaoa |
| lipstick | **un rossetto** | oon roassehttoa |
| make-up remover pads | **dei tamponi per togliere il trucco** | daiee tahmpoanee pair tolyayray eel trookkoa |
| nail brush | **uno spazzolino da unghie** | oonoa spahtsoaleenoa dah oonggeeay |
| nail file | **una lima da unghie** | oonah leemah dah oonggeeay |
| nail polish | **uno smalto** | oonoa smahltoa |
| nail polish remover | **un solvente per le unghie** | oon soalvayntay pair lay oonggeeay |
| nail scissors | **un paio di forbicine per le unghie** | oon paaeeoa dee forbeecheenay pair lay oonggeeay |
| perfume | **un profumo** | oon proafoomoa |
| powder | **della cipria** | dayllah cheepreeah |
| razor | **un rasoio** | oon rahsoaeeoa |
| razor blades | **delle lamette** | dayllay lahmayttay |
| rouge | **del fard** | dayl "fard" |

| | | |
|---|---|---|
| safety pins | **delle spille di sicurezza** | **day**llay **speel**lay dee seekoo**rayt**tsah |
| shaving cream | **una crema da barba** | **oo**nah **krai**mah dah **bahr**bah |
| soap | **una saponetta** | **oo**nah sahpoa**nayt**tah |
| sun-tan cream | **una crema solare** | **oo**nah **krai**mah soa**laa**ray |
| sun-tan oil | **un olio solare** | oon **ol**yoa soa**laa**ray |
| talcum powder | **del talco** | dayl **tahl**koa |
| tissues | **dei fazzolettini di carta** | **dai**ee fahttsoalehttee**nee** dee **kahr**tah |
| toilet paper | **della carta igienica** | **day**llah **kahr**tah ee**jay**neekah |
| toilet water | **dell'acqua di colonia** | dayll**ahk**kwah dee koa**lo**neeah |
| toothbrush | **uno spazzolino da denti** | **oo**noa spahttsoa**lee**noa dah **dehn**tee |
| toothpaste | **un dentifricio** | oon daynteef**ree**choa |
| tweezers | **delle pinzette** | **day**llay peen**tseht**tay |

**For your hair** *Per i vostri capelli*

| | | |
|---|---|---|
| bobby pins | **delle mollette** | **day**llay mol**layt**tay |
| colour shampoo | **uno shampoo colorante** | **oo**noa **shahm**poa koaloa**rahn**tay |
| comb | **un pettine** | oon **payt**teenay |
| dry shampoo | **uno shampo secco** | **oo**noa **shahm**poa **sehk**koa |
| hairbrush | **una spazzola per capelli** | **oo**nah **spaht**tsoalah pair kah**payl**lee |
| hair slide | **un fermaglio** | oon fayr**maa**lyoa |
| hairgrips | **delle mollette** | **day**llay mol**layt**tay |
| hair lotion | **una lozione per capelli** | **oo**nah loatsee**oa**nay pair kah**pehl**lee |
| hairspray | **della lacca** | **day**llah **lahk**kah |
| setting lotion | **una lozione fissativa** | **oo**nah loatsee**oa**nay feessah**tee**vah |
| shampoo for dry/greasy (oily) hair | **dello shampoo per capelli secchi/grassi** | **day**lloa **shahm**poa pair kah**pehl**lee **sayk**kee/**grahs**see |

**For the baby** *Per il vostro bambino*

| | | |
|---|---|---|
| baby food | **degli alimenti per bebè** | **day**lyee ahlee**main**tee pair bay**bay** |
| dummy (pacifier) | **un succhiotto** | oon sookkee**ot**toa |
| feeding bottle | **un biberon** | oon beebay**roan** |
| nappies (diapers) | **dei pannolini** | **dai**ee pahnnoa**lee**nee |

## Clothing *Abbigliamento*

If you want to buy something specific, prepare yourself in advance. Look at the list of clothing on page 116. Get some idea of the colour, material and size you want. They're all listed on the next few pages.

### General *Generalità*

| | | |
|---|---|---|
| I'd like ... | **Vorrei ...** | vor**rai**ee |
| I want ... for a 10-year-old boy/girl. | **Desidero ... per un bambino/una bambina di 10 anni.** | day**zee**dayroa ... pair oon bahm**bee**noa/**oo**nah bahm**bee**nah dee 10 **ahn**nee |
| I want something like this. | **Voglio qualcosa come questo.** | **vo**lyoa kwahl**kaw**sah **koa**may koo**ay**stoa |
| I like the one in the window. | **Mi piace quello in vetrina.** | mee pee**aa**chay koo**ayl**loa een vay**tree**nah |
| How much is that per metre? | **Quanto costa al metro?** | **kwahn**toa **kos**tah ahl **may**troa |

| | | | |
|---|---|---|---|
| 1 centimetre (cm.) | = 0.39 in. | 1 inch = | 2.54 cm. |
| 1 metre (m.) | = 39.37 in. | 1 foot = | 30.5 cm. |
| 10 metres | = 32.81 ft. | 1 yard = | 0.91 m. |

### Colour *Colore*

| | | |
|---|---|---|
| I want something in ... | **Voglio qualcosa di colore ...** | **vo**lyoa kwahl**kaw**sah dee koa**loa**ray |
| I'd like a darker/lighter shade. | **Desidero una tonalità più scura/più chiara.** | day**zee**dayroa **oo**nah toanahlee**tah** pee**oo** **skoo**rah/pee**oo** kee**aa**rah |
| I want something to match this. | **Voglio qualcosa per ravvivare questo.** | **vo**lyoa kwahl**kaw**sah pair rahvvee**vaa**ray koo**ay**stoa |
| I'd like the same colour as ... | **Vorrei lo stesso colore che ...** | vor**rai**ee loa **stays**soa koa**loa**ray kai |
| I don't like the colour. | **Non mi piace il colore.** | noan mee pee**aa**chay eel koa**loa**ray |

| | | |
|---|---|---|
| beige | **beige** | baizh |
| black | **nero** | **nay**roa |
| blue | **blu** | bloo |
| light blue | **azzurro** | ah**dzoor**roa |
| brown | **marrone** | mahr**roa**nay |
| golden | **dorato** | doa**raa**toa |
| green | **verde** | **vayr**day |
| grey | **grigio** | **gree**joa |
| mauve | **lilla** | **leel**lah |
| orange | **arancio** | ah**rahn**choa |
| pink | **rosa** | **raw**zah |
| purple | **viola** | vee**o**lah |
| red | **rosso** | **roas**soa |
| silver | **argentato** | ahrjayn**taa**toa |
| turquoise | **turchese** | toor**kay**zay |
| white | **bianco** | bee**ahng**koa |
| yellow | **giallo** | **jahl**loa |
| light ... | **... chiaro** | kee**aa**roa |
| dark ... | **... scuro** | **skoo**roa |

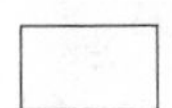

**tinta unita** (**teen**tah oo**nee**tah)

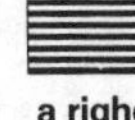

**a righe** (ah **ree**gay)

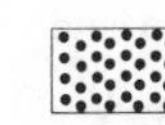

**a pallini** (ah pahl**lee**nee)

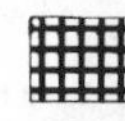

**a quadri** (ah **kwaa**dree)

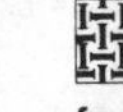

**fantasia** (fahntah**zee**ah)

## Material *Tessuto*

| | | |
|---|---|---|
| Do you have anything in ...? | **Ha qualcosa in ...?** | ah kwahl**kaw**sah een |
| I want a cotton blouse. | **Voglio una blusa di cotone.** | **vol**yoa **oo**nah **bloo**sah dee koa**toa**nay |
| Is that ...? | **È un prodotto ...?** | ai oon proa**doat**toa |
| handmade | **fatto a mano** | **faht**toa ah **maa**noa |
| imported | **importato** | eempoar**taa**toa |
| made here | **nazionale** | nahtseeoa**naa**lay |
| I want something thinner. | **Desidero qualcosa di più fine.** | day**zee**dayroa kwahl**kaw**sah dee pee**oo** **fee**nay |
| Do you have any better quality? | **Ha una qualità migliore?** | ah **oo**nah kwahlee**tah** meel**yoa**ray |
| What's it made of? | **Di che cos'è?** | dee kay ko**sai** |

| | | |
|---|---|---|
| cambric | **la tela battista** | lah **tay**lah baht**tee**stah |
| camel-hair | **il pelo di cammello** | eel **pay**loa dee kahm**mehl**loa |
| chiffon | **lo chiffon** | loa sheef**foan** |
| corduroy | **il velluto a coste** | eel vayl**loo**toa ah **koa**stay |
| cotton | **il cotone** | eel koa**toa**nay |
| crepe | **il crespo** | eel **kray**spoa |
| denim | **la tela di cotone** | lah **tay**lah dee koa**toa**nay |
| felt | **il feltro** | eel **fayl**troa |
| flannel | **la flanella** | lah flah**nehl**lah |
| gabardine | **il gabardine** | eel gahbahr**deen** |
| lace | **il pizzo** | eel **peet**tsoa |
| leather | **la pelle** | lah **pehl**lay |
| linen | **il lino** | eel **lee**noa |
| poplin | **il popeline** | eel poapay**leen** |
| satin | **il raso** | eel **raa**soa |
| silk | **la seta** | lah **say**tah |
| suede | **la renna** | lah **rehn**nah |
| terrycloth | **il tessuto di spugna** | eel tays**soo**toa dee **spoo**ñah |
| velvet | **il velluto** | eel vayl**loo**toa |
| velveteen | **il velluto di cotone** | eel vayl**loo**toa dee koa**toa**nay |
| wool | **la lana** | lah **laa**nah |
| worsted | **il pettinato** | eel paytteen**aa**toa |

| | | |
|---|---|---|
| Is it ...? | **È ...?** | ai |
| pure cotton/wool | **puro cotone/pura lana** | **poo**roa koa**toa**nay/**poo**rah **laa**nah |
| synthetic | **sintetico** | seen**tay**teekoa |
| colourfast | **di colore solido** | dee koa**loa**ray **so**leedoa |
| wrinkle resistant | **ingualcibile** | eengwahl**chee**beelay |
| Is it hand washable/ machine washable? | **Si può lavare a mano/ in lavatrice?** | see pwo lah**vaa**ray ah **maa**noa/een lahvah**tree**chay |
| Will it shrink? | **Si restringe al lavaggio?** | see ray**streen**jay ahl lah**vahd**joa |

## Size *Taglia*

| | | |
|---|---|---|
| I take size 38. | **La mia taglia è il 38.** | lah **mee**ah **tah**lyah ai eel 38 |
| Could you measure me? | **Può prendermi le misure?** | pwo **prehn**dayrmee lay mee**zoo**ray |
| I don't know the Italian sizes. | **Non conosco le misure italiane.** | noan koa**noa**skoa lay mee**zoo**ray eetahlee**aa**nay |

Sizes can vary somewhat from one manufacturer to another, so be sure to try on shoes and clothing before you buy.

**Women** *Donne*

| Dresses/Suits | | | | | | |
|---|---|---|---|---|---|---|
| American | 8 | 10 | 12 | 14 | 16 | 18 |
| British | 10 | 12 | 14 | 16 | 18 | 20 |
| Continental | 36 | 38 | 40 | 42 | 44 | 46 |

| Stockings | | | | | | | Shoes | | | |
|---|---|---|---|---|---|---|---|---|---|---|
| American / British | 8 | 8½ | 9 | 9½ | 10 | 10½ | 6 / 4½ | 7 / 5½ | 8 / 6½ | 9 / 7½ |
| Continental | 0 | 1 | 2 | 3 | 4 | 5 | 37 | 38 | 40 | 41 |

**Men** *Uomini*

| Suits/Overcoats | | | | | | | Shirts | | | |
|---|---|---|---|---|---|---|---|---|---|---|
| American / British | 36 | 38 | 40 | 42 | 44 | 46 | 15 | 16 | 17 | 18 |
| Continental | 46 | 48 | 50 | 52 | 54 | 56 | 38 | 41 | 43 | 45 |

| Shoes | | | | | | | | | |
|---|---|---|---|---|---|---|---|---|---|
| American / British | 5 | 6 | 7 | 8 | 8½ | 9 | 9½ | 10 | 11 |
| Continental | 38 | 39 | 41 | 42 | 43 | 43 | 44 | 44 | 45 |

**A good fit?** *Una buona prova?*

| | | |
|---|---|---|
| Can I try it on? | **Posso provarlo?** | possoa provahrloa |
| Where's the fitting room? | **Dov'è la cabina di prova?** | doavai lah kahbeenah dee prawvah |
| Is there a mirror? | **C'è uno specchio?** | chai oonoa spaykkeeoa |
| It fits very well. | **Va molto bene.** | vah moaltoa bainay |
| It doesn't fit. | **Non va bene.** | noan vah bainay |
| It's too ... | **È troppo ...** | ai troppoa |
| short/long | **corto/lungo** | koartoa/loonggoa |
| tight/loose | **stretto/largo** | strayttoa/lahrgoa |

NUMBERS, see page 147

| | | |
|---|---|---|
| How long will it take to alter? | **Quanto tempo ci vuole per le modifiche?** | **kwahn**toa **tehm**poa chee **vwo**lay pair lay moa**dee**feekay |

## Clothes and accessories *Indumenti e accessori*

| | | |
|---|---|---|
| I'd like a/an/some ... | **Vorrei ...** | vor**rai**ee |
| anorak | **una giacca a vento** | **oo**nah **jahk**kah ah **vayn**toa |
| bathing cap | **una cuffia da bagno** | **oo**nah **koof**feeah dah **baa**ñoa |
| bathing suit | **un costume da bagno** | oon koa**stoo**may dah **baa**ñoa |
| bathrobe | **un accappatoio** | oon ahkkahppah**toa**eeoa |
| blouse | **una blusa** | **oo**nah **bloo**zah |
| bow tie | **una cravatta a farfalla** | **oo**nah krah**vaht**tah ah fahr**fahl**lah |
| bra | **un reggiseno** | oon raydjee**say**noa |
| braces | **delle bretelle** | **dayl**lay bray**tehl**lay |
| briefs | **uno slip** | **oo**noa "slip" |
| cap | **un berretto** | oon bayr**rayt**toa |
| cardigan | **un cardigan** | oon "cardigan" |
| coat | **un cappotto** | oon kahp**pot**toa |
| dress | **un abito** | oon **aa**beetoa |
| dressing gown | **un accappatoio** | oon ahkkahppah**toa**eeoa |
| evening dress (woman's) | **un abito da sera** | oon **aa**beetoa dah **say**rah |
| frock | **un abito** | oon **aa**beetoa |
| garter belt | **un reggicalze** | oon raydjee**kahl**tsay |
| girdle | **un busto** | oon **boo**stoa |
| gloves | **dei guanti** | **dai**ee **gwahn**tee |
| handbag | **una borsetta** | **oo**nah boar**sayt**tah |
| handkerchief | **un fazzoletto** | oon fahtsoa**leht**toa |
| hat | **un cappello** | oon kahp**pehl**loa |
| jacket | **una giacca** | **oo**nah **jahk**kah |
| jeans | **dei jeans** | **dai**ee "jeans" |
| jersey | **una maglietta** | **oo**nah mahl**yeht**tah |
| jumper (Br.) | **un maglione** | oon mahl**yoa**nay |
| kneesocks | **dei calzettoni** | **dai**ee kahltseht**toa**nee |
| nightdress | **una camicia da notte** | **oo**nah kah**mee**chah dah **not**tay |
| overalls | **una tuta** | **oo**nah **too**tah |
| pair of ... | **un paio di ...** | oon **paa**eeoa dee |
| panties | **uno slip** | **oo**noa "slip" |
| pants (Am.) | **dei pantaloni** | **dai**ee pahntah**loa**nee |
| panty girdle | **una guaina** | **oo**nah **gwaa**eenah |
| panty hose | **dei collant** | **dai**ee **kol**lahnt |

| | | |
|---|---|---|
| pullover | **un pullover** | oon "pullover" |
| roll-neck (turtle-neck) | **a collo alto** | ah **kol**loa **ahl**toa |
| round | **a girocollo** | ah jeeroa**kol**loa |
| V-neck | **con scollatura a punta** | kon skollah**too**rah ah **poon**tah |
| pyjamas | **un pigiama** | oon pee**jaa**mah |
| raincoat | **un impermeabile** | oon eempayrmay**aa**beelay |
| scarf | **una sciarpa** | **oo**nah **shahr**pah |
| shirt | **una camicia** | **oo**nah kah**mee**chah |
| shorts | **uno short** | **oo**noa "short" |
| skirt | **una gonna** | **oo**nah **goan**nah |
| slip | **una sottoveste** | **oo**nah soattoa**veh**stay |
| socks | **dei calzini** | **da**iee kahl**tsee**nee |
| stockings | **delle calze da donna** | **day**llay **kahl**tsay dah **don**nah |
| suit (man's) | **un completo** | oon koam**play**toa |
| suit (woman's) | **un tailleur** | oon "tailleur" |
| suspenders (Am.) | **delle bretelle** | **day**llay bray**teh**llay |
| sweater | **un maglione** | oon mah**lyoa**nay |
| sweatshirt | **una blusa** | **oo**nah **bloo**zah |
| swimming trunks/ swimsuit | **un costume da bagno** | oon koa**stoo**may dah **baa**ñoa |
| T-shirt | **una maglietta di cotone** | **oo**nah mah**lyeht**tah dee koa**toa**nay |
| tie | **una cravatta** | **oo**nah krah**vaht**tah |
| tights | **dei collant** | **da**iee kol**lahnt** |
| tracksuit | **una tuta sportiva** | **oo**nah **too**tah spor**tee**vah |
| trousers | **dei pantaloni** | **da**iee pahntah**loa**nee |
| umbrella | **un ombrello** | oon oam**brehl**loa |
| underpants | **delle mutande/uno slip** | **day**llay moo**tahn**day/**oo**noa "slip" |
| undershirt | **una canottiera** | **oo**nah kahnottee**ay**rah |
| vest (Am.) | **un panciotto** | oon pahn**chot**toa |
| vest (Br.) | **una canottiera** | **oo**nah kahnottee**ay**rah |
| waistcoat | **un panciotto** | oon pahn**chot**toa |

| | | |
|---|---|---|
| belt | **la cintura** | lah cheen**too**rah |
| button | **il bottone** | eel boat**toa**nay |
| pocket | **la tasca** | lah **tah**skah |
| press stud (snap fastener) | **il bottone a pressione** | eel boat**toa**nay ah praysseeo**a**nay |
| sleeve | **la manica** | lah **maa**neekah |
| zip (zipper) | **la cerniera** | lah chehrnee**ay**rah |

## Shoes *Scarpe*

| | | |
|---|---|---|
| I'd like a pair of ... | **Vorrei un paio di ...** | vorraiee oon **paa**eeoa dee |
| boots | **stivali** | stee**vaa**lee |
| moccasins | **mocassini** | moakahs**see**nee |
| plimsolls (sneakers) | **scarpe da tennis** | **skahr**pay dah **tain**nees |
| sandals | **sandali** | **sahn**dahlee |
| shoes | **scarpe** | **skahr**pay |
| flat | **basse** | **bahs**say |
| with a heel | **con i tacchi** | koan ee **tahk**kee |
| slippers | **pantofole** | pahn**to**foalay |
| These are too ... | **Queste sono troppo ...** | **kway**stay **soa**noa **trop**poa |
| narrow/wide | **strette/larghe** | **strayt**tay/**lahr**gay |
| large/small | **grandi/piccole** | **grahn**dee/**peek**koalay |
| Do you have a larger/ smaller size? | **Ha un numero più grande/più piccolo?** | ah oon **noo**mayroa pee**oo** **grahn**day/pee**oo** **peek**koaloa |
| Do you have the same in black? | **Ha le stesse in nero?** | ah lay **stehs**say een **nay**roa |
| cloth/leather/ rubber/suede | **in tela/pelle/ gomma/camoscio** | een **tay**lah/**pehl**lay/ **goam**mah/kah**mo**shoa |
| Is it genuine leather? | **È vera pelle?** | ai **vay**rah **pehl**lay |
| I need some shoe polish/shoelaces. | **Mi serve del lucido/ dei lacci.** | mee **sair**vay dayl **loo**cheedoa/**dai**ee **laht**chee |

Shoes worn out? Here's the key to getting them fixed again:

| | | |
|---|---|---|
| Can you repair these shoes? | **Mi può riparare queste scarpe?** | mee pwo reepah**raa**ray koo**ay**stay **skahr**pay |
| Can you stitch this? | **Può attaccare questo?** | pwo ahttahk**kaa**ray koo**ay**stoa |
| I want new soles and heels. | **Desidero suole e tacchi nuovi.** | day**zee**dayroa **swo**lay ay **tahk**kee **nwaw**vee |
| When will they be ready? | **Quando saranno pronte?** | **kwahn**doa sah**rahn**noa **proan**tay |
| I need them ... | **Ne ho bisogno ...** | nay oa beezoañoa |
| as soon as possible | **il più presto possibile** | eel pee**oo** **preh**stoa pos**see**beelay |
| tomorrow | **domani** | doa**maa**nee |

COLOURS, see page 113

## Electrical appliances *Apparecchi elettrici*

In Italy you will usually find 220-volt current, though some older buildings, particularly in Rome, have 125-volt outlets.

| | | |
|---|---|---|
| What's the voltage? | **Qual è il voltaggio?** | kwahl ai eel voal**tahd**joa |
| Do you have a battery for this? | **Ha una pila per questo?** | ah **oo**nah **pee**lah pair koo**ay**stoa |
| This is broken. Can you repair it? | **È rotto. Me lo può riparare?** | ai **roat**toa. may loa pwo reepah**raa**ray |
| Can you show me how it works? | **Può mostrarmi come funziona?** | pwo moa**straar**mee **koa**may foontsee**oa**nah |
| I'd like (to hire) a video cassette. | **Vorrei (noleggiare) una video cassetta.** | vor**rai**ee (noalayd**jaa**ray) **oo**nah **vee**dayoa kahs**seht**tah |
| I'd like a/an/some ... | **Vorrei ...** | vor**rai**ee |
| adaptor | **una presa multipla** | **oo**nah **pray**zah **mool**teeplah |
| amplifier | **un amplificatore** | oon ahmpleefeekah**toa**ray |
| bulb | **una lampadina** | **oo**nah lahmpah**dee**nah |
| clock-radio | **una radio-sveglia** | **oo**nah **raa**deeoa-**svay**lyah |
| electric toothbrush | **uno spazzolino da denti elettrico** | **oo**noa spatsoa**lee**noa dah **dayn**tee ay**leht**treekoa |
| extension lead (cord) | **una prolunga** | **oo**nah proa**loong**gah |
| hair dryer | **un asciugacapelli** | oon ashoogahkah**payl**lee |
| headphones | **una cuffia (d'ascolto)** | **oo**nah **koof**feeah (dahs**koal**toa) |
| (travelling) iron | **un ferro da stiro (da viaggio)** | oon **fehr**roa dah **stee**roa (dah vee**ahd**joa) |
| lamp | **una lampada** | **oo**nah **lahm**pahdah |
| plug | **una spina** | **oo**nah **spee**nah |
| portable ... | **... portatile** | ... poar**taa**teelay |
| radio | **una radio** | **oo**nah **raa**deeoa |
| car radio | **un'autoradio** | oonowtoa**raa**deeoa |
| record player | **un giradischi** | oon jeerah**dee**skee |
| shaver | **un rasoio elettrico** | oon rah**soa**eeoa ay**leht**treekoa |
| speakers | **degli altoparlanti** | **day**lyee ahltoapahr**lahn**tee |
| (cassette) tape recorder | **un registratore (a cassette)** | oon rayjeestrah**toa**ray (ah kas**seht**tay) |
| (colour) television | **un televisore (a colori)** | oon taylayvee**zoa**ray (ah koa**loa**ree) |
| transformer | **un trasformatore** | oon trahsfoarmah**toa**ray |
| video-recorder | **un video registratore** | oon **vee**dayoa rayjeestrah**toa**ray |

## Grocery *Negozio di alimentari*

| | | |
|---|---|---|
| I'd like some bread, please. | **Vorrei del pane, per favore.** | vor**rai**ee dayl **paa**nay pair fah**voa**ray |
| What sort of cheese do you have? | **Che formaggi avete?** | kay foar**mah**djee ah**vay**tay |
| A piece of that one/ the one on the shelf. | **Un pezzo di quello/ quello sullo scaffale.** | oon **peht**soa dee koo**ayl**loa/ koo**ayl**loa **sool**loa skahf**faa**lay |
| I'll have one of those, please. | **Vorrei uno di quelli, per favore.** | vor**rai**ee **oo**noa dee koo**ayl**lee pair fah**voa**ray |
| May I help myself? | **Posso servirmi?** | **pos**soa sayr**veer**mee |
| I'd like ... | **Vorrei ...** | vor**rai**ee |
| a kilo of apples | **un chilo di mele** | oon **kee**loa dee **may**lay |
| half a kilo of tomatoes | **mezzo chilo di pomodori** | **mehd**zoa **kee**loa dee pomo**daw**ree |
| 100 grams of butter | **100 grammi (un etto) di burro** | **chehn**toa **grahm**mee (oon **eht**toa) dee **boor**roa |
| a litre of milk | **un litro di latte** | oon **lee**troa dee **laht**tay |
| half a dozen of eggs | **mezza dozzina di uova** | **mehd**zah doad**zee**nah dee **waw**vah |
| 4 slices of ham | **4 fette di prosciutto** | 4 **feht**tay dee proa**shoot**toa |
| a packet of tea | **un pacchetto di tè** | oon pahk**keht**toa dee tai |
| a jar of jam | **un vasetto di marmellata** | oon vah**zeht**toa dee marmehl**laa**tah |
| a tin (can) of peaches | **una scatola di pesche** | **oo**nah **skaa**toalah dee **pay**skay |
| a tube of mustard | **un tubetto di mostarda** | oon too**beht**toa dee moa**stahr**dah |
| a box of chocolates | **una scatola di cioccolatini** | **oo**nah **skaa**toalah dee chokkoalah**tee**nee |

| | |
|---|---|
| 1 kilogram or kilo (kg.) = 1000 grams (g.) | |
| 100 g. = 3.5 oz. | ½ kg. = 1.1 lbs. |
| 200 g. = 7.0 oz. | 1 kg. = 2.2 lbs. |
| 1 oz. = 28.35 g. | |
| 1 lb. = 453.60 g. | |

| | |
|---|---|
| 1 litre (l.) = 0.88 imp. quarts = 1.06 U.S. quarts | |
| 1 imp. quart = 1.14 l. | 1 U.S. quart = 0.95 l. |
| 1 imp. gallon = 4.55 l. | 1 U.S. gallon = 3.8 l. |

FOOD, see also page 63

## Jeweller's—Watchmaker's *Gioielleria—Orologeria*

| | | |
|---|---|---|
| Could I please see that? | **Potrei vedere quello, per favore?** | potr**aiee** vay**day**ray kooa**yl**loa pair fah**voa**ray |
| Do you have anything in gold? | **Avete qualcosa in oro?** | ah**vay**tay kwahl**kaw**sah een **oroa** |
| How many carats is this? | **Di quanti carati è?** | dee **kwahn**tee kah**raa**tee ai |
| Is this real silver? | **È vero argento?** | ai **vay**roa ahr**jayn**toa |
| Can you repair this watch? | **Può riparare questo orologio?** | pwo reepah**raa**ray koo**ay**stoa oaroa**lo**joa |
| I'd like a/an/some ... | **Vorrei ...** | vor**raiee** |
| alarm clock | **una sveglia** | **oo**nah **svay**lyah |
| bangle | **un braccialetto** | oon brahtchah**leht**toa |
| battery | **una pila** | **oo**nah **pee**lah |
| bracelet | **un braccialetto** | oon brahtchah**leht**toa |
| chain bracelet | **un braccialetto a catena** | oon brahtchah**leht**toa ah kah**tay**nah |
| charm bracelet | **un braccialetto a ciondoli** | oon brahtchah**leht**toa ah **choan**doalee |
| brooch | **una spilla** | **oo**nah **speel**lah |
| chain | **una catenina** | **oo**nah kahtay**nee**nah |
| charm | **un ciondolo** | oon **choan**doaloa |
| cigarette case | **un portasigarette** | oon portahseegah**rayt**tay |
| cigarette lighter | **un accendino** | oon ahtchayn**dee**noa |
| clip | **un fermaglio** | oon fayr**maa**lyoa |
| clock | **un orologio** | oon oaroa**lo**joa |
| cross | **una croce** | **oo**nah **kroa**chay |
| cuckoo clock | **un orologio a cucù** | oon oaroa**lo**joa ah koo**koo** |
| cuff links | **dei gemelli** | **dai**ee jay**mehl**lee |
| cutlery | **delle posate** | **dayl**lay poa**saa**tay |
| earrings | **degli orecchini** | **day**lyee oarayk**kee**nee |
| gem | **una pietra preziosa** | **oo**nah pee**ay**trah pray**tsee**oasah |
| jewel box | **un portagioielli** | oon portahjoee**ehl**lee |
| music box | **un carillon** | oon kahree**yon** |
| necklace | **una collana** | **oo**nah koal**laa**nah |
| pendant | **un pendente** | oon payn**dayn**tay |
| pocket watch | **un orologio da tasca** | oon oaroa**lo**joa dah **tah**skah |
| powder compact | **un portacipria** | oon portah**chee**preeah |
| ring | **un anello** | oon ah**nehl**loa |
| engagement ring | **un anello di fidanzamento** | oon ah**nehl**loa dee feedahntsah**mayn**toa |

| | | |
|---|---|---|
| signet ring | **un anello con stemma** | oon ah**nehl**loa kon **stehm**mah |
| wedding ring | **una fede nuziale** | **oo**nah **fay**day nootsee**aa**lay |
| rosary | **un rosario** | oon raw**zaa**reeoa |
| silverware | **dell'argenteria** | dayllahrjaynta**yree**ah |
| tie clip | **un fermacravatte** | oon fayrmahkrah**vaht**tay |
| tie pin | **uno spillo per cravatta** | **oo**noa **speel**loa pair krah**vaht**tah |
| watch | **un orologio** | oon oaroa**lo**joa |
| automatic | **automatico** | owtoa**maa**teekoa |
| digital | **digitale** | deejee**taa**lay |
| quartz | **al quarzo** | ahl **kwahr**tsoa |
| with a second hand | **con lancetta dei secondi** | kon lahn**cheht**tah **dai**ee say**koan**dee |
| watchstrap | **un cinturino per orologio** | oon cheentoo**ree**noa pair oaroa**lo**joa |
| wristwatch | **un orologio braccialetto** | oon oaroa**lo**joa brahtchah**leht**toa |

| | | |
|---|---|---|
| alabaster | **l'alabastro** | lahlah**bah**stroa |
| amber | **l'ambra** | **lahm**brah |
| amethyst | **l'ametista** | lahmay**tee**stah |
| copper | **il rame** | eel **raa**may |
| coral | **il corallo** | eel koa**rahl**loa |
| crystal | **il cristallo** | eel kree**stahl**loa |
| cut glass | **il vetro tagliato** | eel **vay**troa tah**lyaa**toa |
| diamond | **il diamante** | eel deeah**mahn**tay |
| emerald | **lo smeraldo** | loa smay**rahl**doa |
| enamel | **lo smalto** | loa **smahl**toa |
| gold | **l'oro** | **lo**roa |
| gold plate | **placcato d'oro** | plahk**kaa**toa **do**roa |
| ivory | **l'avorio** | lah**vo**reeoa |
| jade | **la giada** | lah **jaa**dah |
| onyx | **l'onice** | **lo**neechay |
| pearl | **la perla** | lah **pehr**lah |
| pewter | **il peltro** | eel **payl**troa |
| platinum | **il platino** | eel **plaa**teenoa |
| ruby | **il rubino** | eel roo**bee**noa |
| sapphire | **lo zaffiro** | loa dzahf**fee**roa |
| silver | **l'argento** | lahr**jayn**toa |
| silver plate | **placcato d'argento** | plahk**kaa**toa dahr**jayn**toa |
| stainless steel | **l'acciaio inossidabile** | laht**chaa**eeoa eenoas-see**daa**beelay |
| topaz | **il topazio** | eel toa**paa**tseeoa |
| turquoise | **il turchese** | eel toor**kay**zay |

## Optician *Ottico*

| | | |
|---|---|---|
| I've broken my glasses. | **Ho rotto gli occhiali.** | oa **roatt**oa lyee okkee**aa**lee |
| Can you repair them for me? | **Può ripararmeli?** | pwo reepah**raar**maylee |
| When will they be ready? | **Quando saranno pronti?** | **kwahn**doa sah**rahn**noa **proan**tee |
| Can you change the lenses? | **Può cambiare le lenti?** | pwo kahmbee**aa**ray lay **lehn**tee |
| I want tinted lenses. | **Desidero delle lenti colorate.** | day**zee**dayroa **dayl**lay **lehn**tee koaloa**raa**tay |
| The frame is broken. | **La montatura è rotta.** | lah moantah**too**rah ai **roat**tah |
| I'd like a spectacle case. | **Vorrei un astuccio per occhiali.** | vor**rai**ee oon ah**stoot**choa pair okkee**aa**lee |
| I'd like to have my eyesight checked. | **Vorrei farmi controllare la vista.** | vor**rai**ee **fahr**mee koantroal**laa**ray lah **vee**stah |
| I'm short-sighted/ long-sighted. | **Sono miope/presbite.** | **soa**noa **mee**oapay/**preh**zbeetay |
| I want some contact lenses. | **Desidero delle lenti a contatto.** | day**zee**dayroa **dayl**lay **lehn**tee ah koan**taht**toa |
| I've lost one of my contact lenses. | **Ho perso una lente a contatto.** | oa **pehr**soa **oo**nah **lehn**tay ah koan**taht**toa |
| Could you give me another one? | **Può darmene un'altra?** | pwo **daar**mehneh oo**nahl**trah |
| I have hard/soft lenses. | **Ho delle lenti a contatto dure/morbide.** | oa **dayl**lay **lehn**tee ah koan**taht**toa **doo**ray/**mor**beeday |
| Have you any contact-lens liquid? | **Avete del liquido per lenti a contatto?** | ah**vay**tay dayl **lee**kooeedoa pair **lehn**tee ah koan**taht**toa |
| I'd like to buy a pair of sunglasses. | **Vorrei degli occhiali da sole.** | vor**rai**ee **dayl**yee okkee**aa**lee dah **soa**lay |
| May I look in a mirror? | **Posso guardarmi in uno specchio?** | **pos**soa gwahr**daar**mee een **oo**noa **spehk**keeoa |
| I'd like to buy a pair of binoculars. | **Vorrei acquistare un binocolo.** | vor**rai**ee akkooee**staa**ray oon bee**no**koaloa |

## Photography *Fotografia*

| | | |
|---|---|---|
| I want a(n) ... camera. | **Voglio una macchina fotografica ...** | **vol**yoa **oo**nah **mahk**keenah foatoa**graa**feekah |
| automatic | **automatica** | owtoa**maa**teekah |
| inexpensive | **economica** | aykoa**no**meekah |
| simple | **semplice** | **saym**pleechay |
| Show me some cine (movie) cameras, please. | **Per favore, mi faccia vedere alcune cineprese.** | pair fah**voa**ray mee **faht**chah vay**day**ray ahl**koo**nay cheenay**pray**zay |
| I'd like to have some passport photos taken. | **Vorrei che mi facesse delle fotografie d'identità.** | vor**rai**ee kay mee faht**chays**say **dayl**lay foatoa-grah**fee**ay deedaynteet**ah** |

## Film *Pellicola*

| | | |
|---|---|---|
| I'd like a film for this camera. | **Vorrei una pellicola per questa macchina fotografica.** | vor**rai**ee **oo**nah pehl**lee**koalah pair koo**ay**stah **mahk**keenah foatoa**graa**feekah |
| black and white | **in bianco e nero** | een bee**ahng**koa ay **nay**roa |
| colour | **a colori** | ah koa**loa**ree |
| colour negative | **per negativo a colori** | pair naygah**tee**voa ah koa**loa**ree |
| colour slide | **per diapositive** | pair deeahpoazee**tee**vay |
| cartridge | **un rotolo** | oon **ro**toaloa |
| roll film | **una bobina** | **oo**nah boa**bee**nah |
| video cassette | **una video cassetta** | **oo**nah **vee**dayoa kahs**sayt**tah |
| 24/36 exposures | **ventiquattro/trentasei pose** | vaynteek**waht**troa/trayntah**se**hee **poa**zay |
| this size | **questo formato** | koo**ay**stoa foar**maa**toa |
| this ASA/DIN number | **questo numero ASA/DIN** | koo**ay**stoa **noo**mayroa **aa**sah/deen |
| artificial light type | **per luce artificiale** | pair **loo**chay ahrteefee**chaa**lay |
| daylight type | **par luce naturale** | pair **loo**chay nahtoo**raa**lay |
| fast (high-speed) | **rapido** | **raa**peedoa |
| fine grain | **a grana fine** | ah **graa**nah **fee**nay |

## Processing *Sviluppo*

| | | |
|---|---|---|
| How much do you charge for developing? | **Quanto fate pagare per lo sviluppo?** | **kwahn**toa **faa**tay pahg**aa**ray pair loa svee**loop**poa |

NUMBERS, see page 147

| | | |
|---|---|---|
| I want ... prints of each negative. | **Voglio ... stampe per ogni negativa.** | vo**l**yoa ... **stahm**pay pair oañee naygah**tee**vah |
| with a mat finish | **su carta opaca** | soo **kahr**tah oa**paa**kah |
| with a glossy finish | **su carta lucida** | soo **kahr**tah **loo**cheedah |
| Will you please enlarge this? | **Mi può ingrandire questo, per favore?** | mee pwo eenggrahn**dee**ray koo**ay**stoa pair fah**voa**ray |
| When will the photos be ready? | **Quando saranno pronte le fotografie?** | **kwahn**doa sah**rahn**noa **pron**tay lay foatoagrah**fee**ay |

## **Accessories and repairs** *Accessori e riparazioni*

| | | |
|---|---|---|
| I want a/an/some ... | **Vorrei ...** | vor**rai**ee |
| battery | **una pila** | **oo**nah **pee**lah |
| cable release | **uno scatto** | **oo**noa **skaht**toa |
| camera case | **un astuccio (per macchina fotografica)** | oon ah**stoot**choa (pair **mahk**keenah foatoa**graa**feekah) |
| (electronic) flash | **un flash (elettronico)** | oon "flash" (aylayt**tro**neekoa) |
| filter | **un filtro** | oon **feel**troa |
| for black and white | **per bianco e nero** | pair bee**ahng**koa ay **nay**roa |
| for colour | **per foto a colori** | pair **foa**toa ah koa**loa**ree |
| lens | **un obiettivo** | oon oabeeayt**tee**voa |
| telephoto lens | **un teleobiettivo** | oon taylayoabeeayt**tee**voa |
| wide-angle lens | **un grandangolare** | oon grahndahngoa**laa**ray |
| lens cap | **un cappuccio (per obiettivo)** | oon kahp**poot**choa (pair oabeeayt**tee**voa) |
| Can you repair this camera? | **Può riparare questa macchina fotografica?** | pwo reepah**raa**ray koo**ay**stah **mahk**keenah foatoa**graa**feekah |
| The film is jammed. | **La pellicola è bloccata.** | lah pehl**lee**koalah ai bloak**kaa**tah |
| There's something wrong with the ... | **... non funziona.** | noan foontsee**oa**nah |
| exposure counter | **il contatore di esposizioni** | eel koantah**toa**ray dee ayspoazeetsee**oa**nee |
| film winder | **la leva d'avanzamento della pellicola** | lah **lay**vah dahvahntsah**mayn**toa **dayl**lah pehl**lee**koalah |
| flash attachment | **l'attaccatura del flash** | lahttahkkah**too**rah dayl "flash" |
| light meter | **l'esposimetro** | layspoa**zee**maytroa |
| rangefinder | **il telemetro** | eel tay**lay**maytroa |
| shutter | **l'otturatore** | loattoorah**toa**ray |

## **Tobacconist's** *Tabaccheria*

Tobacco is a state monopoly in Italy. You recognize licensed tobacconist's by a large white "T" on a black background. Cigarettes are also sold in some cafés and newsstands.

| | | |
|---|---|---|
| A packet of cigarettes, please. | **Un pacchetto di sigarette, per favore.** | oon pahk**kayt**toa dee seegah**rayt**tay pair fah**voa**ray |
| Do you have any American/English cigarettes? | **Avete sigarette americane/inglesi?** | ah**vay**tay seegah**rayt**tay ahmayree**kaa**nay/eeng**glay**see |
| I'd like a carton. | **Ne vorrei una stecca.** | nay vor**rai**ee **oo**nah **stayk**kah |
| Give me a/some ..., please. | **Per favore, mi dia ...** | pair fah**voa**ray mee **dee**ah |
| candy | **delle caramelle** | **dayl**lay kahrah**mail**lay |
| chewing gum | **della gomma da masticare** | **dayl**lah **goam**mah dah mahstee**kaa**ray |
| chocolate | **del cioccolato** | dayl choakkoa**laa**toa |
| cigarette case | **un portasigarette** | oon portahseegah**rayt**tay |
| cigarette holder | **un bocchino** | oon boak**kee**noa |
| cigarettes | **delle sigarette** | **dayl**lay seegah**rayt**tay |
| filter-tipped/ without filter | **con filtro/ senza filtro** | kon **feel**troa/ **sayn**tsah **feel**troa |
| light/dark tobacco | **tabacco chiaro/ scuro** | tah**bahk**koa kee**aa**roa/ **skoo**roa |
| mild/strong | **leggere/forti** | lay**djay**ray/**for**tee |
| menthol | **al mentolo** | ahl mayn**toa**loa |
| king-size | **formato lungo** | foar**maa**toa **loong**goa |
| cigars | **dei sigari** | **dai**ee **see**gahree |
| lighter | **un accendino** | oon ahtchayn**dee**noa |
| lighter fluid/gas | **della benzina/del gas per accendino** | **dayl**lah bayn**dzee**nah/ dayl gahz pair ahtchayn**dee**noa |
| matches | **dei fiammiferi** | **dai**ee feeahm**mee**fayree |
| pipe | **una pipa** | **oo**nah **pee**pah |
| pipe cleaners | **dei nettapipe** | **dai**ee nayttah**pee**pay |
| pipe tobacco | **del tabacco da pipa** | dayl tah**bahk**koa dah **pee**pah |
| pipe tool | **un curapipe** | oon koorah**pee**pay |
| postcard | **una cartolina** | **oo**nah kahrtoa**lee**nah |
| stamps | **dei francobolli** | **dai**ee frahngkoa**boal**lee |
| sweets | **delle caramelle** | **dayl**lay karah**mail**lay |
| wick | **uno stoppino** | **oo**noa stop**pee**noa |

## Miscellaneous *Diversi*

### Souvenirs *Oggetti ricordo*

Here are some suggestions for articles you might like to bring back as a souvenir or a gift. Italy is particularly noted for its top fashions for men and women, for articles made of silk, leather, olive wood and alabaster, for pottery and embroidered clothes and accessories. Hand-made jewellery of amber, gold and silver are particularly appreciated.

| | | |
|---|---|---|
| antiques | **l'antichità** | lahnteekee**tah** |
| ceramics | **la ceramica** | lah chay**raa**meekah |
| doll | **la bambola** | lah **bahm**boalah |
| flask of Chianti | **il fiasco di Chianti** | eel fee**aa**skoa dee kee**ahn**tee |
| glassware | **gli articoli di vetro** | lyee ahr**tee**koalee dee **veh**troa |
| jewellery | **i gioielli** | ee joee**ehl**lee |
| knitwear | **la maglieria** | lah mahlyay**ree**ah |
| leather work | **la pelletteria** | lah payllayttay**ree**ah |
| needlework | **il ricamo** | eel ree**kaa**moa |
| porcelain | **la porcellana** | lah poarchayl**laa**nah |
| silk | **la seta** | lah **sai**tah |
| woodwork | **il lavoro in legno** | eel lah**voa**roa een **leh**ñoa |

Some typical products of Switzerland are:

| | | |
|---|---|---|
| chocolate | **il cioccolato** | eel choakkoa**laa**toa |
| cuckoo clock | **l'orologio a cucù** | loaroa**lo**joa ah koo**koo** |
| fondue forks/pot | **le forchette/il pentolino per la fonduta** | lay foar**kayt**tay/eel payntoa**lee**noa pair lah foan**doo**tah |
| watch | **l'orologio** | loaroa**lo**joa |

### Records—Cassettes *Dischi—Cassette*

| | | |
|---|---|---|
| Do you have any records by ...? | **Avete dischi di ...?** | ah**vay**tay **dee**skee dee |
| I'd like a ... | **Vorrei ...** | vor**rai**ee |
| cassette | **una cassetta** | oonah kahs**sayt**tah |
| video cassette | **una video cassetta** | oonah **vee**dayoa kahs**sayt**tah |
| compact disc | **un disco compatto** | oon **dee**skoa koam**paht**toa |

| | | |
|---|---|---|
| Have you any songs by ...? | **Avete delle canzoni di ...?** | ah**vay**tay **day**llay kahn**tsoa**nee dee |
| Can I listen to this record? | **Posso ascoltare questo disco?** | **pos**soa ahskoal**taa**ray koo**ay**stoa **dee**skoa |

| | | |
|---|---|---|
| L.P. (33 rpm) | **33 giri** | trayntah**tray jee**ree |
| E.P. (45 rpm) | **super 45 giri** | **soo**pair kwahrahntah**cheeng**kooay **jee**ree |
| single | **45 giri** | kwahrahntah**cheeng**kooay **jee**ree |

| | | |
|---|---|---|
| chamber music | **musica da camera** | **moo**zeekah dah **kaa**mayrah |
| classical music | **musica classica** | **moo**zeekah **klahs**seekah |
| folk music | **musica folcloristica** | **moo**zeekah folklo**ree**steekah |
| instrumental music | **musica strumentale** | **moo**zeekah stroomayn**taa**lay |
| jazz | **jazz** | "jazz" |
| light music | **musica leggera** | **moo**zeekah lay**djai**rah |
| orchestral music | **musica sinfonica** | **moo**zeekah seen**fo**neekah |
| pop music | **musica pop** | **moo**zeekah pop |

## Toys *Giocattoli*

| | | |
|---|---|---|
| I'd like a toy/ game ... | **Vorrei un giocattolo/ un gioco ...** | vor**rai**ee oon joa**kaht**toaloa/oon **joa**koa |
| for a boy | **per un bambino** | pair oon bahm**bee**noa |
| for a 5-year-old girl | **per una bambina di 5 anni** | pair **oo**nah bahm**bee**nah dee 5 **ahn**nee |
| beach ball | **un pallone (da spiaggia)** | oon pahl**loa**nay (dah spee**ahd**jah) |
| bucket and spade (pail and shovel) | **un secchiello e una paletta** | oon saykkee**ayl**loa ay **oo**nah pah**layt**tah |
| building blocks (bricks) | **un gioco di costruzioni** | oon **joa**koa dee koastrootsee**oa**nee |
| card game | **delle carte da gioco** | **day**llay **kahr**tay dah **joa**koa |
| chess set | **degli scacchi** | **day**lyee **skahk**kee |
| doll | **una bambola** | **oo**nah **bahm**boalah |
| electronic game | **un gioco elettronico** | oon **joa**koa aylayt**tro**neekoa |
| flippers | **delle pinne** | **day**llay **peen**nay |
| roller skates | **dei pattini a rotelle** | **dai**ee **paht**teenee ah ro**tehl**lay |
| snorkel | **la maschera da subacqueo** | lah **mahs**kayrah dah soo**bahk**kooayoa |

# Your money: banks—currency

Italy's monetary unit is the *lira* (**lee**rah), plural *lire* (**lee**ray), abbreviated to *L.* or *Lit.* There are coins of 10, 20, 50, 100, 200 and 500 lire. Banknotes come in denomination of 500, 1,000, 2,000, 5,000, 10,000, 50,000 and 100,000 lire.

In Switzerland, the basic unit currency is the *franco* (**frahng**koa) divided into 100 *centesimi* (chayn**tay**zeemee). There are coins of 5, 10, 20 and 50 centimes and of 1, 2 and 5 francs. There are banknotes of 10, 20, 50, 100, 500 and 1,000 francs.

Though hours can vary, banks in Italy are generally open from 8.30 to 1 p.m. and from 2.30 to 3.30 p.m., Monday to Friday.

In Switzerland banks are generally open from 8.30 or 9 a.m. to noon and from 1.30 or 2 to 4.30 or 5 p.m., Monday to Friday. Main branches often remain open during the lunch hours.

In both countries you will find currency-exchange offices *(uffici cambio)* which are often open outside regular banking hours.

Credit cards may be used in an increasing number of hotels, restaurants, shops, etc. Signs are posted indicating which cards are accepted.

Traveller's cheques are accepted by hotels, travel agents and many shops, although the exchange rate is invariably better at a bank. Don't forget to take your passport when going to cash a traveller's cheque. Eurocheques are also accepted.

| | | |
|---|---|---|
| Where's the nearest bank? | **Dov'è la banca più vicina?** | doa**vai** lah **bahng**kah pee**oo** vee**chee**nah |
| Where is the currency exchange? | **Dov'è l'ufficio cambio?** | doa**vai** loo**ffee**choa **kahm**beeoa |

## At the bank *In banca*

| | | |
|---|---|---|
| I want to change some dollars/ pounds. | **Desidero cambiare dei dollari/delle sterline.** | day**zee**dayroa kahmbee**aa**ray **daiee** **dol**lahree/**dayl**lay stayr**lee**nay |
| I want to cash a traveller's cheque/ Eurocheque. | **Voglio incassare un traveller's cheque/ un eurocheque.** | **vol**yoa eengkahs**saa**ray oon "traveller's cheque"/ oon "eurocheque" |
| What's the exchange rate? | **Qual è il corso del cambio?** | kwahl ai eel **koar**soa dayl **kahm**beeoa |
| How much commission do you charge? | **Quanto trattiene di commissione?** | **kwahn**toa trahttee**ay**nay dee koammeessee**oa**nay |
| Can you cash a personal cheque? | **Può cambiare un assegno personale?** | pwo kahmbee**aa**ray oon ahs**say**ñoa payrsoa**naa**lay |
| Can you telex my bank in London? | **Può mandare un telex alla mia banca a Londra?** | pwo mahn**daa**ray oon "telex" **ahl**lah **mee**ah **bahng**kah ah **loan**drah |
| I have a/an/some ... | **Ho ...** | oa |
| bank card | **una carta d'identità bancaria** | **oo**nah **kahr**tah deedayntee**tah** bahng**kaa**reeah |
| credit card | **una carta di credito** | **oo**nah **kahr**tah dee **kray**deetoa |
| introduction from ... | **una lettera di presentazione di ...** | **oo**nah **leht**tayrah dee prayzayntahtsee**oa**nay dee |
| letter of credit | **una lettera di credito** | **oo**nah **leht**tayrah dee **kray**deetoa |
| I'm expecting some money from New York. Has it arrived? | **Aspetto del denaro da New York. È arrivato?** | ahs**peht**toa dayl day**naa**roa dah "New York". ai ahrree**vaa**toa |
| Please give me ... notes (bills) and some small change. | **Per favore, mi dia ... banconote e della moneta.** | pair fah**voa**ray mee **dee**ah ... bahngkoa**no**tay ay **dayl**lah moa**nay**tah |

## Depositing—Withdrawing *Depositi—Prelevamenti*

| | | |
|---|---|---|
| I want to credit this to my account. | **Desidero accreditare questo sul mio conto.** | day**zee**dayroa ahkkraydee**taa**ray koo**ay**stoa sool **mee**oa **koan**toa |
| I want to ... | **Desidero ...** | day**zee**dayroa |
| open an account | **aprire un conto** | ah**pree**ray oon **koan**toa |
| withdraw ... lire | **prelevare ... lire** | praylay**vaa**ray ... **lee**ray |



NUMBERS, see page 147

| | | |
|---|---|---|
| I want to credit this to Mr...'s account. | **Desidero accreditare questo sul conto del signor ...** | day**zee**dayroa ahkkraydee**taa**ray koo**ay**stoa sool **koan**toa dayl see**ñoar** |
| Where should I sign? | **Dove devo firmare?** | **doa**vay **day**voa feer**maa**ray |

**Business terms** *Termini d'affari*

| | | |
|---|---|---|
| My name is ... | **Mi chiamo ...** | mee kee**aa**moa |
| Here's my card. | **Ecco il mio bigliettino.** | **ehk**koa eel **mee**oa beelyayt**tee**noa |
| I have an appointment with ... | **Ho un appuntamento con ...** | oa oon appoontah**mayn**toa kon |
| Can you give me an estimate of the cost? | **Può farmi un preventivo?** | pwo **faar**mee oon prayvayn**tee**voa |
| What's the rate of inflation? | **Qual è il tasso di inflazione?** | kwahl ai eel **tahs**soa dee eenflahtsee**oa**nay |
| Can you provide me with an interpreter/ a secretary? | **Può procurarmi un interprete/una segretaria?** | pwo prokoo**raar**mee oon een**tehr**prehtay/**oo**nah saygray**taa**reeah |
| Where can I make photocopies? | **Dove posso fare delle fotocopie?** | **doa**vay **pos**soa **faa**ray **dayl**lay foto**kaw**peeay |

| | | |
|---|---|---|
| amount | **l'importo** | leem**poar**toa |
| balance | **il bilancio** | eel bee**lahn**choa |
| capital | **il capitale** | eel kahpee**taa**lay |
| cheque book | **il libretto d'assegni** | eel lee**breht**toa dahs**say**ñee |
| contract | **il contratto** | eel koan**traht**toa |
| expenses | **le spese** | lay **spay**say |
| interest | **l'interesse** | leentay**rehs**say |
| investment | **l'investimento** | leenvaystee**mayn**toa |
| invoice | **la fattura** | lah faht**too**rah |
| loss | **la perdita** | lah **payr**deetah |
| mortgage | **l'ipoteca** | leepoa**tay**kah |
| payment | **il pagamento** | eel pahgah**mayn**toa |
| percentage | **la percentuale** | lah payrchayntoo**aa**lay |
| profit | **il profitto** | eel proa**feet**toa |
| purchase | **l'acquisto** | lahkoo**ee**stoa |
| sale | **la vendita** | lah **vayn**deetah |
| share | **l'azione** | lahtsee**oa**nay |
| transfer | **il trasferimento** | eel trahsfayree**mayn**toa |
| value | **il valore** | eel vah**loa**ray |

# At the post office

Post offices in Italy bear the sign *PT* and are normally open from 8.15 a.m. to 1 or 2 p.m., Monday to Friday, Saturday till 12 noon or 1 p.m. Offices in major towns and tourist resorts stay open longer, but often for urgent matters only. Stamps are also sold at tobacconist's *(tabaccaio)* and at some hotel desks. Letter boxes (mailboxes) are red in Italy, and yellow in Switzerland.

Swiss post offices are recognized by a *PTT* sign and are open from 7.30 a.m. to noon and from 1.45 to 6.30 p.m., Monday to Friday, Saturday till 11 a.m.

Note that telephone service in Italy is generally separated from the post office.

| | | |
|---|---|---|
| Where's the nearest post office? | **Dov'è l'ufficio postale più vicino?** | doa**vai** looff**ee**choa poa**staa**lay pee**oo** vee**chee**noa |
| What time does the post office open/close? | **A che ora apre/chiude l'ufficio postale?** | ah kay **oa**rah **aa**pray/kee**oo**day looff**ee**choa poa**staa**lay |
| A stamp for this letter/postcard, please. | **Un francobollo per questa lettera/cartolina, per favore.** | oon frahngkoa**boal**loa pair koo**ay**stah **leht**tayrah/kahrtoa**lee**nah pair fah**voa**ray |
| I want 2 ... -lire stamps. | **Vorrei 2 francobolli da ... lire.** | vorr**ai**ee 2 frahngkoa**boal**lee dah ... **lee**ray |
| What's the postage for a letter to London? | **Qual è l'affrancatura per una lettera per Londra?** | kwahl ai lahffrahngkah**too**rah pair **oo**nah **leht**tayrah pair **loan**drah |
| What's the postage for a postcard to Los Angeles? | **Qual è l'affrancatura per una cartolina per Los Angeles?** | kwahl ai lahffrahngkah**too**rah pair **oo**nah kahrtoa**lee**nah pair "Los Angeles" |
| Where's the letter box (mailbox)? | **Dov'è la cassetta delle lettere?** | doa**vai** lah kahs**seht**tah **dayl**lay **leht**tayray |
| I want to send this parcel. | **Vorrei spedire questo pacco.** | vorr**ai**ee spay**dee**ray koo**ay**stoa **pahk**koa |

| | | |
|---|---|---|
| I want to send this by ... | **Desidero inviare questo per ...** | day**zee**dayroa eenvee**aa**ray koo**ay**stoa pair |
| airmail | **via aerea** | **vee**ah ah**ay**rayah |
| express (special delivery) | **espresso** | ay**sprehs**soa |
| registered mail | **raccomandata** | rahkkoamahn**daa**tah |
| At which counter can I cash an international money order? | **A quale sportello posso riscuotere un vaglia internazionale?** | ah **kwaa**lay spor**tehl**loa **pos**soa rees**kwo**tayray oon **vaa**lyah eentayrnahtseeoa**naa**lay |
| Where's the poste restante (general delivery)? | **Dov'è lo sportello del fermo posta?** | doa**vai** loa spoar**tehl**loa dayl **fayr**moa **pos**tah |
| Is there any mail for me? My name is ... | **C'è della posta per me? Mi chiamo ...** | chai **dayl**lah **pos**tah pair may? mee kee**aa**moa |

| | |
|---|---|
| **FRANCOBOLLI** | STAMPS |
| **PACCHI** | PARCELS |
| **VAGLIA POSTALI** | MONEY ORDERS |

**Telegrams** *Telegrammi*

In Italy and Switzerland, you can either go directly to the post-office to send a telegram or phone it in. Some telegraph offices are open 24 hours a day.

| | | |
|---|---|---|
| I want to send a telegram/telex. | **Vorrei inviare un telegramma/telex.** | vor**rai**ee eenvee**aa**ray oon taylay**grahm**mah/"telex" |
| May I please have a form? | **Può darmi un modulo?** | pwo **daar**mee oon **mo**dooloa |
| How much is it per word? | **Quanto costa ogni parola?** | **kwahn**toa **kos**tah oñee pah**ro**lah |
| How long will a cable to Boston take? | **Quanto tempo ci vorrà per inviare un telegramma a Boston?** | **kwahn**toa **tehm**poa chee vor**rah** pair eenvee**aa**ray oon taylay**grahm**mah ah **bos**ton |
| How much will this telex cost? | **Quanto costerà questo telex?** | **kwahn**toa koastay**rah** koo**ay**stoa "telex" |

## **Telephoning** *Per telefonare*

The telephone system in Italy and Switzerland is virtually entirely automatic. International or long-distance calls can be made from phone boxes, or ask at your hotel. Local calls in Italy can also be made from cafés, where you might have to pay after the call or to buy a *gettone* (token) to put into the phone.

Telephone numbers are given in pairs in Italy so that 12 34 56 would be expressed in Italian, twelve, thirty-four, fifty-six.

| | | |
|---|---|---|
| Where's the telephone? | **Dov'è il telefono?** | doa**vai** eel tay**lay**foanoa |
| I'd like a telephone token. | **Vorrei un gettone (telefonico).** | vor**raiee** oon jayt**toa**nay (taylay**fo**neekoa) |
| Where's the nearest telephone booth? | **Dov'è la cabina telefonica più vicina?** | doa**vai** lah kah**bee**nah taylay**fo**neekah pee**oo** vee**chee**nah |
| May I use your phone? | **Posso usare il suo telefono?** | **pos**soa oo**zaa**ray eel **soo**oa tay**lay**foanoa |
| Do you have a telephone directory for Rome? | **Ha un elenco telefonico di Roma?** | ah oon ay**layng**koa taylay**fo**neekoa dee **roa**mah |
| What's the dialling (area) code for ...? | **Qual è il prefisso di ...?** | kwahl ai eel pray**fees**soa dee |
| How do I get the international operator? | **Come si ottiene il servizio internazionale?** | **koa**may see ottee**ay**nay eel sayr**veet**seeoa eentayrnahtseeoa**naa**lay |

## **Operator** *Centralinista*

| | | |
|---|---|---|
| Good morning, I want Venice 12 34 56. | **Buon giorno. Desidero il 12 34 56 di Venezia.** | bwon **joar**noa. dayzee**day**roa eel 12 34 56 dee vay**nait**seeah |
| Can you help me get this number? | **Mi può aiutare a ottenere questo numero?** | mee pwo aheeoo**taa**ray ah oattay**nay**ray koo**ay**stoa **noo**mayroa |

NUMBERS, see page 147

| | | |
|---|---|---|
| I want to place a ... | **Vorrei fare ...** | vorr**aiee** **faa**ray |
| personal (person-to-person) call | **una telefonata con preavviso** | **oo**nah taylayfoa**naa**tah kon prayahv**vee**zoa |
| reversed charge (collect) call | **una telefonata a carico del destinatario** | **oo**nah taylayfoa**naa**tah ah **kaa**reekoa dayl daysteenah**taa**reeoa |

## Speaking *Al telefono*

| | | |
|---|---|---|
| Hello. This is ... speaking. | **Pronto. Qui parla ...** | **pron**toa. koo**ee** **pahr**lah |
| I want to speak to ... | **Vorrei parlare a ...** | vorr**aiee** pahr**laa**ray ah |
| I want extension ... | **Mi dia la linea interna ...** | mee **dee**ah lah **lee**nayah een**tehr**nah |
| Speak louder/more slowly, please. | **Parli più forte/più lentamente, per favore.** | **pahr**lee pee**oo** **for**tay/pee**oo** layntah**mayn**tay pair fah**voa**ray |

## Bad luck *Sfortuna*

| | | |
|---|---|---|
| Would you please try again later? | **Per favore, vuol provare di nuovo più tardi?** | pair fah**voa**ray vwawl proa**vaa**ray dee **nwaw**voa pee**oo** **tahr**dee |
| Operator, you gave me the wrong number. | **Signorina, mi ha dato il numero sbagliato.** | seeñoa**ree**nah mee ah **daa**toa eel **noo**mayroa zbah**lyaa**toa |
| Operator, we were cut off. | **Signorina, la comunicazione si è interrotta.** | seeñoa**ree**nah lah komoo-neekahtsee**oa**nay see ai eentehr**roat**tah |

### Telephone alphabet

| | | | | | |
|---|---|---|---|---|---|
| A | **Ancona** | ahng**koa**nah | N | **Napoli** | **naa**poalee |
| B | **Bari** | **baa**ree | O | **Otranto** | **oa**trahntoa |
| C | **Catania** | kah**taa**neeah | P | **Palermo** | pah**lehr**moa |
| D | **Domodossola** | doamoa**dos**soalah | Q | **Quarto** | **kwahr**toa |
| E | **Empoli** | **aym**poalee | R | **Roma** | **roa**mah |
| F | **Firenze** | fee**rehn**tsay | S | **Sassari** | **sahs**sahree |
| G | **Genova** | **jai**noavah | T | **Torino** | taw**ree**noa |
| H | **Hotel** | oa**tehl** | U | **Udine** | **oo**deenay |
| I | **Imperia** | eem**pay**reeah | V | **Venezia** | vay**nai**tseeah |
| J | **i lunga** | ee **loong**gah | W | **v doppia** | vee **doap**peeah |
| K | **kappa** | **kahp**pah | X | **ix** | eekss |
| L | **Livorno** | lee**voar**noa | Y | **i greca** | ee **gray**kah |
| M | **Milano** | mee**laa**noa | Z | **zeta** | **dzai**tah |

### Not there *La persona è assente*

| | | |
|---|---|---|
| When will he/she be back? | **Quando ritornerà?** | **kwahn**doa reetoarneh**rah** |
| Will you tell him/her I called? My name is ... | **Vuol dirgli/dirle che ho telefonato? Mi chiamo ...** | vwawl **deer**lyee/**deer**lay kay oa taylayfoa**naa**toa. mee kee**aa**moa |
| Would you ask him/her to call me? | **Può chiedergli/ chiederle di tele-fonarmi?** | pwo kee**ai**dayrlyee/ kee**ai**dayrlay dee taylay-foa**naar**mee |
| Would you please take a message? | **Per favore, può trasmettere un messaggio?** | pair fah**voa**ray pwo trahz**mayt**tayray oon may**ssahd**joa |

### Charges *Costo della telefonata*

| | | |
|---|---|---|
| What was the cost of that call? | **Quanto è costata la telefonata?** | **kwahn**toa ai kos**taa**tah lah taylayfoa**naa**tah |
| I want to pay for the call. | **Desidero pagare la telefonata.** | day**zee**dayroa pah**gaa**ray lah taylayfoa**naa**tah |

| | |
|---|---|
| **C'è una telefonata per lei.** | There's a telephone call for you. |
| **Che numero chiama?** | What number are you calling? |
| **La linea è occupata.** | The line's engaged. |
| **Non risponde.** | There's no answer. |
| **Ha chiamato il numero sbagliato.** | You've got the wrong number. |
| **Il telefono non funziona.** | The phone is out of order. |
| **Un momento!** | Just a moment. |
| **Resti in linea.** | Hold on, please. |
| **Egli/Ella è fuori in questo momento.** | He's/She's out at the moment. |

# Doctor

To be at ease, make sure your health insurance policy covers any illness or accident while on holiday. If not, ask your insurance representative, automobile association or travel agent for details of special health insurance.

## **General** *Generalità*

| | | |
|---|---|---|
| Can you get me a doctor? | **Può chiamarmi un medico?** | pwo keeah**maar**mee oon **mai**deekoa |
| Is there a doctor here? | **C'è un medico qui?** | chai oon **mai**deekoa koo**ee** |
| I need a doctor, quickly! | **Mi serve un medico – presto!** | mee **sayr**vay oon **mai**deekoa – **preh**stoa |
| Where can I find a doctor who speaks English? | **Dove posso trovare un medico che parla inglese?** | **doa**vay **pos**soa troa**vaa**ray oon **mai**deekoa kay **pahr**lah eeng**glay**say |
| Where's the surgery (doctor's office)? | **Dov'è l'ambulatorio del medico?** | doa**vai** lahmboolah**to**reeoa dayl **mai**deekoa |
| What are the surgery (office) hours? | **Quali sono le ore di consultazione?** | **kwah**lee **soa**noa lay **oa**ray dee koansooltahtsee**oa**nay |
| Could the doctor come to see me here? | **Il medico può venire a visitarmi qui?** | eel **mai**deekoa pwo vay**nee**ray ah veezee**taar**mee koo**ee** |
| What time can the doctor come? | **Quando può venire il medico?** | **kwahn**doa pwo vay**nee**ray eel **mai**deekoa |
| Can you recommend a/an ...? | **Può consigliarmi ...?** | pwo koansee**lyaar**mee |
| general practitioner | **un medico generico** | oon **mai**deekoa jeh**nay**reekoa |
| children's doctor | **un pediatra** | oon paydee**aa**trah |
| eye specialist | **un oculista** | oon okoo**lee**stah |
| gynaecologist | **un ginecologo** | oon jeenay**ko**loagoa |
| Can I have an appointment ...? | **Può fissarmi un appuntamento ...?** | pwo fees**saar**mee oon ahppoontah**mayn**toa |
| right now | **subito** | **soo**beetoa |
| tomorrow | **domani** | doa**maa**nee |
| as soon as possible | **il più presto possibile** | eel pee**oo** **preh**stoa pos**see**beelay |

CHEMIST'S (PHARMACY), see page 108

## **Parts of the body** *Parti del corpo*

| | | |
|---|---|---|
| appendix | **l'appendice** | lahppayn**dee**chay |
| arm | **il braccio** | eel **braht**choa |
| artery | **l'arteria** | lahr**tai**reeah |
| back | **la schiena** | lah skee**ai**nah |
| bladder | **la vescica** | lah vay**shee**kah |
| bone | **l'osso** | **los**soa |
| bowels | **l'intestino** | leentay**stee**noa |
| breast | **il petto** | eel **peht**toa |
| chest | **il torace** | eel toa**raa**chay |
| ear | **l'orecchio** | loa**rayk**keeoa |
| eye(s) | **l'occhio (gli occhi)** | **lok**keeoa (lyee **ok**kee) |
| face | **il viso** | eel **vee**zoa |
| finger | **il dito della mano** | eel **dee**toa **dayl**lah **maa**noa |
| foot | **il piede** | eel pee**ay**day |
| genitals | **i genitali** | ee jaynee**taa**lee |
| gland | **la ghiandola** | lah gee**ahn**doalah |
| hand | **la mano** | lah **maa**noa |
| head | **la testa** | lah **teh**stah |
| heart | **il cuore** | eel **kwo**ray |
| intestines | **l'intestino** | leentay**stee**noa |
| jaw | **la mascella** | lah mah**shehl**lah |
| joint | **l'articolazione** | lahrteekoalahtsee**oa**nay |
| kidney | **il rene** | eel **rai**nay |
| knee | **il ginocchio** | eel jee**nok**keeoa |
| leg | **la gamba** | lah **gahm**bah |
| lip | **il labbro** | eel **lahb**broa |
| liver | **il fegato** | eel **fay**gahtoa |
| lung | **il polmone** | eel poal**moa**nay |
| mouth | **la bocca** | lah **boak**kah |
| muscle | **il muscolo** | eel **moo**skoaloa |
| neck | **il collo** | eel **kol**loa |
| nerve | **il nervo** | eel **nehr**voa |
| nervous system | **il sistema nervoso** | eel see**stai**mah nehr**voa**soa |
| nose | **il naso** | eel **naa**soa |
| rib | **la costola** | lah **ko**stoalah |
| shoulder | **la spalla** | lah **spahl**lah |
| skin | **la pelle** | lah **pehl**lay |
| spine | **la spina dorsale** | lah **spee**nah doar**saa**lay |
| stomach | **lo stomaco** | loa **sto**mahkoa |
| tendon | **il tendine** | eel **tehn**deenay |
| throat | **la gola** | lah **goa**lah |
| toe | **il dito del piede** | eel **dee**toa dayl pee**ay**day |
| tongue | **la lingua** | lah **leeng**gwah |
| tonsils | **le tonsille** | lay toan**seel**lay |
| vein | **la vena** | lah **vay**nah |

## Accident—Injury *Incidente—Ferita*

| | | |
|---|---|---|
| There has been an accident. | **C'è stato un incidente.** | chai **staa**toa oon eenchee**dayn**tay |
| My child has had a fall. | **Il mio bambino/ la mia bambina è caduto(a).** | eel **mee**oa bahm**bee**noa/ lah **mee**ah bahm**bee**nah ai kah**doo**toa(ah) |
| He/She has hurt his/ her head. | **Lui/Lei si è fatto(a) male alla testa.** | **loo**ee/**lay**ee see ai **faht**toa(ah) **maa**lay **ahl**lah **teh**stah |
| He's/She's unconscious. | **È svenuto(a).** | ai zvay**noo**toa(ah) |
| He's/She's bleeding heavily. | **Perde molto sangue.** | **payr**day **moal**toa **sahng**gooay |
| He's/She's (seriously) injured. | **È (gravemente) ferito(a).** | ai (grahvai**mayn**tay) fay**ree**toa(ah) |
| His/Her arm is broken. | **Si è rotto(a) il braccio.** | see ai **rot**toa(ah) eel **braht**choa |
| His/Her ankle is swollen. | **Ha la caviglia gonfia.** | ah lah kah**vee**lyah **goan**feeah |
| I've been stung. | **Sono stato punto.** | **soa**noa **staa**toa **poon**toa |
| I've got something in my eye. | **Ho qualcosa nell'occhio.** | oa kwahl**kaw**sah nehl**lok**keeoa |
| I've got a/an ... | **Ho ...** | oa |
| blister | **una vescica** | **oo**nah vay**shee**kah |
| boil | **un foruncolo** | oon foa**roong**koaloa |
| bruise | **una contusione** | **oo**nah koantoozee**oa**nay |
| burn | **una scottatura** | **oo**nah skottah**too**rah |
| cut | **un taglio** | oon **taa**lyoa |
| graze | **un'escoriazione** | oonayskoareeahtsee**oa**nay |
| insect bite | **una puntura d'insetto** | **oo**nah poon**too**rah deen**seht**toa |
| lump | **un bernoccolo** | oon bayr**nok**koaloa |
| rash | **un esantema** | oon ayzahn**teh**mah |
| sting | **una puntura** | **oo**nah poon**too**rah |
| swelling | **un gonfiore** | oon goanfee**oa**ray |
| wound | **una ferita** | **oo**nah fay**ree**tah |
| Could you have a look at it? | **Può esaminarlo?** | pwo ayzahmee**naar**loa |
| I can't move my ... | **Non posso muovere ...** | noan **pos**soa **mwo**vayray |
| It hurts. | **Mi fa male.** | mee fah **maa**lay |

| | |
|---|---|
| **Dove fa male?** | Where does it hurt? |
| **Che genere di dolore è?** | What kind of pain is it? |
| **debole/acuto/lancinante costante/a intervalli** | dull/sharp/throbbing constant/on and off |
| **È ...** | It's ... |
| **rotto/distorto slogato/lacerato** | broken/sprained dislocated/torn |
| **Voglio che faccia una radiografia.** | I want you to have an X-ray taken. |
| **Sarà ingessato.** | You'll get a plaster. |
| **Ha fatto infezione.** | It's infected. |
| **È stato vaccinato(a) contro il tetano?** | Have you been vaccinated against tetanus? |
| **Le darò un antisettico/ un antinevralgico.** | I'll give you an antiseptic/ a painkiller. |

## Illness *Malattia*

| | | |
|---|---|---|
| I'm not feeling well. | **Non mi sento bene.** | noan mee **sayn**toa **bai**nay |
| I'm ill. | **Mi sento male.** | mee **sayn**toa **maa**lay |
| I feel ... | **Mi sento ...** | mee **sayn**toa |
| dizzy<br>nauseous<br>shivery | **stordito(a)**<br>**la nausea**<br>**rabbrividire** | stoar**dee**toa(ah)<br>lah **now**zayah<br>rahbbreevee**dee**ray |
| I've got a fever. | **Ho la febbre.** | oa lah **fehb**bray |
| My temperature is 38 degrees. | **Ho la febbre a 38.** | oa lah **fehb**bray ah 38 |
| I've been vomiting. | **Ho vomitato.** | oa voamee**taa**toa |
| I'm constipated/ I've got diarrhoea. | **Sono costipato(a)/ Ho la diarrea.** | **soa**noa koastee**paa**toa(ah)/ oa lah deeahr**ray**ah |
| My ... hurt(s). | **Ho male al/alla ...** | oa **maa**lay ahl/**ahl**lah |
| I have a nosebleed. | **Mi sanguina il naso.** | mee **sahng**gooeenah eel **naa**soa |

NUMBERS, see page 147

| | | |
|---|---|---|
| I've got (a/an) ... | **Ho ...** | oa |
| asthma | **l'asma** | **lah**zmah |
| backache | **il mal di schiena** | eel mahl dee skee**ai**nah |
| cold | **il raffreddore** | eel rahffrayd**doa**ray |
| cough | **la tosse** | lah **toss**ay |
| cramps | **i crampi** | ee **krahm**pee |
| earache | **il mal d'orecchi** | eel mahl doa**rayk**kee |
| hay fever | **la febbre del fieno** | lah **fehb**bray dayl fee**eh**noa |
| headache | **il mal di testa** | eel mahl dee **teh**stah |
| indigestion | **un'indigestione** | ooneendeejaystee**oa**nay |
| palpitations | **delle palpitazioni** | **dayl**lay pahlpeetahtsee**oa**nee |
| rheumatism | **i reumatismi** | ee rayoomah**tee**zmee |
| sore throat | **il mal di gola** | eel mahl dee **goa**lah |
| stiff neck | **il torcicollo** | eel torchee**kol**loa |
| stomach ache | **il mal di stomaco** | eel mahl dee **sto**mahkoa |
| sunstroke | **un colpo di sole** | oon **koal**poa dee **soa**lay |
| I have difficulties breathing. | **Ho difficoltà a respirare.** | oa deeffeekol**tah** ah rayspee**raa**ray |
| I have a pain in my chest. | **Ho un dolore nel torace.** | oa oon doa**loa**ray nehl toa**raa**chay |
| I had a heart attack ... years ago. | **Ho avuto un attacco cardiaco ... anni fa.** | oa ah**voo**toa oon aht**tahk**koa kahr**dee**ahkoa ... **ahn**nee fah |
| My blood pressure is too high/too low. | **La mia pressione è troppo alta/troppo bassa.** | lah **mee**ah prehssee**oa**nay ai **trop**poa **ahl**tah/**trop**poa **bahs**sah |
| I'm allergic to ... | **Sono allergico a ...** | **soa**noa ahl**layr**jeekoa ah |
| I'm a diabetic. | **Ho il diabete.** | oa eel deeah**beh**tay |

## Women's complaints *Disturbi femminili*

| | | |
|---|---|---|
| I have period pains. | **Ho delle mestruazioni dolorose.** | oa **dayl**lay maystrooahtsee**oa**nee doaloa**raw**say |
| I have a vaginal infection. | **Ho un'infezione vaginale.** | oa ooneenfaytsee**oa**nay vahjee**naa**lay |
| I'm on the pill. | **Prendo la pillola.** | **prehn**doa lah **peel**loalah |
| I haven't had my period for 2 months. | **Non ho avuto le mestruazioni per 2 mesi.** | noan oa ah**voo**toa lay maystrooahtsee**oa**nee pair 2 **mai**see |
| I'm (3 months) pregnant. | **Sono incinta (di 3 mesi).** | **soa**noa een**cheen**tah (dee 3 **mai**see) |

|  |  |
|---|---|
| **Da quanto tempo si sente così?** | How long have you been feeling like this? |
| **È la prima volta che ha questo disturbo?** | Is this the first time you've had this? |
| **Le misuro la pressione/ la febbre.** | I'll take your blood pressure/ temperature. |
| **Tiri su la manica.** | Roll up your sleeve, please. |
| **Si spogli (fino alla vita).** | Please undress (down to the waist). |
| **Per favore, si sdrai qui.** | Please lie down over there. |
| **Apra la bocca.** | Open your mouth. |
| **Respiri profondamente.** | Breathe deeply. |
| **Tossisca, prego.** | Cough, please. |
| **Dove sente il dolore?** | Where do you feel the pain? |
| **Lei ha ...** | You've got (a/an) ... |
| **l'appendicite** | appendicitis |
| **un avvelenamento da cibi** | food poisoning |
| **una cistite** | cystitis |
| **la gastrite** | gastritis |
| **un'infiammazione a ...** | inflammation of ... |
| **l'influenza** | flu |
| **l'itterizia** | jaundice |
| **una malattia venerea** | venereal disease |
| **il morbillo** | measles |
| **la polmonite** | pneumonia |
| **Le farò un'iniezione.** | I'll give you an injection. |
| **Desidero un campione del sangue/dell'urina/delle feci.** | I want a specimen of your blood/urine/stools. |
| **Deve restare a letto per ... giorni.** | You must stay in bed for ... days. |
| **Deve consultare uno specialista.** | I want you to see a specialist. |
| **Deve andare all'ospedale per un controllo generale.** | I want you to go to the hospital for a general check-up. |
| **Deve essere operato(a).** | You'll have to have an operation. |

## **Prescription—Treatment** *Ricetta—Cura*

| | | |
|---|---|---|
| This is my usual medicine. | **Questa è la mia medicina abituale.** | koo**ay**stah ai lah **mee**ah maydee**chee**nah ahbeetoo**aa**lay |
| Can you give me a prescription for this? | **Può farmi una ricetta per questo?** | pwo **faar**mee **oo**nah ree**chayt**tah pair koo**ay**stoa |
| Can you prescribe a/an/some ...? | **Può prescrivermi ...?** | pwo pray**skree**vayrmee |
| antidepressant | **un antidepressivo** | oon ahnteedayprehs**see**voa |
| sleeping pills | **dei sonniferi** | **dai**ee soan**nee**fayree |
| tranquillizer | **un tranquillante** | oon trahngkooeel**lahn**tay |
| I'm allergic to antibiotics/penicilline. | **Sono allergico(a) agli antibiotici/alla penicillina.** | **soa**noa ahl**layr**jeekoa(ah) **ah**lyee ahnteebee**oa**teechee/ **ahl**lah paineecheel**lee**nah |
| I don't want anything too strong. | **Non voglio qualcosa troppo forte.** | noan **vol**yoa kwahl**kaw**sah **trop**poa **foar**tay |
| How many times a day should I take it? | **Quante volte al giorno devo prenderla?** | **kwahn**tay **vol**tay ahl **joar**noa **day**voa **prehn**dayrlah |
| Must I swallow them whole? | **Devo inghiottirle intere?** | **day**voa eenggeeoat**teer**lay een**tay**ray |

☞ ☜

| | |
|---|---|
| **Che cura fa?** | What treatment are you having? |
| **Che medicine prende?** | What medicine are you taking? |
| **Per iniezioni o via orale?** | Injection or oral? |
| **Prenda ... cucchiaini di questa medicina ...** | Take ... teaspoons of this medicine ... |
| **Prenda una compressa con un bicchiere d'acqua ...** | Take one pill with a glass of water ... |
| **ogni ... ore** | every ... hours |
| **... volte al giorno** | ... times a day |
| **prima/dopo ogni pasto** | before/after each meal |
| **al mattino/alla sera** | in the morning/at night |
| **in caso di dolore** | in case of pain |
| **per ... giorni** | for ... days |

CHEMIST'S (PHARMACY), see page 108

## Fee *Onorario*

| | | |
|---|---|---|
| How much do I owe you? | **Quanto le devo?** | **kwahn**toa lay **day**voa |
| May I have a receipt for my health insurance? | **Posso avere una ricevuta per la mia assicurazione malattia?** | **pos**soa ah**vay**ray **oo**nah reechay**voo**tah pair lah **mee**ah asseekoorahtseeoanay mahlaht**tee**ah |
| Can I have a medical certificate? | **Posso avere un certificato medico?** | **pos**soa ah**vay**ray oon chayrteefee**kaa**toa **mai**deekoa |
| Would you fill in this health insurance form, please? | **Potrebbe compilare questo modulo per l'assicurazione malattie, per favore?** | po**trehb**bay koampee**laa**ray koo**ay**stoa **moa**dooloa pair lasseekoorahtsee**oa**nay mahlaht**tee**ay pair fah**voa**ray |

## Hospital *Ospedale*

| | | |
|---|---|---|
| What are the visiting hours? | **Quali sono gli orari di visita?** | **kwah**lee **soa**noa lyee oraaree dee **vee**zeetah |
| When can I get up? | **Quando posso alzarmi?** | **kwahn**doa **pos**soa ahl**tsaar**mee |
| When will the doctor come? | **Quando verrà il dottore?** | **kwahn**doa vayr**rah** eel dot**taw**ray |
| I'm in pain. | **Ho male.** | oa **maa**lay |
| I can't eat/I can't sleep. | **Non ho appetito/ Non riesco a dormire.** | noan oa ahppay**tee**toa/ noan ree**eh**skoa ah doar**mee**ray |
| Can I have a painkiller/some sleeping pills? | **Posso avere un calmante/dei sonniferi?** | **pos**soa ah**vay**ray oon kahl**mahn**tay/**dai**ee soan**nee**fayree |
| Where is the bell? | **Dov'è il campanello?** | doa**vai** eel kahmpah**nehl**loa |

| | | |
|---|---|---|
| nurse | **l'infermiera** | leenfayrmee**ay**rah |
| patient | **il/la paziente** | eel/lah pahtsee**ain**tay |
| anaesthetic | **l'anestetico** | lahnay**stai**teekoa |
| blood transfusion | **la trasfusione di sangue** | lah trahsfoozee**oa**nay dee **sahng**gooay |
| injection | **l'iniezione** | leeneeaytsee**oa**nay |
| operation | **l'operazione** | loapayrahtsee**oa**nay |
| bed | **il letto** | eel **leht**toa |
| bedpan | **la padella** | lah pah**dehl**lah |
| thermometer | **il termometro** | eel tayr**mo**maytroa |

## **Dentist** *Dentista*

| Can you recommend a good dentist? | **Può consigliarmi un buon dentista?** | pwo koanseel**yahr**mee oon bwawn dayn**tee**stah |
|---|---|---|
| Can I make an (urgent) appointment to see Dr ...? | **Desidero un appuntamento (urgente) con il dottor/la dottoressa ...** | day**zee**dayroa oon ahppoontah**mayn**toa (oor**jehn**tay) kon eel doat**toar**/lah doatoa**rehs**sah |
| Can't you possibly make it earlier than that? | **Non è possibile prima?** | noan ai poas**see**beelay **pree**mah |
| I have a broken tooth. | **Mi sono rotto un dente.** | mee **soa**noa **rot**toa oon **dehn**tay |
| I have a toothache. | **Ho mal di denti.** | oa mahl dee **dehn**tee |
| I have an abscess. | **Ho un ascesso.** | oa oon ah**shehs**soa |
| This tooth hurts. | **Mi fa male questo dente.** | mee fah **maa**lay koo**ay**stoa **dehn**tay |
| at the top | **in alto** | een **ahl**toa |
| at the bottom | **in basso** | een **bahs**soa |
| in the front | **davanti** | dah**vahn**tee |
| at the back | **dietro** | dee**eh**troa |
| Can you fix it temporarily? | **Può curarlo provvisoriamente?** | pwo koo**raar**loa proavvee-zoareeah**mayn**tay |
| I don't want it extracted. | **Non voglio un'estrazione.** | noan **vol**yoa oonaystrah-tsee**oa**nay |
| Could you give me an anaesthetic? | **Potrebbe farmi l'anestesia?** | po**trehb**bay **faar**mee lahnaystay**zee**ah |
| I've lost a filling. | **L'otturazione si è staccata.** | loattoorahtsee**oa**nay see ai stahk**kaa**tah |
| The gum ... | **La gengiva ...** | lah jayn**jee**vah |
| is very sore | **è infiammata** | ai eenfeeahm**maa**tah |
| is bleeding | **sanguina** | **sahng**gooeenah |
| I've broken this denture. | **Ho rotto questa dentiera.** | oa **roat**toa koo**ay**stah daynteee**eh**rah |
| Can you repair this denture? | **Può ripararmi questa dentiera?** | pwo reepah**raar**mee koo**ay**stah dayntee**eh**rah |
| When will it be ready? | **Quando sarà pronta?** | **kwahn**doa sah**rah** **proan**tah |

# Reference section

## Where do you come from? *Da dove viene?*

| | | |
|---|---|---|
| Africa | **l'Africa** | **laa**freekah |
| Asia | **l'Asia** | **laa**zeeah |
| Australia | **l'Australia** | low**straa**leeah |
| Europe | **l'Europa** | layoo**ro**pah |
| North America | **l'America del Nord** | lah**mai**reekah dayl nord |
| South America | **l'America del Sud** | lah**mai**reekah dayl sood |
| Algeria | **l'Algeria** | lahljay**ree**ah |
| Austria | **l'Austria** | **low**streeah |
| Belgium | **il Belgio** | eel **beh**ljoa |
| Canada | **il Canada** | eel kahnah**dah** |
| China | **la Cina** | lah **chee**nah |
| Denmark | **la Danimarca** | lah dahnee**mahr**kah |
| England | **l'Inghilterra** | leengeel**teh**rrah |
| Finland | **la Finlandia** | lah feen**lahn**deeah |
| France | **la Francia** | lah **frahn**chah |
| Germany | **la Germania** | lah jayr**maa**neeah |
| Great Britain | **la Gran Bretagna** | lah grahn bray**taa**ñah |
| Greece | **la Grecia** | lah **grai**chah |
| India | **l'India** | **leen**deeah |
| Ireland | **l'Irlanda** | leer**lahn**dah |
| Israel | **Israele** | eesrah**ay**lay |
| Italy | **l'Italia** | lee**taa**leeah |
| Japan | **il Giappone** | eel jahp**poa**nay |
| Luxembourg | **il Lussemburgo** | eel loossaym**boor**goa |
| Morocco | **il Marocco** | eel mah**rok**koa |
| Netherlands | **l'Olanda** | lo**lahn**dah |
| New Zealand | **la Nuova Zelanda** | lah **nwaw**vah dzay**lahn**dah |
| Norway | **la Norvegia** | lah nor**vay**jah |
| Portugal | **il Portogallo** | eel porto**gahl**loa |
| Scotland | **la Scozia** | lah **skot**seeah |
| South Africa | **il Sudafrica** | eel soo**daa**freekah |
| Soviet Union | **l'Unione Sovietica** | looneeoanay soavee**eh**teekah |
| Spain | **la Spagna** | lah **spaa**ñah |
| Sweden | **la Svezia** | lah **sveh**tseeah |
| Switzerland | **la Svizzera** | lah **sveet**tsayrah |
| Tunisia | **la Tunisia** | lah tooneez**ee**ah |
| Turkey | **la Turchia** | lah toor**kee**ah |
| United States | **gli Stati Uniti** | lyee **staa**tee oo**nee**tee |
| Wales | **il Galles** | eel **gahl**layss |
| Yugoslavia | **la Iugoslavia** | lah eeoogoa**slaa**veeah |

## Numbers *Numeri*

| | | |
|---|---|---|
| 0 | **zero** | **dzeh**roa |
| 1 | **uno** | **oo**noa |
| 2 | **due** | **doo**ay |
| 3 | **tre** | tray |
| 4 | **quattro** | **kwaht**troa |
| 5 | **cinque** | **cheeng**kooay |
| 6 | **sei** | **seh**ee |
| 7 | **sette** | **seht**tay |
| 8 | **otto** | **ot**toa |
| 9 | **nove** | **naw**vay |
| 10 | **dieci** | dee**ai**chee |
| 11 | **undici** | **oon**deechee |
| 12 | **dodici** | **doa**deechee |
| 13 | **tredici** | **tray**deechee |
| 14 | **quattordici** | kwaht**tor**deechee |
| 15 | **quindici** | koo**een**deechee |
| 16 | **sedici** | **say**deechee |
| 17 | **diciassette** | deechahs**seht**tay |
| 18 | **diciotto** | dee**chot**toa |
| 19 | **diciannove** | deechahn**naw**vay |
| 20 | **venti** | **vayn**tee |
| 21 | **ventuno** | vayn**too**noa |
| 22 | **ventidue** | vaynteedooay |
| 23 | **ventitre** | vaynteetray |
| 24 | **ventiquattro** | vayntee**kwaht**troa |
| 25 | **venticinque** | vayntee**cheeng**kooay |
| 26 | **ventisei** | vayntee**seh**ee |
| 27 | **ventisette** | vayntee**seht**tay |
| 28 | **ventotto** | vayn**tot**toa |
| 29 | **ventinove** | vayntee**naw**vay |
| 30 | **trenta** | **trayn**tah |
| 31 | **trentuno** | trayn**too**noa |
| 32 | **trentadue** | trayntah**doo**ay |
| 33 | **trentatre** | trayntat**ray** |
| 40 | **quaranta** | kwah**rahn**tah |
| 41 | **quarantuno** | kwahrahn**too**noa |
| 42 | **quarantadue** | kwahrahntah**doo**ay |
| 43 | **quarantatre** | kwahrahntah**tray** |
| 50 | **cinquanta** | cheeng**kwahn**tah |
| 51 | **cinquantuno** | cheengkwahn**too**noa |
| 52 | **cinquantadue** | cheengkwahntah**doo**ay |
| 53 | **cinquantatre** | cheengkwahntah**tray** |
| 60 | **sessanta** | says**sahn**tah |
| 61 | **sessantuno** | sayssahn**too**noa |
| 62 | **sessantadue** | sayssahntah**doo**ay |

| | | |
|---|---|---|
| 63 | **sessantatre** | sayssahntah**tray** |
| 70 | **settanta** | sayt**tahn**tah |
| 71 | **settantuno** | sayttahn**too**noa |
| 72 | **settantadue** | sayttahntah**doo**ay |
| 73 | **settantatre** | sayttahntah**tray** |
| 80 | **ottanta** | ot**tahn**tah |
| 81 | **ottantuno** | ottahn**too**noa |
| 82 | **ottantadue** | ottahntah**doo**ay |
| 83 | **ottantatre** | ottahntah**tray** |
| 90 | **novanta** | noa**vahn**tah |
| 91 | **novantuno** | noavahn**too**noa |
| 92 | **novantadue** | noavahntah**doo**ay |
| 93 | **novantatre** | noavahntah**tray** |
| 100 | **cento** | **chehn**toa |
| 101 | **centouno** | chehntoa**oo**noa |
| 102 | **centodue** | chehntoa**doo**ay |
| 110 | **centodieci** | chehntoadee**ai**chee |
| 120 | **centoventi** | chehntoa**vayn**tee |
| 130 | **centotrenta** | chehntoa**trayn**tah |
| 140 | **centoquaranta** | chehntoakwah**rahn**tah |
| 150 | **centocinquanta** | chehntoacheeng**kwahn**tah |
| 160 | **centosessanta** | chehntoasays**sahn**tah |
| 170 | **centosettanta** | chehntoasayt**tahn**tah |
| 180 | **centottanta** | chehntot**tahn**tah |
| 190 | **centonovanta** | chehntoanoa**vahn**tah |
| 200 | **duecento** | dooay**chehn**toa |
| 300 | **trecento** | tray**chehn**toa |
| 400 | **quattrocento** | kwahttroa**chehn**toa |
| 500 | **cinquecento** | cheengkooay**chehn**toa |
| 600 | **seicento** | sehee**chehn**toa |
| 700 | **settecento** | sehttay**chehn**toa |
| 800 | **ottocento** | otto**chehn**toa |
| 900 | **novecento** | noavay**chehn**toa |
| 1000 | **mille** | **meel**lay |
| 1100 | **millecento** | meellay**chehn**toa |
| 1200 | **milleduecento** | meellaydooay**chehn**toa |
| 2000 | **duemila** | dooay**mee**lah |
| 5000 | **cinquemila** | cheengkooay**mee**lah |
| 10,000 | **diecimila** | deeaichee**mee**lah |
| 50,000 | **cinquantamila** | cheengkwahntah**mee**lah |
| 100,000 | **centomila** | chehntoa**mee**lah |
| 1,000,000 | **un milione** | oon mee**lyoa**nay |
| 1,000,000,000 | **un miliardo** | oon mee**lyahr**doa |

| | | |
|---|---|---|
| first/second | **primo/secondo** | **pree**moa/say**koan**doa |
| third/fourth | **terzo/quarto** | **tehr**tsoa/**kwahr**toa |
| fifth/sixth | **quinto/sesto** | koo**een**toa/**seh**stoa |
| seventh/eighth | **settimo/ottavo** | **seht**teemoa/ott**aa**voa |
| ninth/tenth | **nono/decimo** | **no**noa/**deh**cheemoa |
| once | **una volta** | **oo**nah **vol**tah |
| twice | **due volte** | **doo**ay **vol**tay |
| three times | **tre volte** | tray **vol**tay |
| a half | **un mezzo** | oon **mehd**dzoa |
| half a ... | **mezzo ...** | **mehd**dzoa |
| half of ... | **metà di ...** | may**tah** dee |
| half (adj.) | **mezzo** | **mehd**dzoa |
| a quarter | **un quarto** | oon **kwahr**toa |
| one third | **un terzo** | oon **tehr**tsoa |
| a pair of | **un paio di** | oon **paa**eeoa dee |
| a dozen | **una dozzina** | **oo**nah doad**dzee**nah |
| one per cent | **uno per cento** | **oo**noa pair **chehn**toa |
| 3.4% | **3,4%** | tray **veer**goalah **kwaht**troa pair **chehn**toa |
| 1981 | **millenovecent-ottantuno** | **meel**lay-noavay**chehnt**-ottahn**too**noa |
| 1992 | **millenovecento-novantadue** | **meel**lay-noavay**chehn**toa-noavahntah**doo**ay |
| 2003 | **duemilatre** | dooaymeelah**tray** |

## **Year and age** *Anno ed età*

| | | |
|---|---|---|
| year | **l'anno** | **lahn**noa |
| leap year | **l'anno bisestile** | **lahn**noa beesay**stee**lay |
| decade | **il decennio** | eel deh**chehn**neeoa |
| century | **il secolo** | eel **sai**koloa |
| this year | **quest'anno** | kooay**stahn**noa |
| last year | **l'anno scorso** | **lahn**noa **skoar**soa |
| next year | **l'anno prossimo** | **lahn**noa **pros**seemoa |
| each year | **ogni anno** | oñee **ahn**noa |
| 2 years ago | **2 anni fa** | 2 **ahn**nee fah |
| in one year | **in un anno** | een oon **ahn**noa |
| in the eighties | **negli anni ottanta** | **nay**lyee **ahn**nee otta**hn**tah |
| the 16th century | **il sedicesimo secolo** | eel sehdee**chay**zeemoa **sai**koloa |
| in the 20th century | **nel ventesimo secolo** | nayl vayn**tay**zeemoa **sai**koloa |

| | | |
|---|---|---|
| How old are you? | **Quanti anni ha?** | **kwahn**tee **ahn**nee ah |
| I'm 30 years old. | **Ho trent'anni.** | oa trayn**tahn**nee |
| He/She was born in 1960. | **Lui/Lei è nato(a) nel millenovecento-sessanta.** | looee/laiee ai **nah**toa(ah) nayl meellay-noavay**chehn**-toa-sayss**ahn**tah |
| What is his/her age? | **Quanti anni ha?** | **kwahn**tee **ahn**nee ah |
| Children under 16 are not admitted. | **Vietato ai minori di sedici anni.** | veeay**taa**toa **ahee** meenoa-ree dee **say**deechee **ahn**nee |

## Seasons *Stagioni*

| | | |
|---|---|---|
| spring/summer | **la primavera/l'estate** | lah preemah**vay**rah/lay**staa**tay |
| autumn/winter | **l'autunno/l'inverno** | low**toon**noa/leen**vehr**noa |
| in spring | **in primavera** | een preemah**vay**rah |
| during the summer | **durante l'estate** | doo**rahn**tay lay**staa**tay |
| in autumn | **in autunno** | een ow**toon**noa |
| during the winter | **durante l'inverno** | doo**rahn**tay leen**vehr**noa |
| high season | **alta stagione** | **ahl**tah stah**joa**nay |
| low season | **bassa stagione** | **bahs**sah stah**joa**nay |

## Months *Mesi*

| | | |
|---|---|---|
| January | **gennaio*** | jehn**naa**eeoa |
| February | **febbraio** | fehb**braa**eeoa |
| March | **marzo** | **mahr**tsoa |
| April | **aprile** | ah**pree**lay |
| May | **maggio** | **mah**djoa |
| June | **giugno** | **joo**ñoa |
| July | **luglio** | **lool**yoa |
| August | **agosto** | ah**goa**stoa |
| September | **settembre** | sayt**tehm**bray |
| October | **ottobre** | oat**toa**bray |
| November | **novembre** | noa**vehm**bray |
| December | **dicembre** | dee**chehm**bray |
| in September | **in settembre** | een sayt**tehm**bray |
| since October | **da ottobre** | dah oat**toa**bray |
| the beginning of January | **l'inizio di gennaio** | lee**neet**seeoa dee jehn**naa**eeoa |
| the middle of February | **la metà di febbraio** | lah may**tah** dee fehb**braa**eeoa |
| the end of March | **la fine di marzo** | lah **fee**nay dee **mahr**tsoa |

* The names of months aren't capitalized in Italian.

## Days and Date *Giorni e data*

| | | |
|---|---|---|
| What day is it today? | **Che giorno è oggi?** | kay **joar**noa ai **od**jee |
| Sunday | **domenica*** | doa**may**neekah |
| Monday | **lunedì** | loonay**dee** |
| Tuesday | **martedì** | mahrtay**dee** |
| Wednesday | **mercoledì** | mehrkoalay**dee** |
| Thursday | **giovedì** | joavay**dee** |
| Friday | **venerdì** | vaynayr**dee** |
| Saturday | **sabato** | **saa**bahtoa |
| It's ... | **È ...** | ai |
| July 1 | **il primo luglio** | eel **pree**moa **lool**yoa |
| March 10 | **il 10 marzo** | eel dee**ai**chee **mahr**tsoa |
| in the morning | **al mattino** | ahl mah**ttee**noa |
| during the day | **durante il giorno** | doo**rahn**tay eel **joar**noa |
| in the afternoon | **nel pomeriggio** | nayl poamay**reed**joa |
| in the evening | **alla sera** | **ahl**lah **say**rah |
| at night | **la notte** | lah **not**tay |
| the day before yesterday | **ieri l'altro** | ee**ai**ree **lahl**troa |
| yesterday | **ieri** | ee**ai**ree |
| today | **oggi** | **od**jee |
| tomorrow | **domani** | doa**maa**nee |
| the day after tomorrow | **dopodomani** | dopoadoa**maa**nee |
| the day before | **il giorno prima** | eel **joar**noa **pree**mah |
| the next day | **il giorno seguente** | eel **joar**noa saygoo**ayn**tay |
| two days ago | **due giorni fa** | **doo**ay **joar**nee fah |
| in three days' time | **fra tre giorni** | frah tray **joar**nee |
| last week | **la settimana scorsa** | lah saytteemaanah skoarsah |
| next week | **la settimana prossima** | lah sayttee**maa**nah **pros**seemah |
| for a fortnight (two weeks) | **per quindici giorni** | pair koo**een**deechee **joar**nee |
| birthday | **il compleanno** | eel koamplay**ahn**noa |
| day off | **il giorno di riposo** | eel **joar**noa dee ree**po**soa |
| holiday | **il giorno festivo** | eel **joar**noa fay**stee**voa |
| holidays/vacation | **le vacanze** | lay vah**kahn**tsay |
| week | **la settimana** | lah sayttee**maa**nah |
| weekend | **il fine settimana** | eel **fee**nay sayttee**maa**nah |
| working day | **il giorno feriale** | eel **joar**noa fayree**aa**lay |

* The names of days aren't capitalized in Italian.

## Public holidays *Giorni festivi*

While there may be additional regional holidays in Italy, only national holidays are cited below.

| | | |
|---|---|---|
| January 1 | **Capodanno** or **Primo dell'Anno** | New Year's Day |
| April 25 | **Anniversario della Liberazione (1945)** | Liberation Day |
| May 1 | **Festa del Lavoro** | Labour Day |
| August 15 | **Ferragosto** | Assumption Day |
| November 1 | **Ognissanti** | All Saints' Day |
| December 8 | **L'Immacolata Concezione** | Immaculate Conception |
| December 25 | **Natale** | Christmas Day |
| December 26 | **Santo Stefano** | St. Stephen's Day |
| Movable date: | **Lunedì di Pasqua (Pasquetta)** | Easter Monday |

Except for the 25th April, all the Italian holidays are celebrated in the Ticino, as well as the 19th March *(San Giuseppe),* 1st August (National Holiday), and the usual holidays *Ascensione* (Ascension Day), *Lunedì di Pentecoste* (Whit Monday) and *Corpus Domini.*

## Greetings and wishes *Saluti e auguri*

| | | |
|---|---|---|
| Merry Christmas! | **Buon Natale!** | bwawn nah**taa**lay |
| Happy New Year! | **Buon anno!** | bwawn **ahn**noa |
| Happy Easter! | **Buona Pasqua!** | **bwaw**nah **pah**skwah |
| Happy birthday! | **Buon compleanno!** | bwawn koamplay**ahn**noa |
| Best wishes! | **Tanti auguri!** | **tahn**tee ahoo**goo**ree |
| Congratulations! | **Congratulazioni!** | koangrahtoolahtsee**oa**nee |
| Good luck/All the best! | **Buona fortuna!** | **bwaw**nah foar**too**nah |
| Have a nice trip! | **Buon viaggio!** | bwawn vee**ahd**joa |
| Have a nice holiday! | **Buone vacanze!** | **bwaw**nay vah**kahn**tsay |
| Best regards from ... | **I migliori saluti da ...** | ee mee**lyoa**ree sah**loo**tee dah |
| My regards to ... | **I miei saluti a ...** | ee mee**ai**ee sah**loo**tee ah |

## What time is it? *Che ore sono?*

| | | |
|---|---|---|
| Excuse me. Can you tell me the time? | **Mi scusi. Può dirmi che ore sono?** | mee **skoo**zee. pwo **deer**mee kay **oa**ray **soa**noa |
| It's five past one. | **È l'una e cinque.** | ai **loo**nah ay **cheeng**kooay |
| It's ... | **Sono le ...** | **soa**noa lay |
| ten past two | **due e dieci** | **doo**ay ay dee**ai**chee |
| a quarter past three | **tre e un quarto** | tray ay oon **kwahr**toa |
| twenty past four | **quattro e venti** | **kwaht**troa ay **vayn**tee |
| twenty-five past five | **cinque e venticinque** | **cheeng**kooay ay vaynteeh-**cheeng**kooay |
| half past six | **sei e mezza** | **se**hee ay **mehd**dzah |
| twenty-five to eight | **sette e trentacinque** | **seht**tay ay trayntah-**cheeng**kooay |
| twenty to eight | **otto meno venti** | **ot**toa **mai**noa **vayn**tee |
| a quarter to nine | **nove meno un quarto** | **naw**vay **mai**noa oon **kwahr**toa |
| ten to ten | **dieci meno dieci** | dee**ai**chee **mai**noa dee**ai**chee |
| five to eleven | **undici meno cinque** | **oon**deechee **mai**noa **cheeng**kooay |
| twelve o'clock (noon/midnight) | **dodici (mezzogiorno/ mezzanotte)** | **doa**deechee (mehdzoa**joar**noa/ mehdzah**not**tay) |
| in the morning | **del mattino** | dayl mah**ttee**noa |
| in the afternoon | **del pomeriggio** | dayl poamay**reed**joa |
| in the evening | **della sera** | **dayl**lah **say**rah |
| The train leaves at ... | **Il treno parte alle ...** | eel **tray**noa **pahr**tay **ahl**lay |
| 13.04 (1.04 p.m.) | **tredici e quattro*** | **tray**deechee ay **kwaht**troa |
| 0.40 (0.40 a.m.) | **zero e quaranta** | **dzeh**roa ay kwah**rahn**tah |
| in five minutes | **fra cinque minuti** | frah **cheeng**kooay mee**noo**tee |
| in a quarter of an hour | **fra un quarto d'ora** | frah oon **kwahr**toa **doa**rah |
| half an hour ago | **mezz'ora fa** | mehd**zoa**rah fah |
| about two hours | **circa due ore** | **cheer**kah **doo**ay **oa**ray |
| more than 10 minutes | **più di dieci minuti** | pe**eoo** dee dee**ai**chee mee**noo**tee |
| less than 30 seconds | **meno di trenta secondi** | **mai**noa dee **trayn**tah say**koan**dee |
| The clock is fast/ slow. | **L'orologio è avanti/ indietro.** | loaroa**lo**joa ai ah**vahn**tee/ een**deeay**troa |

* In ordinary conversation, time is expressed as shown above. However, official time uses a 24-hour clock which means that after noon hours are counted from 13 to 24.

## Common abbreviations *Abbreviazioni correnti*

| | | |
|---|---|---|
| A.A.T. | **Azienda Autonoma di Soggiorno, Cura e Turismo** | local tourist board |
| a. | **arrivo** | arrival |
| ab. | **abitanti** | inhabitants, population |
| a.C. | **avanti Cristo** | B.C. |
| A.C.I. | **Automobile Club d'Italia** | Italian Automobile Association |
| a.D. | **anno Domini** | A.D. |
| A.G.I.P. | **Azienda Generale Italiana Petroli** | Italian National Oil Company |
| alt. | **altitudine** | altitude |
| C.I.T. | **Compagnia Italiana Turismo** | Italian Travel Agency |
| c.m. | **corrente mese** | of this month |
| C.P. | **casella postale** | post office box |
| C.so | **Corso** | avenue |
| d.C. | **dopo Cristo** | A.D. |
| ecc. | **eccetera** | etc. |
| E.N.I.T. | **Ente Nazionale italiano per il Turismo** | National Tourist Organization |
| F.F.S. | **Ferrovie Federali Svizzere** | Swiss Federal Railways |
| F.S. | **Ferrovie dello Stato** | Italian State Railways |
| I.V.A. | **Imposta sul Valore Aggiunto** | value added tax (sales tax) |
| Mil. | **militare** | military |
| p. | **partenza; pagina** | departure; page |
| P.T. | **Poste & Telecomunicazioni** | Post & Telecommunications |
| P.za | **Piazza** | square |
| R.A.I. | **Radio Audizioni Italiane** | Italian Broadcasting Company |
| Rep. | **Repubblica** | republic |
| sec. | **secolo** | century |
| Sig. | **Signor** | Mr. |
| Sig.a | **Signora** | Mrs. |
| Sig.na | **Signorina** | Miss |
| S.p.a. | **Società per azioni** | Ltd., Inc. |
| S.P.Q.R. | **Senatus Populusque Romanus** | The Senate and the People of Rome (Latin) |
| S.r.l. | **Società a responsabilità limitata** | limited liability company |
| S./S.ta | **San(to)/Santa** | Saint |
| S.S. | **Sua Santità** | His Holiness |
| T.C.I. | **Touring Club Italiano** | Italian Touring Association |
| V.le | **Viale** | avenue |
| V.U. | **Vigili Urbani** | city police |

## Signs and notices *Cartelli*

| | |
|---|---|
| **Affittasi** | To let, for hire |
| **Al completo** | Full/No vacancies |
| **Aperto da . . . a . . .** | Open from . . . to . . . |
| **Ascensore** | Lift (elevator) |
| **Attenti al cane** | Beware of the dog |
| **Caldo** | Hot |
| **Cassa** | Cash desk |
| **Chiudere la porta** | Close the door |
| **Chiuso** | Closed |
| **Chiuso per ferie/per riposo settimanale** | Closed for holiday/Weekly closing day |
| **Entrare senza bussare** | Enter without knocking |
| **Entrata** | Entrance |
| **Entrata libera** | Free entrance |
| **Freddo** | Cold |
| **Fuori servizio** | Out of order |
| **I trasgressori saranno puniti a norma di legge** | Trespassers will be prosecuted |
| **Informazioni** | Information |
| **In sciopero** | On strike |
| **In vendita** | For sale |
| **Libero** | Vacant |
| **Non disturbare** | Do not disturb |
| **Non toccare** | Do not touch |
| **Occupato** | Occupied |
| **Pericolo (di morte)** | Danger (of death) |
| **Pista per ciclisti** | Path for cyclists |
| **Pittura fresca** | Wet paint |
| **Privato** | Private |
| **Prudenza** | Caution |
| **Riservato** | Reserved |
| **Saldi** | Sales |
| **Signore** | Ladies |
| **Signori** | Gentlemen |
| **Spingere** | Push |
| **Strada privata** | Private road |
| **Suonare, per favore** | Please ring |
| **Svendita** | Sales |
| **Tirare** | Pull |
| **Uscita** | Exit |
| **Uscita di sicurezza** | Emergency exit |
| **Vietato . . .** | . . . forbidden |
| **Vietato fumare** | No smoking |
| **Vietato l'ingresso** | No entrance |
| **Vietato toccare** | Do not touch |

## Emergency *Emergenza*

| | | |
|---|---|---|
| Call the police | **Chiami la polizia** | keeaamee lah poaleetseeah |
| DANGER | **PERICOLO** | payreekoaloa |
| FIRE | **AL FUOCO** | ahl fwawkoa |
| Gas | **Gas** | gaz |
| Get a doctor | **Chiami un medico** | keeaamee oon maideekoa |
| Go away | **Se ne vada** | say nay vaadah |
| HELP | **AIUTO** | aheeootoa |
| Get help quickly | **Chiami aiuti, presto** | keeaamee aheeootee prehstoa |
| I'm ill | **Mi sento male** | mee sayntoa maalay |
| I'm lost | **Mi sono perso(a)** | mee soanoa pehrsoa(ah) |
| Leave me alone | **Mi lasci in pace** | mee laashee een paachay |
| LOOK OUT | **ATTENZIONE** | ahttayntseeoanay |
| Poison | **Veleno** | vaylaynoa |
| POLICE | **POLIZIA** | poaleetseeah |
| Quick | **Presto** | prehstoa |
| STOP | **FERMATEVI** | fayrmaatayvee |
| Stop that man/ woman | **Fermate quell'uomo/ quella donna** | fayrmaatay kooayllwomoa/ kooayllah donnah |
| STOP THIEF | **AL LADRO** | ahl laadroa |

## Emergency telephone numbers *Chiamate di emergenza*

| | | |
|---|---|---|
| **Italy:** | Police, all-purpose emergency number | 113 |
| | Road assistance (Automobile Club d'Italia) | 116 |
| **Switzerland:** | Police, all-purpose emergency number | 117 |
| | Fire | 118 |

## Lost! *In caso di perdite o di furti*

| | | |
|---|---|---|
| Where's the ...? | **Dov'è ...?** | doavai |
| lost-property (lost and found) office | **l'ufficio oggetti smarriti** | looffeechoa oadjehttee zmahrreetee |
| police station | **il posto di polizia** | eel poastoa dee poaleetseeah |
| I want to report a theft. | **Devo denunciare un furto.** | dayvoa daynoonchaaray oon foortoa |
| My ... has been stolen. | **Mi hanno rubato ...** | mee ahnnoa roobaatoa |
| I've lost my ... | **Ho perso ...** | oa pehrsoa |
| handbag | **la mia borsetta** | lah meeah boarsayttah |
| passport | **il mio passaporto** | eel meeoa pahssahpoartoa |
| wallet | **il mio portafogli** | eel meeoa portahfoalyee |

CAR ACCIDENTS, see page 78

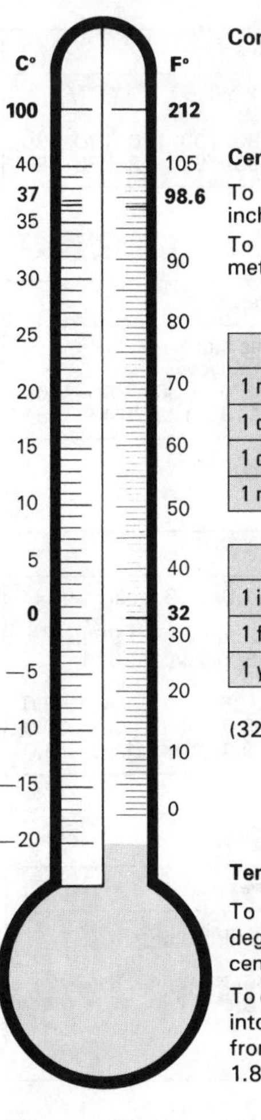


## Conversion tables

### Centimetres and inches

To change centimetres into inches, multiply by .39.

To change inches into centimetres, multiply by 2.54.

| | in. | feet | yards |
|---|---|---|---|
| 1 mm. | 0.039 | 0.003 | 0.001 |
| 1 cm. | 0.39 | 0.03 | 0.01 |
| 1 dm. | 3.94 | 0.32 | 0.10 |
| 1 m. | 39.40 | 3.28 | 1.09 |

| | mm. | cm. | m. |
|---|---|---|---|
| 1 in. | 25.4 | 2.54 | 0.025 |
| 1 ft. | 304.8 | 30.48 | 0.305 |
| 1 yd. | 914.4 | 91.44 | 0.914 |

(32 metres = 35 yards)

### Temperature

To convert centigrade into degrees Fahrenheit, multiply centigrade by 1.8 and add 32.

To convert degrees Fahrenheit into centigrade, subtract 32 from Fahrenheit and divide by 1.8.

## Kilometres into miles

1 kilometre (km.) = 0.62 miles

| km. | 10 | 20 | 30 | 40 | 50 | 60 | 70 | 80 | 90 | 100 | 110 | 120 | 130 |
|---|---|---|---|---|---|---|---|---|---|---|---|---|---|
| miles | 6 | 12 | 19 | 25 | 31 | 37 | 44 | 50 | 56 | 62 | 68 | 75 | 81 |

## Miles into kilometres

1 mile = 1.609 kilometres (km.)

| miles | 10 | 20 | 30 | 40 | 50 | 60 | 70 | 80 | 90 | 100 |
|---|---|---|---|---|---|---|---|---|---|---|
| km. | 16 | 32 | 48 | 64 | 80 | 97 | 113 | 129 | 145 | 161 |

## Fluid measures

1 litre (l.) = 0.88 imp. quart or = 1.06 U.S. quart

1 imp. quart = 1.14 l.
1 imp. gallon = 4.55 l.

1 U.S. quart = 0.95 l.
1 U.S. gallon = 3.8 l.

| litres | 5 | 10 | 15 | 20 | 25 | 30 | 35 | 40 | 45 | 50 |
|---|---|---|---|---|---|---|---|---|---|---|
| imp. gal. | 1.1 | 2.2 | 3.3 | 4.4 | 5.5 | 6.6 | 7.7 | 8.8 | 9.9 | 11.0 |
| U.S. gal. | 1.3 | 2.6 | 3.9 | 5.2 | 6.5 | 7.8 | 9.1 | 10.4 | 11.7 | 13.0 |

## Weights and measures

1 kilogram or kilo (kg.) = 1000 grams (g.)

100 g. = 3.5 oz.
200 g. = 7.0 oz.

½ kg. = 1.1 lb.
1 kg. = 2.2 lb.

1 oz. = 28.35 g.
1 lb. = 453.60 g.



CLOTHING SIZES, see page 115/YARDS AND INCHES, see page 112

# A very basic grammar

## Articles

There are two genders in Italian—masculine (masc.) and feminine (fem.).

### 1. Definite article (the):

| | singular | plural |
|---|---|---|
| masc. | **l'** before a vowel | **gli** |
| | **lo** before **z** or **s + consonant** | **gli** |
| | **il** before all other consonants | **i** |
| | **l'amico** (the friend) | **gli amici** (the friends) |
| | **lo studente** (the student) | **gli studenti** (the students) |
| | **il treno** (the train) | **i treni** (the trains) |
| fem. | **l'** before a vowel | **le** |
| | **la** before a consonant | **le** |
| | **l'arancia** (the orange) | **le arance** (the oranges) |
| | **la casa** (the house) | **le case** (the houses) |

### 2. Indefinite article (a/an):

masc. **un** (**uno** before **z** or **s + consonant***)
**un piatto** (a plate)
**uno specchio** (a mirror)

fem. **una** (**un'** before a vowel)
**una strada** (a street)
**un'amica** (a girl friend)

### 3. Partitive (some/any)

In affirmative sentences and some interrogatives, **some** and **any** are expressed by **di + definite article,** which has the following contracted forms:

| | | |
|---|---|---|
| masc. | **dell'** before a vowel | **degli** |
| | **dello** before **z** or **s + consonant** | **degli** |
| | **del** before other consonants | **dei** |
| fem. | **dell'** before a vowel | **delle** |
| | **della** before a consonant | **delle** |

* When **s** is followed by a vowel, the masculine articles are **il/i** (definite) and **un** (indefinite).

For other contractions of preposition + definite article, see page 163.

| | |
|---|---|
| **Desidero del vino** | I want some wine. |
| **Vorrei delle sigarette.** | I'd like some cigarettes. |
| **Ha degli amici a Roma?** | Have you any friends in Rome? |

### Nouns

Nouns ending in **o** are generally masculine. To form the plural, change **o** to **i**.

| | |
|---|---|
| **il tavolo** (the table) | **i tavoli** (the tables) |

Nouns ending in **a** are usually feminine. To form the plural, change **a** to **e**.

| | |
|---|---|
| **la casa** (the house) | **le case** (the houses) |

Nouns ending in **e**—no rule as to gender. Learn each noun individually. Plurals are formed by changing the **e** to **i**.

| | |
|---|---|
| **il piede** (the foot) | **i piedi** (the feet) |
| **la notte** (the night) | **le notti** (the nights) |

### Adjectives

They agree with the noun they modify in number and gender. There are two basic types—ending in **o** and ending in **e**.

| | singular | plural |
|---|---|---|
| masc. | **leggero** light (in weight) | **leggeri** |
| | **grande** big | **grandi** |
| fem. | **leggera** | **leggere** |
| | **grande** | **grandi** |

They usually follow the noun but certain common adjectives precede the noun.

**un caro amico** (a dear friend)
**una strada lunga** (a long street)

### Demonstratives

| | |
|---|---|
| this | **questo/questa** (contracted to **quest'** before a vowel) |
| these | **questi/queste** (no contraction) |
| that | **quell', quello, quel** (masc.)/**quell', quella*** (fem.) |
| those | **quegli, quei** (masc.)/ **quelle** (fem.) |

### Possessive adjectives and pronouns

These agree in number and gender *with the nouns they modify* (or replace). They are almost always used with the definite article.

| | masculine | | feminine | |
|---|---|---|---|---|
| | singular | plural | singular | plural |
| my, mine | **il mio** | **i miei** | **la mia** | **le mie** |
| your, yours | **il tuo** | **i tuoi** | **la tua** | **le tue** |
| his, her, hers, its | **il suo** | **i suoi** | **la sua** | **le sue** |
| our, ours | **il nostro** | **i nostri** | **la nostra** | **le nostre** |
| your, yours | **il vostro** | **i vostri** | **la vostra** | **le vostre** |
| their, theirs | **il loro** | **i loro** | **la loro** | **le loro** |
| **your, yours (sing.) | **il suo** | **i suoi** | **la sua** | **le sue** |
| **your, yours (plur.) | **il loro** | **i loro** | **la loro** | **le loro** |

Thus, depending on the context, **il suo cane** can mean *his, her* or *your dog,* **la sua casa,** *his, her* or *your house.*

### Personal pronouns

| | Subject | Direct Object | Indirect Object | After a Preposition |
|---|---|---|---|---|
| I | **io** | **mi** | **mi** | **me** |
| you | **tu** | **ti** | **ti** | **te** |
| he, it (masc.) | **lui/egli** | **lo** | **gli** | **lui** |
| she, it (fem.) | **lei/ella** | **la** | **le** | **lei** |
| we | **noi** | **ci** | **ci** | **noi** |
| you | **voi** | **vi** | **vi** | **voi** |
| they (masc.) | **loro/essi** | **li** | **loro** | **loro** |
| they (fem.) | **loro/esse** | **le** | **loro** | **loro** |

* These forms follow the same system as **dell'/dello/della,** etc. (see p. 163).
** This is the formal form—used in addressing people you do not know well.

*Note:* There are two forms for "you" in Italian: **tu** (singular) is used when talking to relatives, close friends and children (and between young people); the plural of **tu** is **voi. Lei** (singular) and **Loro** (plural) are used in all other cases (with the 3rd person singular/plural of the verb).

### Verbs

Here we are concerned only with the infinitive and the present tense.

Learn these two **auxiliary verbs:**

| **essere** (to be) | **avere** (to have) |
|---|---|
| **io* sono** (I am) | **io* ho** (I have) |
| **tu sei** (you are) | **tu hai** (you have) |
| **lui, lei è** (he, she, it is) | **lui, lei ha** (he, she, it has) |
| **lei è** (you are) | **lei ha** (you have) |
| **noi siamo** (we are) | **noi abbiamo** (we have) |
| **voi siete** (you are) | **voi avete** (you have) |
| **essi/esse sono** (they are) | **essi/esse hanno** (they have) |

**C'è/Ci sono** are equivalent to "there is/there are":

| | |
|---|---|
| **C'è una lettera per Lei.** | There's a letter for you. |
| **Ci sono due pacchi per lui.** | There are two parcels for him. |

**Regular verbs** follow one of three patterns (conjugations) depending on the ending of the infinitive.

| | ends in **-are** | ends in **-ere** | ends in **-ire** |
|---|---|---|---|
| Infinitive: | **amare** (to love) | **vendere** (to sell) | **partire** (to leave) |
| **io*** | **amo** | **vendo** | **parto** |
| **tu** | **ami** | **vendi** | **parti** |
| **lui, lei** | **ama** | **vende** | **parte** |
| **noi** | **amiamo** | **vendiamo** | **partiamo** |
| **voi** | **amate** | **vendete** | **partite** |
| **essi/esse** | **amano** | **vendono** | **partono** |

* The subject pronouns are seldom used except for emphasis.

**Irregular verbs:** As in all languages, these have to be learned. Here are four you'll find useful.

| Infinitive: | **andare** (to go) | **potere** (to be able) | **volere** (to want) | **fare** (to make) |
|---|---|---|---|---|
| **io** | **vado** | **posso** | **voglio** | **faccio** |
| **tu** | **vai** | **puoi** | **vuoi** | **fai** |
| **lui/lei** | **va** | **può** | **vuole** | **fa** |
| **noi** | **andiamo** | **possiamo** | **vogliamo** | **facciamo** |
| **voi** | **andate** | **potete** | **volete** | **fate** |
| **essi/esse** | **vanno** | **possono** | **vogliono** | **fanno** |

## Negatives

Negatives are formed by putting **non** before the verb.

**Non vado a Roma.** I am not going to Rome.

## Questions

In Italian, questions are often formed by simply changing the inflexion of your voice. Remember that the personal pronoun is rarely used, either in affirmative sentences or in questions.

**Parlo italiano.** I speak Italian.
**Parla italiano?** Do you speak Italian?

## Prepositions

There is a list of prepositions on page 14. Note the following contractions:

| Definite Article | **a** at, to | **da** by, from | **di** of | **in** in | **su** on | **con** with |
|---|---|---|---|---|---|---|
| **+ il** | **al** | **dal** | **del** | **nel** | **sul** | **col** |
| **+ l'** | **all'** | **dall'** | **dell'** | **nell'** | **sull'** | **coll'** |
| **+ lo** | **allo** | **dallo** | **dello** | **nello** | **sullo** | **con lo** |
| **+ la** | **alla** | **dalla** | **della** | **nella** | **sulla** | **con la** |
| **+ i** | **ai** | **dai** | **dei** | **nei** | **sui** | **coi/con i** |
| **+ gli** | **agli** | **dagli** | **degli** | **negli** | **sugli** | **con gli** |
| **+ le** | **alle** | **dalle** | **delle** | **nelle** | **sulle** | **con le** |

# Dictionary
and alphabetical index

# English–Italian

*f* feminine *m* masculine *pl* plural

**a** un(a) 159
**abbey** abbazia *f* 81
**abbreviation** abbreviazione *f* 154
**able, to be** potere 163
**about** *(approximately)* circa 153
**above** sopra 15, 63
**absces** ascesso *m* 145
**absorbent cotton** cotone idrofilo *m* 109
**accept, to** accettare 62, 102
**accessories** accessori *m/pl* 116, 125
**accident** incidente *m* 78, 79, 139
**accommodation** alloggio *m* 22
**account** conto *m* 130, 131
**ache** dolore *m*, male *m* 141
**adaptor** presa multipla *f* 119
**address** indirizzo *m* 21, 31, 76, 79, 102
**address book** agenda per gli indirizzi *f* 104
**adhesive** adesivo(a) 105
**admission** entrata *f* 82, 89, 155
**Africa** Africa *f* 146
**after** dopo 14, 77
**afternoon** pomeriggio *m* 151, 153
**after-shave lotion** lozione dopobarba *f* 110
**age** età *f* 149; anni *m* 150
**ago** fa 149, 151
**air conditioner** condizionatore d'aria *m* 28
**air conditioning** aria condizionata *f* 23
**airmail** via aerea 133
**airplane** aereo *m* 65
**airport** aeroporto *m* 16, 21, 65
**alabaster** alabastro *m* 122
**alarm clock** sveglia *f* 121
**alcohol** alcool *m* 107
**alcoholic** alcolico(a) 59
**Algeria** Algeria *f* 146
**allergic** allergico(a) 141, 143
**almond** mandorla *f* 54
**alphabet** alfabeto *m* 8
**also** anche 15
**amazing** sorprendente 84
**amber** ambra *f* 122
**ambulance** ambulanza *f* 79
**American** americano(a) 93, 126
**American plan** pensione completa *f* 24
**amethyst** ametista *f* 122
**amount** importo *m* 62, 131
**amplifier** amplificatore *m* 119
**anaesthetic** anestetico *m* 144
**analgesic** analgesico *m* 109
**anchovy** acciuga *f* 41, 46
**and** e 15
**animal** animale *m* 85
**ankle** caviglia *f* 139
**anorak** giacca a vento *f* 116
**another** un(') altro(a) 123
**answer, to** rispondere 136
**antibiotic** antibiotico *m* 143
**antidepressant** antidepressivo *m* 143
**antiques** antichità *f/pl* 83
**antique shop** antiquario *m* 98
**antiseptic** antisettico(a) 109
**antiseptic** antisettico *m* 140
**any** del, della 14
**anyone** qualcuno(a) 11
**anything** qualcosa 17, 25, 113

**aperitif** aperitivo *m* 56
**appendicitis** appendicite *f* 142
**appendix** appendice *f* 138
**appetizer** antipasto *m* 41
**apple** mela *f* 54, 63
**appliance** apparecchio *m* 119
**appointment** appuntamento *m* 30, 131, 137, 145
**apricot** albicocca *f* 54
**April** aprile *m* 150
**archaeology** archeologia *f* 83
**architect** architetto *m* 83
**area code** prefisso *m* 134
**arm** braccio *m* 138, 139
**arrival** arrivo *m* 16, 65
**arrive, to** arrivare 65, 68, 130
**art** arte *f* 83
**artery** arteria *f* 138
**art gallery** galleria d'arte *f* 81, 98
**artichoke** carciofo *m* 41, 52
**artificial** artificiale 124
**artist** artista *m/f* 81, 83
**ashtray** portacenere *m* 27, 36
**Asia** Asia *f* 146
**ask for, to** chiedere 25, 61, 136
**asparagus** asparago *m* 52
**aspirin** aspirina *f* 109
**assorted** assortito(a) 41
**asthma** asma *f* 141
**at** a 14, 163
**at least** come minimo 24
**at once** subito 15; immediatamente 31
**aubergine** melanzana *f* 52
**August** agosto *m* 150
**aunt** zia *f* 93
**Australia** Australia *f* 146
**Austria** Austria *f* 146
**automatic** automatico(a) 20, 122, 124
**autumn** autunno *m* 150
**average** medio(a) 91
**awful** orribile 84

## B

**baby** bambino *m* 24, 111; bebè *m* 111
**baby food** alimenti per bebè *m/pl* 111
**babysitter** babysitter *f* 27
**back** schiena *f* 138
**backache** mal di schiena *m* 141
**bacon** pancetta *f* 38
**bacon and eggs** uova e pancetta *m/pl* 38
**bad** cattivo(a) 13, 95
**bag** borsa *f* 18; sacchetto *m* 103
**baggage** bagagli *m/pl* 18, 26, 31, 71
**baggage cart** carrello portabagagli *m* 18, 71
**baggage check** deposito bagagli *m* 67, 71
**baked** al forno 47, 50
**baker's** panetteria *f* 98
**balance** *(account)* bilancio *m* 131
**balcony** balcone *m* 23
**ball** *(inflated)* pallone *m* 128
**ballet** balletto *m* 88
**ball-point pen** biro *f* 104
**banana** banana *f* 54, 63
**bandage** benda *f* 109
**Band-Aid** cerotto *m* 109
**bangle** braccialetto *m* 121
**bangs** frangia *f* 30
**bank** *(finance)* banca *f* 98, 129
**bank card** carta d'identità bancaria *f* 130
**banknote** banconota *f* 130
**bar** bar *m* 33, 67; *(chocolate)* stecca *f* 64
**barbecued** alla graticola, alla griglia 50
**barber's** barbiere *m* 30, 98
**basil** basilico *m* 53
**basketball** pallacanestro *f* 89
**bass** *(fish)* branzino *m* 46
**bath** *(hotel)* bagno *m* 23, 25, 27
**bathing cap** cuffia da bagno *f* 116
**bathing hut** cabina *f* 91
**bathing suit** costume da bagno *m* 116
**bathrobe** accappatoio *m* 116
**bathroom** bagno *m* 27
**bath salts** sali da bagno *m/pl* 110
**bath towel** asciugamano *m* 27
**battery** pila *f* 119, 121, 125; *(car)* batteria *f* 75, 78
**bay leaf** lauro *m* 53
**be, to** essere 162; trovarsi 11
**beach** spiaggia *f* 90
**bean** fagiolo *m* 52
**beard** barba *f* 31
**beautiful** bello(a) 13, 84
**beauty salon** istituto di bellezza *m* 30, 98
**bed** letto *m* 24, 144
**bed and breakfast** camera e colazione *f* 24
**bedpan** padella *f* 144
**beef** manzo *m* 48

**beer** birra *f* 59, 64
**beet(root)** barbabietola *f* 52
**before** *(place)* davanti a 14; *(time)* prima di 14, 151
**begin, to** iniziare 80, 88; incominciare 87
**beginner** principiante *m/f* 91
**beginning** inizio *m* 150
**behind** dietro 14, 77
**beige** beige 113
**Belgium** Belgio *m* 146
**bell** *(electric)* campanello *m* 144
**bellboy** fattorino *m* 26
**below** al di sotto 15; sotto 63
**belt** cintura *f* 117
**bend** *(road)* curva *f* 79
**berth** cuccetta *f* 69, 70, 71
**best** migliore 152
**better** migliore 13, 25, 101, 113
**beware** attento(a) 155
**between** tra, fra 15
**bicycle** bicicletta *f* 74
**big** grande 13, 101
**bill** conto *m* 31, 62, 102; *(banknote)* banconota *f* 130
**billion** *(Am.)* miliardo *m* 148
**binoculars** binocolo *m* 123
**bird** uccello *m* 85
**birthday** compleanno *m* 151, 152
**biscuit** *(Br.)* biscotto *m* 64
**bitter** amaro(a) 61
**black** nero(a) 113
**black and white** bianco e nero 124, 125
**blackberry** mora *f* 54
**blackcurrant** ribes nero *m* 54
**bladder** vescica *f* 138
**blanket** coperta *f* 27
**bleach** decolorazione *f* 30
**bleed, to** perdere sangue 139; sanguinare 145
**blind** persiana *f* 29
**blister** vescica *f* 139
**blood** sangue *m* 142
**blood pressure** pressione *f* 141
**blood transfusion** trasfusione di sangue *f* 144
**blouse** blusa *f* 116
**blow-dry** asciugatura col fono *f* 30
**blue** blu, azzurro(a) 113
**blueberry** mirtillo *m* 54
**boar** *(wild)* cinghiale *m* 51
**boarding house** pensione *f* 19, 22
**boat** battello *m* 74
**bobby pin** molletta *f* 111
**body** corpo *m* 138
**boil** foruncolo *m* 139
**boiled** lesso(a) 47, 50
**boiled egg** uovo alla coque *m* 38
**bone** osso *m* 138
**book** libro *m* 11, 104
**book, to** prenotare 69
**booking office** ufficio prenotazioni *m* 19, 67
**booklet** blocchetto *m* 72
**bookshop** libreria *f* 98, 104
**boot** stivale *m* 118
**born** nato(a) 150
**botanical gardens** giardino botanico *m* 81
**botany** botanica *f* 83
**bottle** bottiglia *f* 17, 57
**bottle-opener** apribottiglia *m* 106
**bottom** basso *m* 145
**bowels** intestino *m* 138
**bow tie** cravatta a farfalla *f* 116
**box** scatola *f* 120
**boxing** pugilato *m* 89
**boy** *(child)* bambino *m* 112, 128
**boyfriend** ragazzo *m* 93
**bra** reggiseno *m* 116
**bracelet** braccialetto *m* 121
**braces** *(suspenders)* bretelle *f/pl* 116
**brains** *(food)* cervello *m* 48
**braised** brasato(a) 50
**brake** freno *m* 78
**brake fluid** olio dei freni *m* 75
**brandy** brandy *m* 59
**bread** pane *m* 36, 38, 64
**break, to** rompere 29, 119, 123, 145; rompersi 139, 145
**break down, to** avere un guasto 78
**breakdown** guasto *m* 78
**breakdown van** carro attrezzi *m* 78
**breakfast** colazione *f* 24, 34, 38
**breast** petto *m* 138
**breathe, to** respirare 141
**bridge** ponte *m* 85
**briefs** slip *m* 116
**bring, to** portare 12
**bring down, to** portare giù 31
**British** britannico(a) 93
**broken** rotto(a) 29, 119, 140
**brooch** spilla *f* 121
**brother** fratello *m* 93
**brown** marrone 113
**bruise** contusione *f* 139
**brush** spazzola f 111

**Brussels sprouts** cavolini di Bruxelles *m/pl* 52
**bubble bath** bagnoschiuma *m* 110
**bucket** secchio *m* 106; secchiello *m* 128
**build, to** costruire 83
**building** edificio *m* 81, 83
**building blocks/bricks** gioco di costruzioni *m* 128
**bulb** lampadina *f* 28, 75, 119
**burn** scottatura *f* 139
**burn out, to** *(bulb)* bruciare 28
**bus** autobus *m* 18, 19, 65, 72, 73; pullman *m* 72, 80
**business** affari *m/pl* 16, 131
**business trip** viaggio d'affari *m* 93
**bus stop** fermata dell'autobus *f* 72, 73
**busy** impegnato(a) 96
**but** ma, però 15
**butane gas** gas butano *m* 32, 106
**butcher's** macelleria *f* 98
**butter** burro *m* 36, 38, 64
**button** bottone *m* 29, 117
**buy, to** comprare 82, 104; acquistare 123

## C

**cabana** cabina *f* 91
**cabbage** cavolo *m* 52
**cabin** *(ship)* cabina *f* 74
**cable** telegramma *m* 133
**cable car** funivia *f* 74
**cable release** scatto *m* 125
**café** caffè *m* 33
**caffein-free** decaffeinato 38, 60
**cake** dolce *m* 55; torta *f* 55, 64
**cake shop** pasticceria *f* 98
**calculator** calcolatrice *f* 105
**calendar** calendario *m* 104
**call** *(phone)* telefonata *f* 135, 136
**call, to** chiamare 11, 78, 156; telefonare 136
**cambric** tela battista *f* 114
**camel-hair** pelo di cammello *m* 114
**camera** macchina fotografica *f* 124, 125
**camera case** astuccio (per macchina fotografica) *m* 125
**camera shop** negozio di apparecchi fotografici *m* 98
**camp, to** campeggiare 32
**campbed** letto da campo *m* 106
**camping** campeggio *m* 32
**camping equipment** materiale da campeggio *m* 106
**camp site** campeggio *m* 32
**can** *(of peaches)* scatola *f* 120
**can** *(to be able)* potere 11, 12, 163
**Canada** Canada *m* 146
**cancel, to** annullare 65
**candle** candela *f* 106
**candy** caramella *f* 126
**can opener** apriscatole *m* 106
**cap** berretto *m* 116
**caper** cappero *m* 53
**capital** *(finance)* capitale *m* 131
**car** macchina *f* 19, 20, 75, 76, 78; automobile *f* 78
**carafe** caraffa *f* 57
**carat** carato *m* 121
**caravan** roulotte *f* 32
**caraway** cumino *m* 53
**carbon paper** carta carbone *f* 104
**carburettor** carburatore *m* 78
**card** carta *f* 93; *(visiting)* bigliettino *m* 131
**card game** carte da gioco *f/pl* 128
**cardigan** cardigan *m* 116
**car hire** autonoleggio *m* 19, 20
**car park** parcheggio *m* 77
**car racing** corsa automobilistica *f* 89
**car radio** autoradio *f* 119
**car rental** autonoleggio *m* 20
**carrot** carota *f* 52
**carry, to** portare 21
**cart** carrello *m* 18
**carton** *(of cigarettes)* stecca (di sigarette) *f* 17
**cartridge** *(camera)* rotolo *m* 124
**case** *(instance)* caso *m* 143; *(cigarettes etc)* astuccio *m* 123, 125
**cash, to** incassare 130; riscuotere 133
**cash desk** cassa *f* 103, 155
**cashier** cassiere(a) *m/f* 103
**cassette** cassetta *f* 119, 127
**castle** castello *m* 81
**catacomb** catacomba *f* 81
**catalogue** catalogo *m* 82
**cathedral** cattedrale *f* 81
**Catholic** cattolico(a) 84
**cauliflower** cavolfiore *m* 52
**caution** prudenza *f* 155
**cave** grotta *f* 81
**celery** sedano *m* 52
**cellophane tape** nastro adesivo *m* 104

**cemetery** cimitero *m* 81
**centimetre** centimetro *m* 112
**centre** centro *m* 19, 21, 76, 81
**century** secolo *m* 149
**ceramics** ceramica *f* 83, 127
**cereal** cereali *m/pl* 38
**certificate** certificato *m* 144
**chain** catena *f* 79
**chain** *(jewellery)* catenina *f* 121
**chain bracelet** braccialetto a catena *m* 121
**chair** sedia *f* 36, 106
**chamber music** musica da camera *f* 128
**change** *(money)* moneta *f* 77, 130; resto *m* 62
**change, to** cambiare 61, 65, 68, 73, 75, 123; *(money)* 18, 130
**chapel** cappella *f* 81
**charcoal** carbonella *f* 106
**charge** tariffa *f* 20; prezzo *m* 89; costo *m* 136
**charge, to** fare pagare 24; *(commission)* trattenere 130
**charm** *(trinket)* ciondolo *m* 121
**charm bracelet** braccialetto a ciondoli *m* 121
**cheap** buon mercato 13; economico(a) 101
**check** assegno *m* 130; *(restaurant)* conto *m* 62
**check, to** controllare 75, 123; *(luggage)* far registrare 71
**check book** libretto d'assegni *m* 131
**check in, to** *(airport)* presentarsi 65
**check out, to** partire 31
**checkup** *(medical)* controllo *m* 142
**cheers!** salute! cin-cin! 56
**cheese** formaggio *m* 53, 63, 64
**chef** chef *m* 40
**chemist's** farmacia *f* 98, 108
**cheque** assegno *m* 130
**cheque book** libretto d'assegni *m* 131
**cherry** ciliegia *f* 54
**chess** scacchi *m/pl* 93, 128
**chest** torace *m* 138, 141
**chestnut** castagna *f* 54
**chewing gum** gomma da masticare *f* 126
**chicken** pollo *m* 51, 63
**chick-pea** cece *m* 52
**chicory** indivia *f* 52; *(Am.)* cicoria *f* 52
**chiffon** chiffon *m* 114
**child** bambino(a) *m/f* 24, 61, 82, 93, 139
**children's doctor** pediatra *m/f* 137
**China** Cina *f* 146
**chips** patatine fritte *f/pl* 63, 64
**chives** cipollina *f* 53
**chocolate** cioccolato *m* 126, 127; *(hot)* cioccolata (calda) *f* 38, 60
**chocolate bar** stecca di cioccolato *f* 64
**choice** scelta *f* 40
**chop** braciola *f* 48
**Christmas** Natale *m* 152
**church** chiesa *f* 81, 84
**cigar** sigaro *m* 126
**cigarette** sigaretta *f* 17, 95, 126
**cigarette case** portasigarette *m* 121, 126
**cigarette lighter** accendino *m* 121
**cine camera** cinepresa *f* 124
**cinema** cinema *m* 86, 96
**cinnamon** cannella *f* 53
**circle** *(theatre)* galleria *f* 87
**city** città *f* 81
**clam** vongola *f* 45, 47
**classical** classico(a) 128
**clean** pulito(a) 61
**clean, to** pulire 29, 76
**cleansing cream** crema detergente *f* 110
**cliff** scogliera *f* 85
**clip** fermaglio *m* 121
**clock** orologio *m* 121, 153
**clog, to** otturare 28
**close** *(near)* vicino(a) 78, 98
**close, to** chiudere 11, 82, 108, 132
**closed** chiuso(a) 155
**clothes** abiti *m/pl* 29; indumenti *m/pl* 116
**clothes peg** molletta da bucato *f* 106
**clothing** abbigliamento *m* 112
**cloud** nuvola *f* 94
**clove** chiodo di garofano *m* 53
**coach** *(bus)* pullman *m* 72
**coat** cappotto *m* 116
**coconut** noce di cocco *f* 54
**cod** baccalà *m* 46, 47; *(fresh)* merluzzo *m* 46
**coffee** caffè *m* 38, 60, 64
**coin** moneta *f* 83
**cold** freddo(a) 13, 25, 61, 94, 155
**cold** *(illness)* raffreddore *m* 108, 141
**cold cuts** affettati *m/pl* 64
**colour** colore *m* 103, 112, 124, 125

**colour chart** tabella dei colori *f* 30
**colour negative** negativo a colori *m* 124
**colour shampoo** shampoo colorante *m* 111
**colour slide** diapositiva *f* 124
**colour television** *(set)* televisore a colori *m* 119
**comb** pettine *m* 111
**come, to** venire 36, 92, 95, 137, 146
**comedy** commedia *f* 86
**commission** commissione *f* 130
**common** *(frequent)* corrente 154
**compact disc** disco compatto *m* 127
**compartment** scompartimento *m* 70
**compass** bussola *f* 106
**complaint** reclamo *m* 61
**concert** concerto *m* 88
**concert hall** sala dei concerti *f* 81, 88
**conductor** *(orchestra)* maestro *m* 88
**confectioner's** pasticceria *f* 98
**confirm, to** confermare 65
**confirmation** conferma *f* 23
**congratulations** congratulazioni *f/pl* 152
**connection** *(train)* coincidenza *f* 65, 68
**constant** costante 140
**constipated** costipato(a) 140
**contact lens** lente a contatto *f* 123
**contain, to** contenere 37
**contraceptive** antifecondativo *m* 109
**contract** contratto *m* 131
**control** controllo *m* 16
**convent** convento *m* 81
**cookie** biscotto *m* 64
**cool box** ghiacciaia *f* 106
**copper** rame *m* 122
**coral** corallo *m* 122
**corduroy** velluto a coste *m* 114
**cork** tappo *m* 61
**corkscrew** cavatappi *m* 106
**corner** angolo *m* 21, 36, 77
**corn plaster** cerotto callifugo *m* 109
**cost** preventivo *m* 131
**cost, to** costare 10, 80, 133, 136
**cotton** cotone *m* 114
**cotton wool** cotone idrofilo *m* 109
**cough** tosse *f* 108, 141
**cough, to** tossire 142
**cough drops** pasticche per la tosse *f/pl* 109
**counter** sportello *m* 133
**countryside** campagna *f* 85
**court house** palazzo di giustizia *m* 81
**cousin** cugino(a) *m/f* 93
**cover charge** coperto *m* 62
**crab** granchio *m* 46
**cramp** crampo *m* 141
**crayfish** gambero *m* 46
**crayon** pastello *m* 104
**cream** panna *f* 55, 60; *(toiletry)* crema *f* 110
**credit** credito *m* 130
**credit, to** accreditare 130, 131
**credit card** carta di credito *f* 20, 31, 62, 102, 130
**crockery** stoviglie *f/pl* 107
**crisps** patatine fritte *f/pl* 64
**cross** croce *f* 121
**crossing** *(by sea)* traversata *f* 74
**crossroads** incrocio *m* 77
**cruise** crociera *f* 74
**crystal** cristallo *m* 122
**cuckoo clock** orologio a cucù *m* 121
**cucumber** cetriolo *m* 52
**cuff link** gemelli *m/pl* 121
**cuisine** cucina *f* 35
**cup** tazza *f* 36, 107
**currency** valuta *f* 129
**currency exchange** ufficio cambio *m* 18, 67, 129
**current** corrente *f* 90
**curtain** tenda *f* 28
**curve** *(road)* curva *f* 79
**custard** crema *f* 55
**customs** dogana *f* 16, 122
**cut** *(wound)* taglio *m* 139
**cut off, to** *(phone)* interrompere 135
**cut glass** vetro tagliato *m* 122
**cuticle remover** prodotto per togliere le pellicine *m* 110
**cutlery** posate *f/pl* 107, 121
**cuttlefish** seppia *f* 47
**cycling** ciclismo *m* 89
**cystitis** cistite *f* 142

## D

**dairy** latteria *f* 98
**dance, to** ballare 88, 96
**danger** pericolo *m* 155, 156
**dangerous** pericoloso(a) 90
**dark** buio(a) 25; scuro(a) 101, 112, 113
**date** data *f* 25, 151; *(fruit)* dattero *m* 54
**daughter** figlia *f* 93
**day** giorno *m* 16, 20, 24, 32, 80, 151

**daylight** luce naturale *f* 124
**day off** giorno di riposo *m* 151
**death** morte *f* 155
**decade** decennio *m* 149
**December** dicembre *m* 150
**decision** decisione *f* 25, 102
**deck** *(ship)* ponte *m* 74
**deck-chair** sedia a sdraio *f* 91
**declare, to** dichiarare 16, 17
**deer** cervo *m* 51
**delay** ritardo *m* 69
**delicatessen** salumeria *f* 98
**delicious** delizioso(a) 62
**deliver, to** consegnare 102
**delivery** consegna *f* 102
**denim** tela di cotone *f* 114
**dentist** dentista *m/f* 145
**denture** dentiera *f* 145
**deodorant** deodorante *m* 110
**department** *(museum, shop)* reparto *m* 83, 100
**department store** grande magazzino *m* 98
**departure** partenza *f* 65
**deposit** *(car hire)* cauzione *f* 20; *(bank)* deposito *m* 130
**deposit, to** *(bank)* depositare 130
**dessert** dessert *m* 40, 55; dolce *m* 39, 55
**detour** *(traffic)* deviazione *f* 79
**develop, to** sviluppare 124
**diabetes** diabete *m* 141
**diabetic** diabetico(a) *m/f* 37
**dialling code** prefisso *m* 134
**diamond** diamante *m* 122
**diaper** pannolino *m* 111
**diarrhoea** diarrea *f* 140
**dictionary** dizionario *m* 104
**diet** dieta *f* 37
**difficult** difficile 13
**difficulty** difficoltà *f* 28, 102, 141
**digital** digitale 122
**dine, to** cenare 94
**dining-car** carrozza ristorante *f* 66, 68, 71
**dining-room** sala da pranzo *f* 27
**dinner** cena *f* 34
**direct** diretto(a) 65
**direct, to** indicare 12
**direction** direzione *f* 76
**director***(theatre)* regista *m* 86
**directory** *(phone)* elenco *m* 134
**disabled** andicappato(a) 82
**disc** disco *m* 77, 127
**discotheque** discoteca *f* 88, 96
**disease** malattia *f* 142
**dish** piatto *m* 36, 37, 40
**dishwashing detergent** detersivo per lavare i piatti *m* 106
**disinfectant** disinfettante *m* 109
**dislocate, to** slogare 140
**dissatisfied** scontento(a) 103
**district** *(town)* quartiere *m* 81
**disturb, to** disturbare 155
**diversion** *(traffic)* deviazione *f* 79
**dizzy** stordito(a) 140
**do, to** fare 163
**doctor** medico *m* 79, 137; dottore *m* (dottoressa *f*) 144, 145
**doctor's office** ambulatorio *m* 137
**dog** cane *m* 155
**doll** bambola *f* 127, 128
**dollar** dollaro *m* 18, 130
**door** porta *f* 155
**double** doppio(a) 59
**double bed** letto matrimoniale *m* 23
**double room** camera doppia *f* 19, 23
**down** giù 15
**downstairs** di sotto 15
**down there** laggiù 77
**downtown** centro *m* 81
**dozen** dozzina *f* 120, 149
**draught beer** birra alla spina *f* 59
**drawing paper** carta da disegno *f* 104
**drawing pin** puntina *f* 104
**dress** abito *m* 116
**dressing gown** accappatoio *m* 116
**drink** bevanda *f* 40, 56, 59, 60, 61; bicchiere *m* 95
**drink, to** bere 35, 36
**drinking water** acqua potabile *f* 32
**drip, to** *(tap)* sgocciolare 28
**drive, to** guidare, andare 21, 76
**driving licence** patente *f* 20
**drop** *(liquid)* goccia *f* 109
**drugstore** farmacia *f* 98, 108
**dry** secco(a) 30, 57, 111
**dry cleaner's** lavanderia a secco *f* 29, 98; tintoria *f* 38
**dry shampoo** shampoo secco *m* 111
**duck** anatra *f* 48
**dull** *(pain)* debole 140
**dummy** succhiotto *m* 111
**during** durante 14, 150, 151
**duty** *(customs)* dazio *m* 17
**duty-free shop** negozio duty-free *m* 19
**dye** tintura *f* 30, 111

## E

**each** ogni 149
**ear** orecchio *m* 138
**earache** mal d'orecchi *m* 141
**ear drops** gocce per le orecchie *f/pl* 109
**early** presto 13, 31
**earring** orecchino *m* 121
**east** est *m* 77
**Easter** Pasqua *f* 152
**easy** facile 13
**eat, to** mangiare 36
**eel** anguilla *f* 44
**egg** uovo *m* (*pl* uova *f*) 38, 64
**eggplant** melanzana *f* 52
**eight** otto 147
**eighteen** diciotto 147
**eighth** ottavo(a) 149
**eighties** anni ottanta *m/pl* 149
**eighty** ottanta 148
**elastic** elastico(a) 109
**elastic bandage** benda elastica *f* 109
**Elastoplast** cerotto *m* 109
**electrical** elettrico(a) 119
**electrical appliance** apparecchio elettrico *m* 119
**electrician** elettricista *m* 98
**electricity** elettricità *f* 32
**electronic** elettronico(a) 125, 128
**elevator** ascensore *m* 27, 100
**eleven** undici 147
**embark, to** imbarcare 74
**emerald** smeraldo *m* 122
**emergency** emergenza *f* 156
**emergency exit** uscita di sicurezza *f* 27, 99, 155
**emery board** limetta per unghie *f* 110
**empty** vuoto(a) 13
**enamel** smalto *m* 122
**end** fine *f* 150
**endive** cicoria *f* 52; *(Am.)* indivia *f* 52
**engagement ring** anello di fidanzamento *m* 121
**engine** *(car)* motore *m* 78
**England** Inghilterra *f* 146
**English** inglese 11, 80, 82, 84, 104, 105, 126, 137
**enjoyable** piacevole 31
**enjoy oneself, to** divertirsi 96
**enlarge, to** ingrandire 125
**enough** abbastanza 14
**enquiry** informazione *f* 68
**entrance** entrata *f* 67, 99, 155
**entrance fee** entrata *f* 82
**envelope** busta *f* 27, 104
**equipment** equipaggiamento *m*, tenuta *f* 91; materiale *m* 106
**eraser** gomma *f* 104
**escalator** scala mobile *f* 100
**escalope** scaloppina *f* 49
**Europe** Europa *f* 146
**evening** sera *f* 87, 96, 151, 153; serata *f* 95, 96
**evening dress** abito da sera *m* 88, 116
**everything** tutto 31
**examine, to** esaminare 139
**excellent** eccellente 84
**exchange, to** cambiare 103
**exchange rate** corso del cambio *m* 18, 130
**excursion** gita *f* 80
**excuse, to** scusare 10
**exercise book** quaderno *m* 104
**exhaust pipe** tubo di scappamento *m* 78
**exhibition** esposizione *f* 81
**exit** uscita *f* 67, 99, 155
**expect, to** aspettare 130
**expense** spesa *f* 131
**expensive** caro(a) 13, 19, 24, 101
**exposure** *(photography)* posa *f* 124
**exposure counter** contatore di esposizioni *m* 125
**express** espresso 133
**expression** espressione *f* 9
**expressway** autostrada *f* 76
**extension cord/lead** prolunga *f* 119
**extra** supplemento *m* 40
**extract, to** *(tooth)* estrarre 145
**eye** occhio *m* (*pl* occhi) 138, 139
**eye drops** gocce per gli occhi *f/pl* 109
**eye pencil** matita per occhi *f* 110
**eye shadow** ombretto *m* 110
**eyesight** vista *f* 123
**eye specialist** oculista *m/f* 137

## F

**face** viso *m* 138
**face-pack** maschera di bellezza *f* 30
**face powder** cipria *f* 110
**factory** fabbrica *f* 81
**fair** fiera *f* 81
**fall** caduta *f* 139; *(autumn)* autunno *m* 150
**family** famiglia *f* 93
**fan** ventilatore *m* 28

**fan belt** cinghia del ventilatore *f* 75
**far** lontano(a) 13
**fare** prezzo *m* 21
**farm** fattoria *f* 85
**fast** rapido(a) 124
**fat** *(meat)* grasso *m* 37
**father** padre *f* 93
**February** febbraio *m* 150
**fee** *(doctor)* onorario *m* 144
**feeding bottle** biberon *m* 111
**feel, to** *(physical state)* sentirsi 140
**felt** feltro *m* 114
**felt-tip pen** pennarello *m* 104
**fennel** finocchio *m* 52
**ferry** traghetto *m* 74
**fever** febbre *f* 140
**few** pochi(e) 14; *(a)* alcuni(e) 14
**field** campo *m* 85
**fifteen** quindici 147
**fifth** quinto(a) 149
**fifty** cinquanta 147
**fig** fico *m* 54
**file** *(tool)* lima *f* 110
**fill in, to** compilare 26, 144
**fillet** filetto *m* 48
**filling** *(tooth)* otturazione *f* 145
**filling station** stazione di rifornimento *f* 75
**film** *(movie)* film *m* 86; *(camera)* pellicola *f* 124, 125
**filter** filtro *m* 125
**filter-tipped** con filtro 126
**find, to** trovare 10, 11, 100, 137
**fine** *(OK)* bene 25
**fine arts** belle arti *f/pl* 83
**fine grain** *(film)* a grana fine 124
**finger** dito *m* 138
**fire** fuoco *m* 156
**first** primo(a) 68, 73, 149
**first-aid kit** cassetta del pronto soccorso *f* 106
**first class** prima classe *f* 69
**first course** primo piatto *m* 40
**first name** nome *m* 25
**fish** pesce *m* 46
**fish, to** pescare 90
**fishing** pesca *f* 90
**fishing tackle** arnese da pesca *m* 106
**fishmonger's** pescheria *f* 98
**fit, to** andare bene 115
**fitting room** cabina di prova *f* 115
**five** cinque 147
**fix, to** riparare 75; curare 145
**fizzy** *(mineral water)* gasato(a) 60
**flannel** flanella *f* 114
**flash** *(photography)* flash *m* 125
**flash attachment** attaccatura del flash *f* 125
**flashlight** lampadina tascabile *f* 106
**flask** fiasco *m* 127
**flat** basso(a) 118
**flat** *(apartment)* appartamento *m* 22
**flat tyre** foratura *f* 75; gomma sgonfia *f* 78
**flea market** mercato delle pulci *m* 81
**flight** volo *m* 65
**flight number** numero del volo *m* 65
**flippers** pinne *f/pl* 128
**floor** piano *m* 27
**floor show** varietà *m* 88
**florist's** fiorista *m/f* 98
**flour** farina *f* 37
**flower** fiore *m* 85
**flu** influenza *f* 142
**fog** nebbia *f* 94
**folding chair** sedia pieghevole *f* 107
**folding table** tavola pieghevole *f* 107
**folk music** musica folcloristica *f* 128
**food** cibo *m* 37
**food box** contenitore per il cibo *m* 142
**food poisoning** avvelenamento da cibo *m* 142
**foot** piede *m* 138
**football** calcio *m* 89
**foot cream** crema per i piedi *f* 110
**footpath** sentiero *m* 85
**for** per 15, 143
**forbid, to** vietare 155
**forecast** previsione *f* 94
**foreign** straniero(a) 59
**forest** foresta *f* 85
**fork** forchetta *f* 36, 61, 107, 127
**form** *(document)* modulo *m* 133; scheda *f* 25, 26
**fortnight** quindici giorni *m/pl* 151
**fortress** fortezza *f* 81
**forty** quaranta 147
**foundation cream** fondo tinta *m* 110
**fountain** fontana *f* 81
**fountain pen** penna stilografica *f* 104
**four** quattro 147
**fourteen** quattordici 147
**fourth** quarto(a) 149
**frame** *(glasses)* montatura *f* 123
**France** Francia *f* 146
**free** libero(a) 13, 70, 82, 96, 155

**French bean** fagiolino *m* 52
**French fries** patatine fritte *f/pl* 63
**fresh** fresco(a) 54, 61
**Friday** venerdì *m* 151
**fried** fritto(a) 47, 50
**fried egg** uovo fritto *m* 38
**friend** amico(a) *m/f* 95
**fringe** frangia *f* 30
**frock** abito *m* 116
**from** da 14, 163
**front** davanti 75
**fruit** frutta *f* 54
**fruit cocktail** macedonia di frutta *f* 54
**fruit juice** succo di frutta *m* 38, 60
**frying-pan** padella *f* 106
**full** pieno(a) 13; completo(a) 155; intero(a) 80
**full board** pensione completa *f* 20
**full insurance** assicurazione completa *f* 20
**furniture** mobilio *m* 83
**furrier's** pellicceria *f* 98

## G

**gabardine** gabardine *m* 114
**gallery** galleria *f* 81, 98
**game** gioco *m* 128; *(food)* cacciagione *f* 50
**garage** garage *m* 26, 78
**garden** giardino *m* 81, 85
**garlic** aglio *m* 53
**gas** gas *m* 156
**gasoline** benzina *f* 75, 78
**gastritis** gastrite *f* 142
**gauze** garza *f* 109
**general** generale 26, 100
**general delivery** fermo posta *m* 133
**general practitioner** medico generico *m* 137
**genitals** genitali *m/pl* 138
**gentleman** signore *m* 155
**genuine** vero(a) 118
**geology** geologia *f* 83
**Germany** Germania *f* 146
**get, to** *(find)* trovare 10, 21, 32; *(call)* chiamare 31, 137; *(obtain)* ottenere 134; procurarsi 89, 90
**get back, to** ritornare 80
**get off, to** scendere 73
**get to, to** andare a 19; arrivare a 70
**get up, to** alzarsi 144
**gherkin** cetriolino *m* 52, 64
**gin and tonic** gin e tonico *m* 60
**ginger** zenzero *m* 53
**girdle** busto *m* 116
**girl** *(child)* bambina *f* 112, 128
**girlfriend** ragazza *f* 93
**give, to** dare 12, 123, 135
**glad** *(to know you)* piacere 92
**gland** ghiandola *f* 138
**glass** bicchiere *m* 36, 57, 60, 61, 143
**glasses** occhiali *m/pl* 123
**glassware** articolo di vetro *m* 127
**gloomy** malinconico(a) 84
**glossy** *(finish)* lucido(a) 125
**glove** guanto *m* 116
**glue** colla *f* 105
**go, to** andare 95, 96, 163
**go away, to** andarsene 156
**gold** oro *m* 121, 122
**golden** dorato(a) 113
**gold plate** placcato d'oro *m* 122
**golf** golf *m* 89
**good** buono(a) 13, 101
**good-bye** arrivederci 9
**goods** merci *f/pl* 16
**goose** oca *f* 51
**gooseberry** uva spina *f* 54
**go out, to** uscire 96
**gram** grammo *m* 120
**grammar book** grammatica *f* 105
**grape** uva *f* 54, 64
**grapefruit** pompelmo *m* 54
**grapefruit juice** succo di pompelmo *m* 38, 60
**gray** grigio(a) 113
**graze** escoriazione *f* 139
**greasy** grasso(a) 30, 111
**Great Britain** Gran Bretagna *f* 146
**Greece** Grecia *f* 146
**green** verde 113
**green bean** fagiolino *m* 52
**greengrocer's** negozio di frutta e verdura *m* 98
**green salad** insalata verde *f* 52
**greeting** saluto *m* 9, 152
**grey** grigio(a) 113
**grilled** alla griglia 47; ai ferri 50
**grocery** negozio di alimentari *m* 98, 120
**group** gruppo *m* 82
**guide** guida *f* 80
**guidebook** guida turistica *f* 82, 104, 105
**guinea fowl** faraona *f* 51
**gum** *(teeth)* gengiva *f* 145
**gynaecologist** ginecologo(a) *m/f* 137

**H**

**hair** capelli *m/pl* 30, 111
**hairbrush** spazzola per capelli *f* 111
**haircut** taglio dei capelli *m* 30
**hairdresser's** parrucchiere *m* 27, 30, 98
**hair dryer** asciugacapelli *m* 119
**hair lotion** lozione per capelli *f* 111
**hair slide** fermaglio *m* 111
**hairspray** lacca *f* 30, 111
**half** metà *f*, mezzo *m* 149
**half a day** mezza giornata *f* 80
**half a dozen** mezza dozzina *f* 120
**half an hour** mezz'ora *f* 153
**half board** mezza pensione *f* 24
**half price** *(ticket)* metà tariffa *f* 69
**hall** *(large room)* sala *f* 81, 88
**ham** prosciutto *m* 41, 48, 63, 64
**hammer** martello *m* 106
**hammock** amaca *f* 106
**hand** mano *f* 138
**handbag** borsetta *f* 116, 156
**hand cream** crema per le mani *f* 110
**handicrafts** artigianato *m* 83
**handkerchief** fazzoletto *m* 116
**handmade** fatto(a) a mano 113
**hanger** attaccapanni *m* 27
**hangover** mal di testa *m* 108
**happy** felice, buon(a) 152
**harbour** porto *m* 81
**hard** duro(a) 123
**hard-boiled egg** uovo sodo *m* 38
**hardware shop** negozio di ferramenta *m* 99
**hare** lepre *f* 51
**hat** cappello *m* 116
**have, to** avere 162
**hay fever** febbre del fieno *f* 108, 141
**hazelnut** nocciola *f* 54
**he** egli, lui 161
**head** testa *f* 138, 139
**headache** mal di testa *m* 141
**headlight** faro *m* 79
**headphones** cuffia (d'ascolto) *f* 119
**health** salute *f* 56
**health food shop** negozio di cibi dietetici *m* 99
**health insurance** assicurazione malattie *f* 144
**heart** cuore *m* 138
**heart attack** attacco cardiaco *m* 141
**heating** riscaldamento *m* 23, 28
**heavy** pesante 13, 101
**heel** tacco *m* 118
**height** altitudine *f* 85
**helicopter** elicottero *m* 74
**hello!** *(phone)* pronto 135
**help** aiuto *m* 156
**help, to** aiutare 13, 21, 100, 134; *(oneself)* servirsi 120
**her** suo, sua (*pl* suoi, sue) 161
**herbs** odori *m/pl* 53
**herb tea** tisana *f* 60
**here** qui, ecco 13
**herring** aringa *f* 46
**high** alto(a) 90, 141
**high season** alta stagione *f* 150
**high tide** alta marea *f* 90
**hill** collina *f* 85
**hire** noleggio *m* 20, 74
**hire, to** noleggiare 19, 20, 74, 90, 91, 119; affittare 155
**his** suo, sua (*pl* suoi, sue) 161
**history** storia *f* 83
**hitchhike, to** fare l'autostop 74
**hold on!** *(phone)* resti in linea! 136
**hole** buco *m* 29
**holiday** giorno festivo *m* 151
**holidays** vacanze *f/pl* 151; ferie *f/pl* 155
**home address** domicilio *m* 25
**honey** miele *m* 38
**hors d'oeuvre** antipasto *m* 41
**horse riding** corsa di cavalli *f* 89
**hospital** ospedale *m* 144
**hot** caldo(a) 14, 25, 38, 94
**hotel** albergo *m* 19, 21, 22; hotel *m* 22, 80
**hotel guide** guida degli alberghi *f* 19
**hotel reservation** prenotazione d'albergo *f* 19
**hot water** acqua calda *f* 23, 28
**hot-water bottle** borsa dell'acqua calda *f* 27
**hour** ora *f* 153
**house** casa *f* 83, 85
**how** come 10
**how far** quanto dista 10, 76, 85, 100
**how long** quanto tempo 10, 24
**how many** quanti 10
**how much** quanto 10, 24
**hundred** cento 148
**hungry, to be** aver fame 12, 35
**hurry** *(to be in a)* avere fretta 21
**hurt, to** fare male 139, 145; *(oneself)* farsi male 139
**husband** marito *m* 93
**hydrofoil** aliscafo *m* 74

**I**

**I** io 161
**ice** ghiaccio *m* 94
**ice-cream** gelato *m* 55, 64
**ice-cream parlour** gelateria *f* 33
**ice cube** cubetto di ghiaccio *m* 27
**iced coffee** caffè freddo *m* 60
**ice pack** elemento refrigerante *m* 106
**iced tea** tè freddo *m* 60
**ill** malato(a) 140
**illness** malattia *f* 160
**important** importante 12
**impressive** impressionante 84
**in** in 13, 163
**include, to** comprendere 20, 24, 32, 62, 80; includere 31
**India** India *f* 146
**indigestion** indigestione *f* 141
**indoor** *(swimming pool)* coperto(a) 90
**inexpensive** economico(a) 35, 124
**infection** infezione *f* 141
**inflammation** infiammazione *f* 142
**inflation** inflazione *f* 131
**inflation rate** tasso d'inflazione *m* 131
**influenza** influenza *f* 142
**information** informazione *f* 67, 155
**injection** iniezione *f* 142, 144
**injure, to** ferire 139
**injured** ferito(a) 79, 139
**injury** ferita *f* 139
**ink** inchiostro *m* 105
**inn** locanda *f* 22, 33; osteria *f* 33
**inquiry** informazione *f* 68
**insect bite** puntura d'insetto *f* 108, 139
**insect repellent** crema contro gli insetti *f* 109
**insect spray** spray insetticida *m* 109
**inside** dentro 15
**instead** invece 37
**instrumental** *(music)* strumentale 128
**insurance** assicurazione *f* 20, 79, 144
**interest** interesse *m* 80, 131
**interested, to be** interessarsi 83, 96
**interesting** interessante 84
**international** internazionale 133, 134
**interpreter** interprete *m/f* 131
**intersection** incrocio *m* 77
**introduce, to** presentare 92
**introduction** presentazione *f* 92, 130
**investment** investimento *m* 131
**invitation** invito *m* 94
**invite, to** invitare 94
**invoice** fattura *f* 131
**iodine** tintura di iodio *f* 109
**Ireland** Irlanda *f* 146
**iron** *(laundry)* ferro da stiro *m* 119
**iron, to** stirare 29
**ironmonger's** negozio di ferramenta *m* 99
**Israel** Israele *m* 146
**Italian** italiano(a) 10, 11, 95, 104, 114
**Italy** Italia *f* 146
**its** suo, sua (*pl* suoi, sue) 161
**ivory** avorio *m* 122

**J**

**jacket** giacca *f* 116
**jade** giada *f* 122
**jam** marmellata *f* 38
**jam, to** incastrare 28; bloccare 125
**January** gennaio *m* 150
**Japan** Giappone *m* 146
**jar** vasetto *m* 120
**jaundice** itterizia *f* 142
**jaw** mascella *f* 138
**jeans** jeans *m/pl* 116
**jersey** maglietta *f* 116
**jewel** gioiello *m* 121
**jewel box** portagioielli *m* 121
**jeweller's** gioielleria *f* 99, 121
**jewellery** gioielli *m/pl* 127
**joint** articolazione *f* 138
**journey** percorso *m* 72
**juice** succo *m* 38, 60
**July** luglio *m* 150
**jumper** *(sweater)* maglione *m* 116
**June** giugno *m* 116
**just** *(only)* soltanto 100

**K**

**kerosene** petrolio *m* 106
**key** chiave *f* 26
**kidney** rognone *m* 48; rene *m* 138
**kilogram** chilogrammo *m* 120
**kilometre** chilometro *m* 20
**kind** gentile 95
**kind** *(type)* genere *m* 140
**knapsack** zaino *m* 106
**knee** ginocchio *m* 138
**kneesocks** calzettoni *m/pl* 116
**knife** coltello *m* 36, 61, 107
**knitwear** maglieria *f* 127
**knock, to** bussare 155
**know, to** sapere 16; conoscere 96, 114

**L**

**label** etichetta *f* 105
**lace** pizzo *m* 114
**lady** signora *f* 155
**lake** lago *m* 81, 85, 90
**lamb** agnello *m* 48
**lamp** lampada *f* 46
**landmark** punto di riferimento *m* 85
**landscape** paesaggio *m* 92
**lantern** lanterna *f* 106
**large** grande 101, 118
**lark** allodola *f* 51
**last** ultimo(a) 13, 68, 73; scorso(a) 149, 151
**last name** cognome *m* 25
**late** tardi 13
**later** più tardi 135
**laugh, to** ridere 95
**launderette** lavanderia automatica *f* 99
**laundry** *(place)* lavanderia *f* 29, 99; *(clothes)* biancheria *f* 29
**laundry service** servizio di lavanderia *m* 23
**laxative** lassativo *m* 109
**lead** *(theatre)* ruolo principale *m* 86
**lead-free** senza piombo 75
**leap year** anno bisestile *m* 149
**leather** pelle *f* 114, 118
**leather goods** pelletteria *f* 127
**leave, to** partire 31, 68, 74, 162; lasciare 156; *(deposit)* depositare 26, 71
**leek** porro *m* 52
**left** sinistra 21, 63, 69, 77
**left-luggage office** deposito bagagli *m* 67, 71
**leg** gamba *f* 138
**lemon** limone *m* 37, 38, 54, 55, 60, 64
**lemonade** limonata *f* 60
**lemon juice** succo di limone *m* 60
**lens** *(glasses)* lente *f* 123; *(camera)* obiettivo *m* 125
**lens cap** cappuccio per obiettivo *m* 125
**lentil** lenticchia *f* 52
**less** meno 14
**lesson** lezione *f* 91
**let, to** *(hire out)* affittare 155
**letter** lettera *f* 132
**letter box** cassetta delle lettere *f* 132
**letter of credit** lettera di credito *f* 130
**lettuce** lattuga *f* 52
**level crossing** passaggio a livello *m* 79
**library** biblioteca *f* 81, 99
**lie down, to** sdraiarsi 142
**life belt** cintura di salvataggio *f* 74
**life boat** canotto di salvataggio *m* 74
**lifeguard** bagnino *m* 90
**lift** ascensore *m* 27, 100
**light** leggero(a) 13, 55, 57, 101, 128; *(colour)* chiaro(a) 101, 112, 113
**light** luce *f* 28, 124; *(cigarette)* fiammifero *m* 95
**lighter** accendino *m* 126
**lighter fluid** benzina per accendino *f* 126
**lighter gas** gas per accendino *m* 126
**light meter** esposimetro *m* 125
**like, to** volere 12, 20, 23; desiderare 103; piacere 25, 61, 92, 96, 102, 112
**lime** cedro *m* 54
**line** linea *f* 73, 136
**linen** *(cloth)* lino *m* 114
**lip** labbro *m* 138
**lipsalve** burro cacao *m* 110
**lipstick** rossetto *m* 110
**liqueur** liquore *m* 59
**liquid** liquido *m* 123
**listen, to** ascoltare 128
**litre** litro *m* 57, 75, 120
**little** *(a)* un po' 14
**live, to** vivere 83
**liver** fegato *m* 48, 138
**lobster** aragosta *f* 46
**local** locale 36, 60
**London** Londra *f* 130
**long** lungo(a) 115
**long-sighted** presbite 123
**look, to** guardare 123
**look for, to** cercare 12
**look out!** attenzione! 156
**loose** *(clothes)* largo(a) 115
**lose, to** perdere 123, 156
**loss** perdita *f* 131
**lost** perduto(a) 12; perso(a) 156
**lost and found office** ufficio oggetti smarriti *m* 67, 156
**lost property office** ufficio oggetti smarriti *m* 67, 156
**lot** *(a)* molto 14
**lotion** lozione *f* 110
**loud** *(voice)* forte 135
**love, to** amare 162

**lovely** bello(a) 94
**low** basso(a) 90, 141
**lower** inferiore 69, 70
**low season** bassa stagione *f* 150
**low tide** bassa marea *f* 90
**luck** fortuna *f* 152
**luggage** bagagli *m/pl* 18, 26, 31, 71
**luggage locker** custodia automatica dei bagagli *f* 18, 67, 71
**luggage trolley** carrello portabagagli *m* 18, 71
**lump** *(bump)* bernoccolo *m* 139
**lunch** pranzo *m* 34, 80, 94
**lung** polmone *m* 138

## M

**mackerel** sgombro *m* 47
**magazine** rivista *f* 105
**magnificent** magnifico(a) 84
**maid** cameriera *f* 26
**mail, to** spedire 28
**mail** posta *f* 28, 133
**mailbox** cassetta delle lettere *f* 132
**main** principale 80
**make, to** fare 131, 163
**make up, to** rifare 28; preparare 108
**make-up remover pad** tampone per togliere il trucco *m* 110
**man** uomo *m* (*pl* uomini) 115
**manager** direttore *m* 26
**manicure** manicure *f* 30
**many** molti(e) 14
**map** carta geografica *f* 76, 105; pianta *f* 105
**March** marzo *m* 150
**marinated** marinato(a) 47
**marjoram** maggiorana *f* 63
**market** mercato *m* 81, 99
**marmalade** marmellata d'arance *f* 38
**married** sposato(a) 93
**marrow** midollo *m* 48
**mass** *(church)* messa *f* 84
**mat** *(finish)* opaco(a) 125
**match** fiammifero *m* 106, 126; *(sport)* partita *f*, incontro *m* 89
**match, to** *(colour)* ravvivare 112
**material** *(cloth)* tessuto *m* 113
**matinée** spettacolo del pomeriggio *m* 87
**mattress** materasso *m* 106
**mauve** lilla 113
**May** maggio *m* 150
**may** *(can)* potere 11, 12, 163
**meadow** prato *m* 85
**meal** pasto *m* 24, 34, 62, 143
**mean, to** significare 10, 25
**means** mezzo *m* 74
**measles** morbillo *m* 142
**measure, to** prendere le misure 114
**meat** carne *f* 48, 49, 61
**meatball** polpetta *f* 48
**mechanic** meccanico *m* 78
**mechanical pencil** portamine *m* 105
**medical** medico(a) 144
**medicine** medicina *f* 83, 143
**medium** *(meat)* a puntino 50
**meet, to** incontrare 96
**melon** melone *m* 54
**mend, to** riparare 75; *(clothes)* rammendare 29
**menthol** *(cigarettes)* mentolo *m* 126
**menu** menù *m* 36, 39, 40
**message** messaggio *m* 28, 136
**methylated spirits** alcool metilico *m* 106
**metre** metro *m* 112
**mezzanine** *(theatre)* galleria *f* 87
**middle** mezzo *m* 69; metà *f* 87, 150
**midnight** mezzanotte *f* 153
**mileage** chilometraggio *m* 20
**milk** latte *m* 38, 60, 64
**milkshake** frullato di latte *m* 60
**million** milione *m* 148
**mineral water** acqua minerale *f* 60
**minister** *(religion)* pastore *m* 84
**minute** minuto *m* 153
**mirror** specchio *m* 115, 123
**miscellaneous** diverso(a) 127
**Miss** Signorina *f* 9
**miss, to** mancare 18, 29, 61
**mistake** errore *m* 31, 61, 62
**mixed** misto(a) 55
**moccasin** mocassino *m* 118
**modified American plan** mezza pensione *f* 24
**moisturizing cream** crema idratante *f* 110
**moment** momento *m* 136
**monastery** monastero *m* 81
**Monday** lunedì *m* 151
**money** denaro *m* 129, 130
**money order** vaglia *m* 133
**month** mese *m* 16, 150
**monument** monumento *m* 81
**moon** luna *f* 94
**moped** motorino *m* 74
**more** più 14

**morning** mattino *m* 151, 153
**mortgage** ipoteca *f* 131
**mosque** moschea *f* 84
**mosquito net** zanzariera *f* 106
**motel** motel *m* 22
**mother** madre *f* 93
**motorbike** moto *f* 74
**motorboat** barca a motore *f* 91
**motorway** autostrada *f* 76
**mountain** montagna *f* 85
**moustache** baffi *m/pl* 31
**mouth** bocca *f* 138
**mouthwash** gargarismo *m* 109
**move, to** muovere 139
**movie** film *m* 86
**movie camera** cinepresa *f* 124
**movies** cinema *m* 86, 96
**Mr.** Signor *m* 9
**Mrs.** Signora *f* 9
**much** molto(a) 14
**mug** boccale *m* 107
**muscle** muscolo *m* 138
**museum** museo *m* 81
**mushroom** fungo *m* 52
**music** musica *f* 83, 128
**musical** commedia musicale *f* 86
**mussel** cozza *f* 46
**must, to** dovere 95
**mustard** senape *f* 37, 64
**my** mio, mia (*pl* miei, mie) 161

## N

**nail** *(human)* unghia *f* 110
**nail file** lima da unghie *f* 110
**nail polish** smalto *m* 110
**nail polish remover** solvente per le unghie *m* 110
**nail scissors** forbicine per le unghie *f/pl* 110
**name** nome *m* 23, 25, 79; cognome *m* 25
**napkin** tovagliolo *m* 36, 105, 106
**nappy** pannolino *m* 111
**narrow** stretto(a) 118
**nationality** cittadinanza *f* 25; nazionalità *f* 92
**natural** naturale 83
**natural history** storia naturale *f* 83
**nausea** nausea *f* 140
**near** vicino(a) 13; vicino a 14
**nearby** qui vicino 77, 84
**nearest** il (la) più vicino(a) 78, 98
**neat** *(drink)* liscio(a) 56, 59
**neck** collo *m* 30, 138
**necklace** collana *f* 121
**need, to** aver bisogno 29, 118; essere necessario 90; servire 118
**needle** ago *m* 27
**needlework** ricamo *m* 127
**negative** negativo *m* 125
**nephew** nipote *m* 93
**nerve** nervo *m* 138
**nervous** nervoso(a) 138
**never** mai 15
**new** nuovo(a) 13
**newsagent's** giornalaio *m* 99
**newspaper** giornale *m* 104, 105
**newsstand** edicola *f* 19, 67, 99 104
**New Year** Capodanno *m* 152
**New Zealand** Nuova Zelanda *f* 146
**next** prossimo(a) 65, 68, 73, 76, 149; seguente 151
**next to** accanto a 14, 77
**niece** nipote *f* 93
**night** notte *f* 24, 151
**nightclub** night-club *m* 88
**night cream** crema da notte *f* 110
**nightdress** camicia da notte *f* 116
**nine** nove 147
**nineteen** diciannove 147
**ninety** novanta 148
**ninth** nono(a) 149
**no** no 9
**noisy** rumoroso(a) 25
**nonalcoholic** analcolico(a) 60
**none** nessuno(a) 15
**nonsmoker** *(compartment)* non fumatori *m/pl* 70
**noon** mezzogiorno *m* 31, 153
**normal** normale 30
**north** nord *m* 77
**North America** America del Nord *f* 140
**nose** naso *m* 138
**nosebleed** emorragia nasale *f* 140
**nose drops** gocce nasali *f/pl* 109
**not** non 15, 163
**note** *(banknote)* banconota *f* 130
**notebook** taccuino *m* 105
**note paper** carta da lettere *m* 105
**nothing** nulla 15, 17; niente 15
**notice** *(sign)* cartello *m* 155
**November** novembre *m* 150
**now** adesso 15
**number** numero *m* 26, 65, 135, 136, 147
**nurse** infermiera *f* 144
**nutmeg** noce moscata *f* 53

**O**

**occupied** occupato(a) 13, 155
**October** ottobre *m* 150
**octopus** polpo *m* 46
**offer, to** offrire 95
**office** ufficio *m* 19, 67, 99, 132, 133, 156
**oil** olio *m* 37, 64, 75, 111
**oily** grasso(a) 30, 111
**old** vecchio(a), anziano(a) 13
**old town** città vecchia *f* 81
**olive** oliva *f* 41
**omelet** frittata *f* 42
**on** su 14, 163
**once** una volta 149
**one** uno(a) 147
**one-way** *(ticket)* andata *f* 69
**on foot** a piedi 76
**onion** cipolla *f* 52
**only** soltanto 15, 80
**on request** a richiesta 73
**on time** in orario 68
**onyx** onice *m* 122
**open** aperto(a) 13, 82, 155
**open, to** aprire 10, 17, 82, 108, 131, 132, 142
**open-air** all'aperto 90
**opera** opera *f* 88
**opera house** teatro dell'opera *m* 81, 88
**operation** operazione *f* 144
**operator** centralinista *m/f* 134
**operetta** operetta *f* 88
**opposite** di fronte 77
**optician** ottico *m* 99, 123
**or** o 15
**oral** orale 143
**orange** arancio 113
**orange** arancia *f* 54, 64
**orange juice** succo d'arancia *m* 38, 60
**orangeade** aranciata *f* 60
**orchestra** orchestra *f* 88; *(seats)* poltrona *f* 87
**orchestral music** musica sinfonica *f* 128
**order** *(goods, meal)* ordinazione *f* 40, 102
**order, to** *(goods, meal)* ordinare 61, 102, 103
**oregano** origano *m* 53
**ornithology** ornitologia *f* 83
**our** nostro(a) 161
**out of order** fuori servizio 155
**out of stock** esaurito(a) 103
**outlet** *(electric)* presa *f* 27
**outside** fuori 15; all'aperto 36
**oval** ovale 101
**over there** laggiù 69
**overalls** tuta *f* 116
**overdone** troppo cotto(a) 61
**overheat, to** *(engine)* surriscaldare 78
**overtake, to** sorpassare 79
**owe, to** dovere 144
**overwhelming** sbalorditivo(a) 84
**oyster** ostrica *f* 41, 46

**P**

**pacifier** succhiotto *m* 111
**packet** pacchetto *m* 120, 126
**page** pagina *f* 77
**page** *(hotel)* fattorino *m* 26
**pail** secchio *m* 106; secchiello *m* 128
**pain** dolore *m* 140, 141; male *m* 144
**painkiller** antinevralgico *m* 140; calmante *m* 144
**paint** pittura *f* 155
**paint, to** dipingere 83
**paintbox** scatola di colori *f* 105
**painter** pittore *m* 83
**painting** pittura *f* 83
**pair** paio *m* 116, 118, 149
**pajamas** pigiama *m* 117
**palace** palazzo *m* 81
**palpitation** palpitazione *f* 141
**panties** slip *m* 116
**pants** *(trousers)* pantaloni *m/pl* 116
**panty girdle** guaina *f* 116
**panty hose** collant *m* 116
**paper** carta *f* 105
**paperback** libro tascabile *m* 105
**paper napkin** tovagliolo di carta *m* 107
**paraffin** *(fuel)* petrolio *m* 106
**parcel** pacco *m* 132
**pardon?** prego? 10
**parents** genitori *m/pl* 93
**park** parco *m* 81
**park, to** parcheggiare 26, 77
**parking** parcheggio *m* 77, 79
**parking disc** disco di sosta *m* 77
**parking meter** parchimetro *m* 77
**parliament** parlamento *m* 81
**parsley** prezzemolo *m* 53
**part** parte *f* 138
**partridge** pernice *f* 51

**party** *(social gathering)* ricevimento *m* 95
**pass** *(mountain)* passo *m* 85
**pass, to** *(car)* sorpassare 79
**passport** passaporto *m* 16, 17, 25, 26, 156
**passport photo** fotografia d'identità *f* 124
**pass through, to** essere di passaggio 16
**pasta** pasta *f* 44
**paste** *(glue)* colla *f* 105
**pastry** pasticcino *m* 64
**pastry shop** pasticceria *f* 99
**patch, to** *(clothes)* rappezzare 29
**path** sentiero *m* 85; pista *f* 155
**patient** paziente *m/f* 144
**pay, to** pagare 31, 62, 102
**payment** pagamento *m* 102, 131
**pea** pisello *m* 52
**peach** pesca *f* 54
**peak** picco *m* 85
**peanut** arachide *f* 54
**pear** pera *f* 54
**pearl** perla *f* 122
**pedestrian** pedonale 79
**peg** *(tent)* picchetto *m* 107
**pen** penna *f* 105
**pencil** matita *f* 105
**pencil sharpener** temperamatite *m* 105
**pendant** pendente *m* 121
**penicilline** penicillina *f* 143
**penknife** temperino *m* 107
**pensioner** pensionato *m* 82
**people** gente *f* 93
**pepper** pepe *m* 37; *(sweet)* peperone *m* 52
**per cent** per cento 149
**percentage** percentuale *f* 131
**perch** pesce persico *m* 46
**per day** per un giorno 20, 89; al giorno 32
**perform, to** *(theatre)* rappresentare 86
**perfume** profumo *m* 110
**perfume shop** profumeria *f* 108
**perhaps** forse 15
**per hour** all'ora 77; per un'ora 89
**period** *(monthly)* mestruazioni *f/pl* 141
**period pains** mestruazioni dolorose *f/pl* 141
**permanent wave** permanente *f* 30
**permit** permesso *m* 90
**per night** per una notte 24
**per person** per persona 32
**person** persona *f* 32
**personal** personale 17
**personal call** telefonata con preavviso *f* 135
**personal cheque** assegno personale *m* 130
**person-to-person call** telefonata con preavviso *f* 135
**per week** per una settimana 20, 24
**petrol** benzina *f* 75, 78
**pewter** peltro *m* 122
**pheasant** fagiano *m* 51
**photo** fotografia *f* 82, 124, 125
**photocopy** fotocopia *f* 131
**photograph, to** fotografare, fare delle fotografie 82
**photographer** fotografo *m* 99
**photography** fotografia *f* 124
**phrase** espressione *f* 11
**pick up, to** prendere 80, 96
**pickles** sottaceti *m/pl* 41, 64
**picnic** picnic *m* 63
**picnic basket** cestino da picnic *m* 107
**picture** quadro *m* 83; *(photo)* fotografia *f* 82
**piece** pezzo *m* 120
**pig** porcellino *m*, porchetta *f* 46
**pigeon** piccione *m* 51
**pill** pillola *f* 141; compressa *f* 143
**pillow** guanciale *m* 27
**pin** spillo *m* 111, 122
**pineapple** ananas *m* 54
**pink** rosa 113
**pipe** pipa *f* 126
**pipe cleaner** nettapipe *m* 126
**pipe tobacco** tabacco da pipa *m* 126
**pipe tool** curapipe *m* 126
**pizza** pizza *f* 42, 63
**pizza parlour** pizzeria *f* 33
**place** luogo *m* 25; posto *m* 76
**place of birth** luogo di nascita *m* 25
**plane** aereo *m* 65
**planetarium** planetario *m* 82
**plaster, to** ingessare 140
**plastic** plastica *f* 107
**plastic bag** sacchetto di plastica *m* 107
**plate** piatto *m* 36, 61, 107
**platform** *(station)* binario *m* 67, 68, 69, 70
**platinum** platino *m* 122

**play** *(theatre)* commedia *f* 86
**play, to** interpretare 86; suonare 88; giocare 89, 93
**playground** parco giochi *m* 32
**playing card** carte da gioco *f/pl* 105
**please** per favore, per piacere 9
**plimsolls** scarpe da tennis *f/pl* 118
**plug** *(electric)* spina *f* 28
**plum** prugna *f* 54, 64
**pneumonia** polmonite *f* 142
**poached** affogato(a) 47
**pocket** tasca *f* 117
**pocket watch** orologio da tasca *m* 121
**point** punto *m* 80
**point, to** *(show)* indicare 11
**poison** veleno *m* 156
**poisoning** avvelenamento *m* 142
**pole** *(ski)* bastone *m* 91
**police** polizia *f* 78, 156
**police station** posto di polizia *m* 99, 156
**polish** *(nails)* smalto *m* 110
**pond** stagno *m* 85
**pop music** musica pop *f* 28
**poplin** popeline *m* 114
**porcelain** porcellana *f* 127
**pork** maiale *m* 48
**port** porto *m* 74; *(wine)* porto *m* 59
**portable** portatile 119
**porter** facchino *m* 18, 26, 71
**portion** porzione *f* 37, 61
**Portugal** Portogallo *m* 146
**possible** possibile 137
**post** *(letters)* posta *f* 28, 133
**post, to** spedire 28
**postage** affrancatura *f* 132
**postage stamp** francobollo *m* 28, 126, 132
**postcard** cartolina *f* 105, 126, 132
**poste restante** fermo posta *m* 133
**post office** ufficio postale *m* 99, 132
**potato** patata *f* 52
**pottery** terracotta *f* 83
**poultry** pollame *m* 50
**pound** *(money)* sterlina *f* 18, 130; *(weight)* libbra *f* 120
**powder** cipria *f* 110
**powder compact** portacipria *m* 121
**prawns** scampi *m/pl* 47
**preference** preferenza *f* 101
**pregnant** incinta 141
**premium** *(gasoline)* super 75
**prescribe, to** prescrivere 143
**prescription** ricetta *f* 108, 143
**press, to** *(iron)* stirare a vapore 29
**press stud** bottone a pressione *m* 117
**pressure** pressione *f* 75, 142
**price** prezzo *m* 24
**priest** prete *m* 84
**print** *(photo)* stampa *f* 125
**private** privato(a) 80, 91, 155
**processing** *(photo)* sviluppo *m* 124
**profession** professione *f* 25
**profit** profitto *m* 131
**programme** programma *m* 87
**prohibit, to** vietare 79, 91, 155
**pronunciation** pronuncia *f* 6
**propelling pencil** portamine *m* 105
**Protestant** protestante 84
**provide, to** procurare 131
**prune** prugna secca *f* 54
**public holiday** giorno festivo *m* 152
**pull, to** tirare 155
**pullover** pullover *m* 117
**pumpkin** zucca *f* 52
**puncture** foratura *f* 75
**purchase** acquisto *m* 131
**pure** puro(a) 114
**purple** viola 113
**push, to** spingere 155
**put, to** mettere 24
**pyjamas** pigiama *m* 117

## Q

**quail** quaglia *f* 51
**quality** qualità *f* 103, 113
**quantity** quantità *f* 14, 103
**quarter** quarto *m* 149; *(part of town)* quartiere *m* 81
**quarter of an hour** quarto d'ora *m* 153
**quartz** quarzo *m* 122
**question** domanda *f* 10, 163
**quick** rapido(a) 13; presto 156
**quickly** presto 137, 156
**quiet** tranquillo(a) 23, 25
**quince** cotogna *f* 54

## R

**rabbi** rabbino *m* 84
**rabbit** coniglio *m* 51
**race course/track** ippodromo *m* 90
**racket** *(sport)* racchetta *f* 90
**radiator** radiatore *m* 78
**radio** *(set)* radio *f* 23, 28, 119
**radish** ravanello *m* 52

**railroad crossing** passaggio a livello *m* 79
**railway** ferrovia *f* 154
**railway station** stazione *f* 19, 21, 67, 70
**rain** pioggia *f* 94
**rain, to** piovere 94
**raincoat** impermeabile *m* 117
**raisin** uva passa *f* 54
**rangefinder** telemetro *m* 125
**rare** *(meat)* al sangue 50, 61
**rash** esantema *m* 139
**raspberry** lampone *m* 54
**rate** tariffa *f* 20; tasso *m* 131
**razor** rasoio *m* 110
**razor blade** lametta *f* 110
**reading-lamp** lampada *f* 27
**ready** pronto(a) 29, 118, 123, 125, 145
**real** vero(a) 121
**rear** dietro 75
**receipt** ricevuta *f* 103, 144
**reception** ricevimento *m* 23
**receptionist** capo ricevimento *m* 26
**recommend, to** consigliare 35, 36, 40, 80, 86, 88, 137, 145
**record** *(disc)* disco *m* 127, 128
**record player** giradischi *m* 119
**rectangular** rettangolare 101
**red** rosso(a) 57, 113
**redcurrant** ribes *m* 54
**red mullet** triglia *f* 46
**reduction** riduzione *f* 24, 82
**refill** ricambio *m* 105
**refund, to** rimborsare 103
**regards** saluti *m/pl* 152
**register, to** *(luggage)* far registrare 71
**registered mail** raccomandato(a) 133
**registration** registrazione *f* 25
**registration form** scheda *f* 25, 26
**regular** *(petrol)* normale 75
**religion** religione *f* 83
**religious service** funzione religiosa *f* 84
**rent, to** noleggiare 19, 20, 74, 89, 91, 119; affittare 155
**rental** noleggio *m* 20, 74
**repair** riparazione *f* 125
**repair, to** riparare 29, 118, 119, 121, 123, 125, 145
**repeat, to** ripetere 11
**report, to** denunciare 156
**reservation** prenotazione *f* 19, 23, 65, 69
**reservations office** ufficio prenotazioni *m* 19, 67
**reserve, to** prenotare 19, 23, 87; riservare 36
**restaurant** ristorante *m* 19, 32, 33, 35, 67
**return** *(ticket)* andata e ritorno 69
**return, to** *(give back)* rendere 103
**reverse the charges, to** telefonare a carico del destinatario 135
**rheumatism** reumatismo *m* 141
**rib** costola *f* 48, 138
**ribbon** nastro *m* 105
**rice** riso *m* 45
**right** destra 63, 69, 77; *(correct)* giusto 13, 70
**ring** *(on finger)* anello *m* 121
**ring, to** suonare 155
**river** fiume *m* 85, 90
**road** strada *f* 76, 77, 85
**road assistance** assistenza stradale *f* 78
**road map** carta stradale *f* 105
**road sign** segnale stradale *m* 79
**roast** arrosto 48, 50
**roast beef** rosbif *m* 48
**rock** masso *m* 79
**roll** *(bread)* panino *m* 38, 64
**roller skates** pattini a rotelle *m/pl* 128
**roll film** bobina *f* 124
**roll-neck** a collo alto 117
**room** camera *f* 19, 23, 24, 25, 28; *(space)* posto *m* 32
**room number** numero della stanza *m* 26
**room service** servizio nella stanza *m* 23
**rope** corda *f* 107
**rosary** rosario *m* 122
**rosé** rosatello 57
**rosemary** rosmarino *m* 53
**rouge** fard *m* 110
**round** rotondo(a) 101
**round-neck** a girocollo 117
**roundtrip** *(ticket)* andata e ritorno 69
**rowing-boat** barca a remi *f* 91
**royal** reale 82
**rubber** gomma *f* 105, 118
**ruby** rubino *m* 122
**rucksack** zaino *m* 107
**ruin** rovina *f* 82
**ruler** *(for measuring)* riga *f* 105
**rum** rum *m* 60
**running water** acqua corrente *f* 23

**S**

**safe** *(not dangerous)* sicuro(a), senza pericolo 90
**safe** cassaforte *f* 26
**safety pin** spillo di sicurezza *m* 111
**saffron** zafferano *m* 53
**sage** salvia *f* 53
**sailing-boat** barca a vela *f* 91
**salad** insalata *f* 52, 64
**salami** salame *m* 41, 63, 64
**sale** vendita *f* 131; *(bargains)* saldi *m/pl* 100, svendita *f* 155
**sales tax** I.V.A. *f* 24, 102
**salmon** salmone *m* 41, 46
**salt** sale *m* 37, 64
**salty** salato(a) 61
**sand** sabbia *f* 90
**sandal** sandalo *m* 118
**sandwich** panino imbottito *m* 63
**sanitary napkin** assorbente igienico *m* 109
**sardine** sardina *f* 41, 47
**satin** raso *m* 114
**Saturday** sabato *m* 151
**sauce** salsa *f* 44
**saucepan** casseruola *f* 107
**saucer** piattino *m* 107
**sausage** salsiccia *f* 48, 64
**scallop** arsella *f* 46
**scarf** sciarpa *f* 117
**scenic route** strada panoramica *f* 85
**scissors** forbici *f/pl* 107; forbicine *f/pl* 110
**scooter** motoretta *f* 74
**Scotland** Scozia *f* 146
**Scottish** scozzese 93
**scrambled eggs** uova strapazzate *f/pl* 38
**screwdriver** cacciavite *m* 107
**sculptor** scultore *m* 83
**sculpture** scultura *f* 83
**sea** mare *m* 23, 85,
**sea bass** spigola *f* 47
**sea bream** orata *f* 46
**seafood** frutti di mare *m/pl* 46
**season** stagione *f* 40, 150
**seasoning** condimento *m* 37
**seat** posto *m* 69, 70, 87
**seat belt** cintura di sicurezza *f* 75
**second** secondo 149
**second** secondo *m* 153
**second class** seconda classe *f* 69
**second hand** lancetta dei secondi *f* 122
**second-hand** d'occasione 104
**secretary** segretaria *f* 27, 131
**see, to** guardare 11
**sell, to** vendere 162
**send, to** mandare 31, 78, 102, 103; spedire 132; inviare 133
**send up, to** portare su 26
**separately** separatamente 62
**September** settembre *m* 150
**seriously** *(wounded)* gravemente 139
**service** servizio *m* 24, 62, 98, 100; *(religion)* funzione *f* 84
**serviette** tovagliolo *m* 36
**set** *(hair)* messa in piega *f* 30
**set menu** menù (a prezzo fisso) *m* 36, 40
**setting lotion** fissatore *m* 30; lozione fissativa *f* 111
**seven** sette 147
**seventeen** diciassette 147
**seventh** settimo 149
**seventy** settanta 148
**sew, to** attaccare 29
**shade** *(colour)* tonalità *f* 112
**shampoo** shampoo *m* 30, 111
**shape** forma *f* 103
**share** *(finance)* azione *f* 131
**sharp** *(pain)* acuto(a) 140
**shave, to** radere 31
**shaver** rasoio (elettrico) *m* 27, 119
**shaving cream** crema da barba *f* 111
**she** ella, lei 161
**shelf** scaffale *m* 100, 120
**ship** nave *f* 74
**shirt** camicia *f* 117
**shiver, to** rabbrividire 140
**shoe** scarpa *f* 118
**shoelace** laccio *m* 118
**shoemaker's** calzolaio *m* 99
**shoe polish** lucido *m* 118
**shoe shop** negozio di scarpe *m* 99
**shop** negozio *m* 98
**shopping** acquisti *m/pl* 97
**shopping area** zona dei negozi *f* 19, 82, 100
**short** corto(a) 30, 115,
**shorts** short *m* 117
**short-sighted** miope 123
**shoulder** spalla *f* 138
**shovel** paletta *f* 49, 128
**show** spettacolo *m* 86, 87
**show, to** mostrare 11, 12, 100, 101, 103, 119

**shower** doccia *f* 23, 32
**shrimp** gamberetto *m* 41, 46
**shrink, to** restringersi 114
**shut** chiuso(a) 13
**shutter** *(window)* imposta *f* 29; *(camera)* otturatore *m* 125
**sick, to be** *(ill)* sentirsi male 140, 156
**sickness** *(illness)* malattia *f* 140
**side** lato *m* 30
**sideboards/burns** basette *f/pl* 31
**sightseeing** visita turistica *f* 80
**sightseeing tour** giro turistico *m* 80
**sign** *(notice)* cartello *m* 155; *(road)* segnale *m* 79
**sign, to** firmare 26, 131
**signature** firma *f* 25
**signet ring** anello con stemma *m* 122
**silk** seta *f* 114, 127
**silver** argentato(a) 113
**silver** argento *m* 121, 122
**silver plate** placcato d'argento 122
**silverware** argenteria *f* 122
**simple** semplice 124
**since** da 15, 150
**sing, to** cantare 88
**single** scapolo *m*, nubile *f* 93
**single** *(ticket)* andata 69
**single room** camera singola *f* 19, 23
**sister** sorella *f* 93
**sit down, to** sedersi 95
**six** sei 147
**sixteen** sedici 147
**sixth** sesto 149
**sixty** sessanta 147
**size** formato *m* 124; *(clothes)* taglia *f*, misura *f* 114, 115; *(shoes)* numero *m* 118
**skates** pattini *m/pl* 91
**skating rink** pista di pattinaggio *f* 91
**ski** sci *m* 91
**ski, to** sciare 91
**ski boot** scarpone da sci *m* 91
**skier** sciatore *m* (sciatrice *f*) 91
**skiing** sci *m* 89, 91
**ski lift** sciovia *m* 91
**skin** pelle *f* 138
**skirt** gonna *f* 117
**ski run** pista di sci *f* 91
**sky** cielo *m* 94
**sled** slitta *f* 91
**sleep, to** dormire 144
**sleeping bag** sacco a pelo *m* 107
**sleeping-car** vagone letto *m* 66, 68, 69, 70
**sleeping pill** sonnifero *m* 109, 143, 144
**sleeve** manica *f* 117
**slice** fetta *f* 55, 63, 120
**slide** *(photo)* diapositiva *f* 124
**slip** sottoveste *f* 117
**slipper** pantofola *f* 118
**slow** lento(a) 13
**slow down, to** rallentare 79
**slowly** lentamente 11, 21, 135
**small** piccolo(a) 13, 25, 101, 118
**smoke, to** fumare 95
**smoked** affumicato(a) 41, 47
**smoker** *(compartment)* fumatori *m/pl* 70
**snack** spuntino *m* 63
**snack bar** snack bar *m* 67
**snail** lumaca *f* 46
**snap fastener** bottone a pressione *m* 117
**sneakers** scarpe da tennis *f/pl* 118
**snorkel** maschera da subacqueo *f* 128
**snow** neve *f* 94
**snow, to** nevicare 94
**soap** saponetta *f* 27, 111
**soccer** calcio *m* 89
**sock** calzino *m* 117
**socket** *(outlet)* presa *f* 27
**soft** morbido(a) 123
**soft drink** bibita *f* 64
**soft-boiled** *(egg)* molle 38
**sold out** *(theatre)* esaurito 87
**sole** suola *f* 118; *(fish)* sogliola *f* 47
**soloist** solista *m/f* 88
**some** del, della (*pl* dei, delle) 14
**someone** qualcuno 95
**something** qualcosa 36, 55, 108, 112, 113, 139
**son** figlio *m* 93
**song** canzone *f* 128
**soon** presto 15
**sore** *(painful)* infiammato(a) 145
**sore throat** mal di gola *m* 141
**sorry** *(I'm)* mi dispiace 11, 16
**sort** genere *m* 86
**sound-and-light show** spettacolo suoni e luci *m* 86
**soup** minestra *f*, zuppa *f* 43
**south** sud *m* 77
**South Africa** Sudafrica *m* 146
**South America** America del Sud *f* 146
**souvenir** oggetto ricordo *m* 127
**souvenir shop** negozio di ricordi *m* 99
**Soviet Union** Unione Sovietica *f* 146

**spade** paletta *f* 128
**Spain** Spagna *f* 146
**spare tyre** ruota di scorta *f* 75
**spark(ing) plug** candela *f* 76
**sparkling** *(wine)* spumante 57
**speak, to** parlare 11, 135
**speaker** *(loudspeaker)* altoparlante *f*
**specialist** specialista *m/f* 142
**speciality** specialità *f* 40, 60
**specimen** *(medical)* campione *m* 142
**spectacle case** astuccio per occhiali *m* 123
**spell, to** sillabare 11
**spend, to** spendere 101
**spice** spezia *f* 53
**spinach** spinacio *m* 52
**spine** spina dorsale *f* 138
**spiny lobster** aragosta *f* 46
**spit-roasted** allo spiedo 50
**spoon** cucchiaio *m* 36, 61, 107
**sport** sport *m* 89
**sporting goods shop** negozio di articoli sportivi *m* 99
**sprain, to** distorcere 140
**spring** *(season)* primavera *f* 150; *(water)* sorgente *f* 85
**square** piazza *f* 82
**squid** calamaro *m* 46
**stadium** stadio *m* 82
**staff** personale *m* 26
**stain** macchia *f* 29
**stainless steel** acciaio inossidabile *m* 107, 122
**stalls** *(theatre)* poltrona *f* 87
**stamp** *(postage)* francobollo *m* 28, 126, 132
**staple** graffetta *f* 105
**star** stella *f* 94
**start, to** iniziare 80, 88; *(car)* partire 78
**starter** antipasto *m* 41
**station** stazione *f* 19, 21, 67, 70, 73
**stationer's** cartoleria *f* 99, 104
**statue** statua *f* 82
**stay** soggiorno *m* 31, 92
**stay, to** restare 16, 24; trattenersi 26; soggiornare 93
**steak** bistecca *f* 48
**steal, to** rubare 156
**steamed** cotto(a) a vapore 47
**stew** spezzatino *m* 49
**stewed** in umido 50
**stiff neck** torcicollo *m* 141
**still** *(mineral water)* naturale 60
**sting** puntura *f* 139
**sting, to** pungere 139
**stitch, to** *(clothes)* cucire 29; *(shoes)* attaccare 118
**stock exchange** borsa valori *f* 82
**stocking** calza da donna *f* 117
**stomach** stomaco *m* 138
**stomach ache** mal di stomaco *m* 141
**stools** feci *f/pl* 142
**stop** *(bus)* fermata *f* 72, 73
**stop!** fermatevi! 156
**stop, to** fermarsi 21, 68, 70, 72
**stop thief!** al ladro! 156
**store** negozio *m* 98
**straight** *(drink)* liscio 56, 59
**straight ahead** diritto 21, 77
**strange** strano 84
**strawberry** fragola *f* 54, 55
**street** strada *f* 25
**streetcar** tram *m* 72
**street map** pianta della città *f* 19, 105
**strike** sciopero *m* 155
**string** spago *m* 105
**strong** forte 143
**student** studente(essa) *m* 82, 93
**stuffed** farcito(a) 50
**subway** *(railway)* metropolitana *f* 73
**suede** renna *f* 114; camoscio *m* 118
**sugar** zucchero *m* 37, 64
**suit** *(man)* completo *m* 117; *(woman)* tailleur *m* 117
**suitcase** valigia *f* 18
**summer** estate *f* 150
**sun** sole *m* 94
**sunburn** scottatura solare *f* 108
**Sunday** domenica *f* 151
**sunglasses** occhiali da sole *m/pl* 123
**sunshade** *(beach)* ombrellone *m* 91
**sunstroke** colpo di sole *m* 141
**sun-tan cream** crema solare *f* 111
**sun-tan oil** olio solare *m* 111
**super** *(petrol)* super 75
**superb** superbo 84
**supermarket** supermercato *m* 99
**suppository** supposta *f* 109
**surfboard** sandolino *m* 91
**surgery** *(consulting room)* ambulatorio *m* 137
**surname** cognome *m* 25
**suspenders** *(Am.)* bretelle *f/pl* 117
**swallow, to** inghiottire 143
**sweater** maglione *m* 117

**sweatshirt** blusa *f* 117
**Sweden** Svezia *f* 146
**sweet** dolce 57, 61
**sweet** caramella *f* 126
**sweetener** dolcificante *f* 37
**swell, to** gonfiare 139
**swelling** gonfiore *m* 139
**swim, to** nuotare 90
**swimming** nuoto *m* 89; balneazione *f* 91
**swimming pool** piscina *f* 32, 90
**swimming trunks** costume da bagno *m* 117
**swimsuit** costume da bagno *m* 117
**Swiss** svizzero(a) 18
**switch** interruttore *m* 29
**switchboard operator** centralinista *m/f* 26
**switch on, to** *(light)* accendere 79
**Switzerland** Svizzera *f* 146
**swollen** gonfio(a) 139
**swordfish** pesce spada *m* 46
**synagogue** sinagoga *f* 84
**synthetic** sintetico 114
**system** sistema *m* 138

## T

**table** tavolo *m* 36; tavola *f* 107
**tablet** pastiglia *f* 109
**tailor's** sartoria *f* 99
**take, to** prendere 18, 25, 73, 102; durare 72; portare 114
**take away, to** *(carry)* portare via 63, 102
**talcum powder** talco *m* 111
**tampon** tampone igienico *m* 109
**tangerine** mandarino *m* 54
**tap** *(water)* rubinetto *m* 28
**tape recorder** registratore *m* 119
**tax** tassa *f* 32; I.V.A. *f* 24, 102
**taxi** taxi *m* 19, 21, 31
**tea** tè *m* 38, 60, 64
**tear, to** lacerare 140
**tearoom** sala da tè *f* 34
**teaspoon** cucchiaino *m* 107, 143
**telegram** telegramma *m* 133
**telegraph office** ufficio telegrafico *m* 133
**telephone** telefono *m* 28, 78, 79, 134
**telephone, to** telefonare 134
**telephone booth** cabina telefonica *f* 134
**telephone call** telefonata *f* 135, 136
**telephone directory** elenco telefonico *m* 134
**telephone number** numero di telefono *m* 96, 135, 136
**telephoto lens** teleobiettivo *m* 125
**television** *(set)* televisore *m* 23, 28, 119
**telex** telex *m* 133
**telex, to** mandare un telex 130
**tell, to** dire 12, 73, 76, 136, 153
**temperature** temperatura *f* 90; *(fever)* febbre *f* 140, 142
**temporary** provvisoriamente 145
**ten** dieci 147
**tendon** tendine *m* 138
**tennis** tennis *m* 89
**tennis court** campo da tennis *m* 89
**tennis racket** racchetta da tennis *f* 89
**tent** tenda *f* 32, 107
**tenth** decimo 149
**tent peg** picchetto per tenda *m* 107
**tent pole** palo per tenda *m* 107
**term** *(word)* termine *m* 131
**terrace** terrazza *f* 36
**terrifying** terrificante 84
**terrycloth** tessuto di spugna *m* 114
**tetanus** tetano *m* 140
**than** di 14
**thank you** grazie 9
**that** quello, quella 10, 100, 161
**the** il, lo, la (*pl* i, gli, le) 159
**theatre** teatro *m* 82, 86
**theft** furto *m* 156
**their** il, la loro (*pl* i, le loro) 161
**then** poi, in seguito 15
**there** là 13; ecco 13
**thermometer** termometro *m* 109, 144
**these** questi, queste 63, 160
**they** essi, loro 161
**thief** ladro *m* 156
**thin** fine 113
**think, to** pensare 62, 94
**third** terzo 149
**third** terzo *m* 149
**thirsty, to be** aver sete 12
**thirteen** tredici 147
**thirty** trenta 147
**this** questo, questa 10, 100, 160
**those** quegli, quei, quelle 160; quelli, quelle 63, 120
**thousand** mille 148
**thread** filo *m* 27

**three** tre 147
**throat** gola *f* 138, 141
**throat lozenge** pasticca per la gola *f* 109
**through train** treno diretto *m* 68, 69
**thrush** tordo *m* 51
**thumbtack** puntina *f* 105
**thunder** tuono *m* 94
**thunderstorm** temporale *m* 94
**Thursday** giovedì *m* 151
**thyme** timo *m* 53
**ticket** biglietto *m* 65, 69, 72, 87, 89
**ticket office** biglietteria *f* 67
**tide** marea *f* 90
**tie** cravatta *f* 117
**tie clip** fermacravatte *m* 122
**tie pin** spillo per cravatta *m* 122
**tight** *(clothes)* stretto(a) 115
**tights** collant *m* 117
**time** tempo *m* 80; *(clock)* ora *f* 137, 153; *(occasion)* volta *f* 143
**timetable** orario ferroviario *m* 68
**tin** *(can)* scatola *f* 120
**tinfoil** foglio d'alluminio *m* 107
**tin opener** apriscatole *m* 107
**tint** sfumatura *f* 111
**tinted** colorato(a) 123
**tip** mancia *f* 62
**tire** ruota *f* 75; gomma *f* 76
**tired** stanco(a) 12
**tissue** *(handkerchief)* fazzoletto di carta *m* 111
**tissue paper** carta velina *f* 105
**to** a 14, 163
**toast** pane tostato *m* 38
**tobacco** tabacco *m* 126
**tobacconist's** tabaccheria *f* 99, 126
**today** oggi 29, 151
**toe** dito del piede *m* 138
**toilet paper** carta igienica *f* 111
**toiletry** articoli da toilette *m/pl* 110
**toilets** gabinetti *m/pl* 27, 32, 37, 67
**token** *(telephone)* gettone *m* 134
**toll** pedaggio *m* 75
**tomato** pomodoro *m* 52
**tomato juice** succo di pomodoro *m* 60
**tomb** tomba *f* 82
**tomorrow** domani 29, 151
**tongue** lingua *f* 48, 138
**tonic water** acqua tonica *f* 60
**tonight** stasera 29, 96; questa sera 86, 87
**tonsil** tonsilla *f* 138
**too** troppo(a) 14; *(also)* anche 15
**tooth** dente *m* 145
**toothache** mal di denti *m* 145
**toothbrush** spazzolino da denti *m* 111, 119
**toothpaste** dentifricio *m* 111
**top** cima *f* 30; alto *m* 145
**topaz** topazio *m* 122
**torch** *(flashlight)* lampadina tascabile *f* 107
**torn** lacerato(a) 140
**touch, to** toccare 155
**tough** duro(a) 61
**tourist office** azienda di soggiorno e turismo *f*, ufficio turistico *m* 22, 80
**tourist tax** tassa di soggiorno *f* 32
**towards** verso 14
**towel** asciugamano *m* 27
**town hall** municipio *m* 82
**tow truck** carro attrezzi *m* 78
**toy** giocattolo *m* 128
**toy shop** negozio di giocattoli *m* 99
**tracksuit** tuta sportiva *f* 117
**traffic** traffico *m* 76
**traffic light** semaforo *m* 77
**trailer** roulotte *f* 32
**train** treno *m* 66, 68, 69, 70, 73
**tram** tram *m* 72
**tranquillizer** tranquillante *m* 109, 143
**transfer** *(bank)* trasferimento *m* 131
**transformer** trasformatore *m* 119
**translate, to** tradurre 11
**transport** trasporto *m* 74
**travel, to** viaggiare 92
**travel agent** agenzia di viaggi *f* 99
**traveller's cheque** traveller's cheque *m* 18, 62, 102, 130
**travel sickness** mal d'auto *m* 108
**treatment** cura *f* 143
**tree** albero *m* 85
**tremendous** fantastico(a) 84
**trim, to** *(beard)* spuntare 31
**trip** viaggio *m* 93, 152; percorso *m* 72
**tripe** trippe *f/pl* 49
**trolley** carrello *m* 18, 71
**trousers** pantaloni *m/pl* 117
**trout** trota *f* 47
**truffle** tartufo *m* 52
**try, to** provare 115; *(sample)* assaggiare 60
**T-shirt** maglietta di cotone *f* 117
**tube** tubetto *m* 120
**Tuesday** martedì *m* 151
**tumbler** bicchiere *m* 107
**tuna** tonno *m* 41, 47

**Tunisia** Tunisia *f* 146
**tunnel** galleria *f* 79
**tunny** tonno *m* 41, 47
**turbot** rombo *m* 46
**Turkey** Turchia *f* 146
**turkey** tacchino *m* 51
**turn, to** *(change direction)* girare 21, 77
**turquoise** turchese 113
**turquoise** turchese *m* 122
**turtleneck** a collo alto 117
**tweezers** pinzette *f/pl* 111
**twelve** dodici 147
**twenty** venti 147
**twice** due volte 149
**twin bed** due letti *m/pl* 23
**two** due 147
**typewriter** macchina per scrivere *f* 27, 105
**typewriter ribbon** nastro per macchina da scrivere *m* 105
**typing paper** carta per macchina da scrivere *f* 105
**tyre** ruota *f* 75; gomma *f* 76

## U

**ugly** brutto(a) 13, 84
**umbrella** ombrello *m* 117; *(beach)* ombrellone *m* 91
**uncle** zio *m* 93
**unconscious** svenuto(a) 139
**under** sotto 15
**underdone** *(meat)* al sangue 50; poco cotto(a) 61
**underground** *(railway)* metropolitana *f* 73
**underpants** mutande *f/pl*, slip *m* 117
**undershirt** canottiera *f* 117
**understand, to** capire 11, 16
**undress, to** spogliare 142
**United States** Stati Uniti *m/pl* 146
**university** università 82
**until** fino a 14
**up** su, in alto 15
**upper** superiore 69
**upset stomach** mal di stomaco *m* 108
**upstairs** di sopra 15
**urgent** urgente 12, 145
**urine** urina *f* 142
**use** uso *m* 17
**use, to** usare 78, 134
**useful** utile 15
**usherette** maschera *f* 87
**usual** abituale 143

## V

**vacancy** camera libera *f* 23
**vacant** libero 13, 155
**vacation** vacanze *f/pl* 151
**vaccinate, to** vaccinare 140
**vacuum flask** thermos *m* 107
**vaginal** vaginale 141
**valley** valle *f* 85
**value** valore *m* 131
**value-added tax** I.V.A. *f* 24, 102, 154
**vanilla** vaniglia *f* 55
**VAT** (sales tax) I.V.A. *f* 24, 102, 154
**veal** vitello *m* 48
**vegetable** verdura *f* 52
**vegetable store** negozio di frutta e verdura *m* 99
**vegetarian** vegetariano *m* 37
**vein** vena *f* 138
**velvet** velluto *m* 114
**velveteen** velluto di cotone *m* 114
**venereal disease** malattia venerea *f* 142
**venison** selvaggina *f* 51
**vermouth** vermouth *m* 59
**very** molto 15
**vest** canottiera *f* 117; *(Am.)* panciotto *m* 117
**video cassette** video cassetta *f* 119, 124, 127
**video recorder** video registratore *m* 119
**view** vista *f* 23, 25
**village** villaggio *m* 76, 85; paese *m* 85
**vinegar** aceto *m* 37
**vineyard** vigna *f* 85
**visit, to** visitare 84
**visiting hours** orari di visita *m/pl* 144
**vitamin pills** vitamine *f/pl* 109
**V-neck** con scollatura a punta 117
**volleyball** pallavolo *f* 89
**voltage** voltaggio *m* 27, 119
**vomit, to** vomitare 140

## W

**waistcoat** panciotto *m* 117
**wait, to** aspettare 21, 95
**waiter** cameriere *m* 26, 36
**waiting-room** sala d'aspetto *f* 67
**waitress** cameriera *f* 26, 36
**wake, to** svegliare 26
**Wales** Galles *m* 146
**walk, to** camminare 74; andare a piedi 85
**wall** muro *m* 85

**wallet** portafogli *m* 156
**walnut** noce *f* 54
**want, to** volere 18, 35, 163; *(wish)* desiderare 12
**warm** caldo(a) 94
**wash, to** lavare 29, 114
**wash-basin** lavabo *m* 28
**washing powder** detersivo *m* 107
**watch** orologio *m* 122, 127
**watchmaker's** orologiaio *m* 99; orologeria *f* 121
**watchstrap** cinturino per orologio *m* 122
**water** acqua *f* 23, 28, 32, 38, 75, 90
**waterfall** cascata *f* 85
**water flask** borraccia *f* 107
**watermelon** anguria *f* 54, cocomero *m* 54
**water-ski** sci nautico *m* 91
**way** strada *f* 76
**we** noi 161
**weather** tempo *m* 93
**weather forecast** previsioni del tempo *f/pl* 94
**wedding ring** fede nuziale *f* 122
**Wednesday** mercoledì *m* 151
**week** settimana *f* 16, 24, 80, 151
**weekend** fine settimana *m* 151
**well** pozzo 85; *(healthy)* bene 9, 140
**well-done** *(meat)* ben cotto(a) 50
**west** ovest *m* 77
**what** che cosa 10, 12; quanto 20; quale 20, 21
**wheel** ruota *f* 78
**when** quando, a che ora 10
**where** dove 10
**which** quale 10
**whipped cream** panna montata *f* 55
**whisky** whisky *m* 17, 59
**white** bianco(a) 57, 113
**whiting** merlano *m* 46
**who** chi 10
**why** perchè 10
**wick** stoppino *m* 126
**wide** largo(a) 118
**wide-angle lens** grandangolare *m* 125
**wife** moglie *f* 93
**wild boar** cinghiale *m* 51
**wind** vento *m* 94
**window** finestra *f* 28, 36; *(train)* finestrino *m* 69; *(shop)* vetrina *f* 100, 112
**windscreen/shield** parabrezza *m* 76
**wine** vino *m* 56, 57, 61
**wine list** lista dei vini *f* 57
**wine merchant** vinaio *m* 99
**winter** inverno *m* 150
**winter sports** sport invernali *m/pl* 91
**wipers** tergicristalli *m/pl* 76
**wish** augurio *m* 152
**with** con 14, 163
**withdraw, to** *(bank)* prelevare 131
**without** senza 14
**woman** donna *f* 115
**wonderful** magnifico(a) 96
**wood** bosco *m* 85
**wood alcohol** alcool metilico *m* 107
**woodwork** lavoro in legno *m* 127
**woodcock** beccaccia *f* 51
**wool** lana *f* 114
**word** parola *f* 11, 15, 133
**work** lavoro *m* 79
**work, to** *(function)* funzionare 28, 119
**working day** giorno feriale *m* 151
**worse** peggiore 13
**wound** ferita *f* 139
**wrinkle resistant** ingualcibile 114
**wristwatch** orologio braccialetto *m* 122
**write, to** scrivere 11, 101
**writing pad** blocco per appunti *m* 105
**writing-paper** carta da lettere *f* 27
**wrong** sbagliato(a) 13, 135

## X

**X-ray** *(photo)* radiografia *f* 140

## Y

**year** anno *m* 149
**yellow** giallo 113
**yes** sì 9
**yesterday** ieri 151
**yet** ancora 15
**yoghurt** yogurt *m* 64
**you** tu, voi 161
**young** giovane 13
**your** tuo(a) (*pl* tuoi, tue) 161; vostro(a) (*pl* vostri(e)) 161
**youth hostel** ostello della gioventù *m* 22, 32
**Yugoslavia** Iugoslavia *f* 146

## Z

**zero** zero *m* 147
**zip(per)** cerniera *f* 117
**zoo** zoo *m* 82
**zoology** zoologia *f* 83

# Indice italiano

AUSTRIA
SWITZERLAND
HUNGARY
ALTO ADIGE
Trento
TRENTINO
Udine
Trieste
Aosta
LOMBARDIA
Venezia
PIEMONTE
Milano
VENETO
Torino
EMILIA-
ROMAGNA
YUGOSLAVIA
FRANCE
Genova
LIGURIA
Bologna
Firenze
Ancona
TOSCANA
Perugia
ADRIATIC
MARCHE
UMBRIA
Isola d'Elba
L'Aquila
LAZIO
ABRUZZI
Corsica
MOLISE
Roma
Campobasso
Bari
Napoli
Ischia
CAMPANIA
PUGLIA
Potenza
Capri
LUCANIA
SARDEGNA
Cagliari
CALABRIA
Catanzaro
Lipari
MEDITERRANEAN
Reggio Cal.
Egadi
Palermo
SICILIA
Catania
N
ALGERIA
TUNISIA

# BERLITZ® Books for travellers

## TRAVEL GUIDES

They fit your pocket in both size and price. Modern, up-to-date, Berlitz gets all the information you need into 128 lively pages with colour maps and photos throughout. What to see and do, where to shop, what to eat and drink, how to save.

| | |
|---|---|
| **AFRICA** | Kenya<br>Morocco<br>South Africa<br>Tunisia |
| **ASIA, MIDDLE EAST** | China (256 pages)<br>Hong Kong<br>India (256 pages)*<br>Japan (256 pages)*<br>Singapore<br>Sri Lanka<br>Thailand<br>Egypt<br>Jerusalem and the Holy Land<br>Saudi Arabia |
| **AUSTRAL-ASIA** | New Zealand |
| **BRITISH ISLES** | Channel Islands<br>London<br>Ireland<br>Oxford and Stratford<br>Scotland |
| **BELGIUM** | Brussels |

*in preparation

## PHRASE BOOKS

World's bestselling phrase books feature all the expressions and vocabulary you'll need, and pronunciation throughout. 192 pages, 2 colours.

Arabic
Chinese
Danish
Dutch
Finnish
French
German
Greek
Hebrew
Hungarian
Italian
Japanese
Norwegian
Polish
Portuguese
Russian
Serbo-Croatian
Spanish (Castilian)
Spanish (Lat. Am.)
Swahili
Swedish
Turkish
European Phrase Book
European Menu Reader

| | |
|---|---|
| **FRANCE** | Brittany<br>French Riviera<br>Loire Valley<br>Paris |
| **GERMANY** | Berlin<br>Munich<br>The Rhine Valley |
| **AUSTRIA and SWITZERLAND** | Tyrol<br>Vienna<br>Geneva/French-speaking areas<br>Zurich/German-speaking areas<br>Switzerland (192 pages) |
| **GREECE, CYPRUS & TURKEY** | Athens<br>Corfu<br>Crete<br>Rhodes<br>Greek Islands of the Aegean<br>Peloponnese<br>Salonica and Northern Greece<br>Cyprus<br>Istanbul |
| **ITALY and MALTA** | Florence<br>Italian Adriatic<br>Italian Riviera<br>Rome<br>Sicily<br>Venice<br>Malta |
| **NETHERLANDS and SCANDINAVIA** | Amsterdam<br>Copenhagen<br>Helsinki<br>Oslo and Bergen<br>Stockholm |
| **PORTUGAL** | Algarve<br>Lisbon<br>Madeira |
| **SPAIN** | Barcelona and Costa Dorada<br>Canary Islands<br>Costa Blanca<br>Costa Brava<br>Costa del Sol and Andalusia<br>Ibiza and Formentera<br>Madrid<br>Majorca and Minorca |
| **EASTERN EUROPE** | Budapest<br>Dubrovnik and Southern Dalmatia<br>Hungary (192 pages)<br>Istria and Croatian Coast<br>Moscow & Leningrad<br>Split and Dalmatia |
| **NORTH AMERICA** | U.S.A. (256 pages)<br>California<br>Florida<br>Hawaii<br>New York<br>Toronto<br>Montreal |
| **CARIBBEAN, LATIN AMERICA** | Puerto Rico<br>Virgin Islands<br>Bahamas<br>Bermuda<br>French West Indies<br>Jamaica<br>Southern Caribbean<br>Mexico City<br>Rio de Janeiro<br>Caribbean Cruise Guide (368 pages) |
| **EUROPE** | Business Travel Guide – Europe (368 pages)<br>Pocket Guide to Europe<br>Cities of Europe |

**Most titles with British and U.S. destinations are available in French, German, Spanish and as many as 7 other languages.**

## DICTIONARIES

Bilingual with 12,500 concepts each way. Highly practical for travellers, with pronunciation shown plus menu reader, basic expressions and useful information. Over 330 pages.

| | |
|---|---|
| Danish | Italian |
| Dutch | Norwegian |
| Finnish | Portuguese |
| French | Spanish |
| German | Swedish |

**Berlitz Books, a world of information in your pocket! At all leading bookshops and airport newsstands.**

BERLITZ® Presents...
THE BERLITZ BASIC LANGUAGE PROGRAM
Available in:
French • Spanish
German • Italian
BERLITZ® BASIC ITALIAN
BERLITZ® BASIC GERMAN
BERLITZ® BASIC SPANISH
BERLITZ® BASIC FRENCH
BERLITZ® CASSETTE COURSE
BASIC FRENCH
BERLITZ®
BASIC FRENCH
FRENCH ZERO
BERLITZ
french
english
anglais
français
BERLITZ
FRENCH
FOR TRAVELLERS

From: ____________________

____________________

____________________

Affix First
Class or
Air Mail
Stamp

To:

____________________

____________________

____________________

11603.

## ORDER FORM

1. Name ______________________________

Address ______________________________

______________________________

2. Complete the address on the adjoining envelope for either:

**Berlitz Publications, Inc.**
**P.O. Box 506**
**Delran, N.J. 08370-0506**
**U.S.A.**

**Cassell Ltd.**
**1 St. Anne's Road**
**Eastbourne**
**East Sussex, BN21 3UN**
**U.K.**

3. Calculate:

**In the U.S.A.**

_____ European
$14.95 set = $_____
_____ Singles at
$9.95 each = $_____
_____ Courses at
$59.95 each = $_____
TOTAL $_____
(NJ residents add sales tax)

**In the U.K.**

_____ European
£10.95 set = £_____
_____ Singles at
£5.95 each = £_____
_____ Courses at
£35.00 each = £_____
TOTAL £_____
(VAT is included)

4. Indicate method of payment, please:

☐ Check or money order enclosed made payable to Berlitz

☐ American Express ☐ Master Charge

☐ Diners Club ☐ Visa

Credit Card No. ______________________________

Expiration Date ______________________________

Interbank No. ______________________________
(Master Charge Only. Located above your name.)

Signature ______________________________

**Note: Credit card holders – it's faster ordering by phone. See numbers on reverse side.**

5. Detach this order form. Insert check or money order in envelope. Please allow up to 4 weeks for delivery. (We pay postage.) Order Berlitz travel guides, phrase books and dictionaries through your bookseller. 11603.